PLANNING METROPOLITAN AUSTRALIA

Australia has long been a highly (sub)urbanized nation, but the major distinctive feature of its contemporary settlement pattern is that the great majority of Australians live in a small number of large metropolitan areas focused on the state capital cities. The development and application of effective urban policy at a regional scale is a significant global challenge given the complexities of urban space and governance. Building on the editors' previous collection *The Australian Metropolis: A Planning History* (2000), this new book examines the recent history of metropolitan planning in Australia since the beginning of the twenty-first century. After a historical prelude, the book is structured around a series of six case studies of metropolitan Melbourne, Sydney, Adelaide, Perth, the fast-growing metropolitan region of South-East Queensland centred on Brisbane, and the national capital of Canberra. These essays are contributed by some of Australia's leading urbanists. Set against a dynamic background of economic change, restructured land uses, a more diverse population, and growing spatial and social inequality, the book identifies a broad planning consensus around the notion of making Australian cities more contained, compact and resilient. But it also observes a continuing gulf between the simplified aims of metropolitan strategies and our growing understanding of the complex functioning of the varied communities in which most people live. This book reflects on the raft of planning challenges presented at the metropolitan scale, looks at what the future of Australian cities might be, and speculates about the prospects of more effective metropolitan planning arrangements.

Stephen Hamnett is Emeritus Professor of Urban and Regional Planning at the University of South Australia in Adelaide and a Commissioner of the Environment, Resources and Development Court of South Australia.

Robert Freestone is Professor of Planning in the Faculty of Built Environment at the University of New South Wales in Sydney, Australia.

Metropolitan planning and governance have risen in importance given the critical role that cities and metros play in resolving pressing economic, social and environmental challenges throughout the world. This book is a distinctive contribution to the literature given its comprehensive look at the metropolitan areas of one nation.

Bruce J. Katz, Centennial Scholar, Brookings Institution

Convincingly identifies the drivers of growth, change, economic dysfunctions, inequality but also opportunities that all Australian metropolitan areas will need to address in the near future. The book unravels how the major cities tackle conflicting pressures and expectations, mainly with strategic plans, and identifies and assesses the different initiatives underway.

Louis Albrechts, Professor of Planning, University of Leuven

This book shows why effective planning at the metropolitan level has been such a hard nut to crack for Australian State Governments. The contributors comprehensively chart the avalanche of often short-lived metropolitan strategies generated across the country since the turn of the century and expertly identify where they came up short. This is essential reading for anybody interested in a sustainable, prosperous and inclusive future for our cities.

Marcus Spiller, Founding Partner, SGS Economics & Planning

Planning, History and Environment Series

Editor:

Ann Rudkin, Alexandrine Press, Marcham, UK

Editorial Board:

Professor Arturo Almandoz, Universidad Simón Bolivar, Caracas, Venezuela and Pontificia
Universidad Católica de Chile, Santiago, Chile
Professor Nezar AlSayyad, University of California, Berkeley, USA
Professor Scott A. Bollens, University of California, Irvine, USA
Professor Robert Bruegmann, University of Illinois at Chicago, USA
Professor Meredith Clausen, University of Washington, Seattle, USA
Professor Yasser Elsheshtawy, UAE University, Al Ain, UAE
Professor Robert Freestone, University of New South Wales, Sydney, Australia
Professor John R. Gold, Oxford Brookes University, Oxford, UK
Professor Michael Hebbert, University College London, UK

Selection of published titles

Planning Europe's Capital Cities: Aspects of nineteenth century development by Thomas Hall
Selling Places: The marketing and promotion of towns and cities, 1850–2000 by Stephen V. Ward
The Australian Metropolis: A planning history edited by Stephen Hamnett and Robert Freestone
Utopian England: Community experiments 1900–1945 by Dennis Hardy
Urban Planning in a Changing World: The twentieth century experience edited by Robert Freestone
Council Housing and Culture: The history of a social experiment by Alison Ravetz
Planning Latin America's Capital Cities, 1850–1950 edited by Arturo Almandoz
Exporting American Architecture, 1870–2000 by Jeffrey W. Cody
The Making and Selling of Post-Mao Beijing by Anne-Marie Broudehoux
Planning Middle Eastern Cities: An urban kaleidoscope in a globalizing world edited by Yasser Elsheshtawy
Globalizing Taipei: The political economy of spatial development edited by Reginald Yin-Wang Kwok
New Urbanism and American Planning: The conflict of cultures by Emily Talen
Remaking Chinese Urban Form: Modernity, scarcity and space. 1949–2005 by Duanfang Lu
Planning Twentieth Century Capital Cities edited by David L.A. Gordon
Planning the Megacity: Jakarta in the twentieth century by Christopher Silver
Designing Australia's Cities: Culture, commerce and the city beautiful, 1900–1930 by Robert Freestone
Ordinary Places, Extraordinary Events: Citizenship, democracy and urban space in Latin America edited by Clara Irazábal (**paperback 2015**)
The Evolving Arab City: Tradition, modernity and urban development edited by Yasser Elsheshtawy
Stockholm: The making of a metropolis by Thomas Hall
Dubai: Behind an urban spectacle by Yasser Elsheshtawy (**paperback 2013**)
Capital Cities in the Aftermath of Empires: Planning in central and southeastern Europe edited by Emily Gunzburger Makaš and Tanja Damljanović Conley (**paperback 2015**)
Lessons in Post-War Reconstruction: Case studies from Lebanon in the aftermath of the 2006 war edited by Howayda Al-Harithy

Orienting Istanbul: Cultural capital of Europe? edited by Deniz Göktürk, Levent Soysal and İpek Türeli
The Making of Hong Kong: From vertical to volumetric by Barrie Shelton, Justyna Karakiewicz and Thomas Kvan (**paperback 2014**)
Urban Coding and Planning edited by Stephen Marshall
Planning Asian Cities: Risks and resilience edited by Stephen Hamnett and Dean Forbes (**paperback 2013**)
Staging the New Berlin: Place marketing and the politics of reinvention post-1989 by Claire Colomb
City and Soul in Divided Societies by Scott A. Bollens
Learning from the Japanese City: Looking east in urban design, 2nd edition by Barrie Shelton
The Urban Wisdom of Jane Jacobs edited by Sonia Hirt with Diane Zahm (**paperback 2014**)
Of Planting and Planning: The making of British colonial cities, 2nd edition by Robert Home
Healthy City Planning: Global health equity from neighbourhood to nation by Jason Corburn
Good Cities, Better Lives: How Europe discovered the lost art of urbanism by Peter Hall
The Planning Imagination: Peter Hall and the study of urban and regional planning edited by Mark Tewdwr-Jones, Nicholas Phelps and Robert Freestone
Garden Suburbs of Tomorrow? A new future for cottage estates by Martin Crookston (**paperback 2016**)
Sociable Cities: The 21st-century reinvention of the Garden City by Peter Hall and Colin Ward
Modernization, Urbanization and Development in Latin America, 1900s–2000s by Arturo Almandoz
Planning the Great Metropolis: The 1929 Regional Plan of New York and Its Environs by David A. Johnson (**paperback 2015**)
Remaking the San Francisco–Oakland Bay Bridge: A case of shadowboxing with nature by Karen Trapenberg Frick (**paperback 2016**)
Great British Plans: Who made them and how they worked by Ian Wray
Homeland: Zionism as a housing regime, 1860–2011 by Yael Allweil
Olympic Cities: City agendas, planning and the world's games 1896–2016, 3rd edition edited by John R. Gold and Margaret M. Gold
Globalizing Seoul: The city's cultural and urban change by Jieheerah Yun
Planning Metropolitan Australia edited by Stephen Hamnett and Robert Freestone

PLANNING METROPOLITAN AUSTRALIA

edited by

Stephen Hamnett

and

Robert Freestone

LONDON AND NEW YORK

First published 2018
by Routledge
2 Park Square, Milton Park, Abingdon, Oxfordshire OX14 4RN

and by Routledge
711 Third Avenue, New York, NY 10017

Routledge is an imprint of the Taylor & Francis Group, an informa business

© 2018 Selection and editorial matter: Stephen Hamnett and Robert Freestone; individual chapters: the contributors

This book was commissioned and edited by Alexandrine Press, Marcham, Oxfordshire

The rights of the authors have been asserted in accordance with sections 77 and 78 of the Copyright, Designs and Patents Act 1988.

All rights reserved. No part of this book may be reprinted or reproduced or utilized in any form or by any electronic, mechanical or other means, now known or hereafter invented, including photocopying and recording, or in any information storage or retrieval system, without permission in writing from the publishers.

The publisher makes no representation, express or implied, with regard to the accuracy of the information contained in this book and cannot accept any legal responsibility or liability for any errors or omissions that may be made.

Trademark notice: Product or corporate names may be trademarks or registered trademarks, and are used only for identification and explanation without intent to infringe.

British Library Cataloguing in Publication Data
A catalogue record of this book is available from the British Library

Library of Congress Cataloging in Publication Data
A catalogue record for this book has been requested

ISBN: 978–1–138–24107–7 (hbk)
ISBN: 978–1–315–28137–7 (ebk)

Typeset in Aldine and Swiss by PNR Design, Didcot

 Printed in the United Kingdom by Henry Ling Limited

Contents

The Contributors		vii
Chapter 1	The Metropolitan Perspective *Stephen Hamnett and Robert Freestone*	1
Chapter 2	Beginnings: The Evolution of Metropolitan Planning to the Late Twentieth Century *Robert Freestone and Christine Garnaut*	26
Chapter 3	Melbourne: Growing Pains for the Liveable City *Robin Goodman*	51
Chapter 4	Sydney: Growth, Globalization and Governance *Raymond Bunker, Robert Freestone and Bill Randolph*	76
Chapter 5	Adelaide: Tough Times in the City of Light *Stephen Hamnett and Jon Kellett*	101
Chapter 6	Perth: From 'Large Provincial City' to 'Globalizing City' *Paul J. Maginn and Neil Foley*	124
Chapter 7	South East Queensland: Change and Continuity in Planning *Paul Burton*	148
Chapter 8	Canberra: 'Normalization' or 'the Pride of Time'? *Karl Friedhelm Fischer and James Weirick*	170
Chapter 9	The Metropolitan Condition *Brendan Gleeson*	195
Index		212

The Contributors

The Editors

Stephen Hamnett is Emeritus Professor of Urban and Regional Planning at the University of South Australia in Adelaide and a Commissioner of the Environment, Resources and Development Court of South Australia. Recent works include *Planning Asian Cities: Risks and Resilience* (2013) (with Dean Forbes), published in the *Planning, History and Environment* series, and a collection of essays on *Australian Cities in the 21st Century* (2016), co-edited and authored with Paul J. Maginn and published in the journal *Built Environment*.

Robert Freestone is Professor of Planning in the Faculty of Built Environment at the University of New South Wales, Sydney. His other edited books include *Dialogues in Urban and Regional Planning 6* (2017), *Place and Placelessness Revisited* (2016), *Exhibitions and the Development of Modern Planning Culture* (2014), *The Planning Imagination: Peter Hall and the Study of Urban and Regional Planning* (2014), and *Urban Planning in a Changing World* (2000).

The Contributors

Raymond Bunker is Visiting Associate Professor at the City Futures Research Centre at the University of New South Wales, Sydney.

Paul Burton is Professor of Urban Management and Planning and Director of the Cities Research Institute at Griffith University, Gold Coast, Queensland.

Karl Friedhelm Fischer is a Visiting Professorial Fellow in the Faculty of Built Environment at the University of New South Wales, Sydney.

Neil Foley is an urban planning consultant and teaches in the Urban and Regional Planning Program at the University of Western Australia, Perth.

Christine Garnaut is Associate Research Professor in Planning and Architectural History in the School of Art, Architecture and Design at the University of South Australia, Adelaide.

Brendan Gleeson is Professor of Urban Policy Studies and Director of the Melbourne Sustainable Society Institute at the University of Melbourne.

Robin Goodman is Professor of Urban Planning at RMIT University, Melbourne.

Jon Kellett is Professor of Planning and Property at the University of Adelaide.

Paul J. Maginn is Program Co-ordinator for the Masters in Urban and Regional Planning Program at the University of Western Australia, Perth.

Bill Randolph is Professor and Director of the City Futures Research Centre at the University of New South Wales, Sydney.

James Weirick is Professor of Landscape Architecture and Director of the Urban Development and Design Program at the University of New South Wales, Sydney.

Chapter 1

The Metropolitan Perspective

Stephen Hamnett and *Robert Freestone*

While the notion of metropolitan planning is not new, there has been a recently renewed focus internationally on the burgeoning growth of large extended metropolitan regions and their continuing policy challenges (see, for example, Roberts *et al.*, 1998; Laquian, 2005; Ross, 2009; Hall, 2011; Sassen, 2011; Xu and Yeh, 2011; Rosan, 2016; Lang and Török, 2017). Katz and Bradley (2013, p. 1) have written about a 'metropolitan revolution' in the USA which rests on 'a simple but profound truth: cities and metropolitan areas are the engines of economic prosperity and social transformation'.

Murphy (2012, p. 156) has defined the essence of metropolitan planning as the adoption of 'a synoptic view of large urbanised regions' which aspires to integrate related issues of population growth, economic development, the planning of transport and infrastructure, growing environmental concerns and increasing socio-spatial inequality. The same author also notes a 'renaissance of planning' at the metropolitan scale in Australia in the early decades of the twenty-first century, expressed in a series of new planning strategies for the major metropolitan regions centred on the mainland state capitals. These regions are the paramount feature of Australia's settlement structure. More than half of the national population now resides in Greater Sydney, Greater Melbourne and the evolving conurbation of South-East Queensland.

The main focus of this book is on the spatial strategies employed to manage growth and change in these metropolitan regions – the circumstances which have produced them, their achievements and their shortcomings. There is also an examination of the extent to which these strategies share distinctive common elements (see Bunker and Searle, 2009; McCosker and Searle, 2016) as well as of the subtle ways in which they differ, one from another, in, for example, the relative importance attached to economic, social and environmental objectives over time; the balance drawn between global ambitions and the need to be responsive to local communities and interest groups; their depth of analysis; and in the formats and visual language that they adopt to express their proposals and aspirations.

The next part of this chapter sets Australian metropolitan plans against a broader backcloth by briefly examining the recent international literature on strategic spatial planning and by pointing to some distinctive features of Australian plans when compared to the more fluid and 'relational' plans characteristic of European and other developed countries in the early twenty-first century. The structure of the book is then outlined and this is followed by a contextual discussion of the changing nature of Australia's society and economy as the prelude to an analysis of recent trends in the growth, changing composition and distribution of the Australian population. This provides further details of the dominance of the larger metropolitan regions and also of the changes occurring across and within these regions. Australia's vulnerability to climate change-related events and other environmental threats is considered next, as is the apparent inability of Australia's federal system of government to develop a coherent response to these threats, and this leads into a more specific discussion of the nature of, and challenges to, governance at the metropolitan scale. Having established this context, the chapter then examines in more detail the characteristics, aims and leading policies of twenty-first century Australian metropolitan plans and shows how these plans, and planning systems more generally, have been shaped by the dominant ideology and practices referred to as 'neoliberalism'. This is followed by an assessment of the achievements of metropolitan plans and leads to an overall conclusion that there remains a significant gap between the ambitions of the plans and the evolving character of the metropolitan regions.

Strategic Spatial Planning

A rich literature has developed in recent decades about emerging styles of strategic spatial planning, led in particular by European planning theorists (see, for example, Albrechts, 2006, 2011, 2017; Healey, 2007; Hillier, 2007; Albrechts *et al.*, 2017). The essence of strategic spatial planning is defined succinctly by Albrechts (2011, p. 79) as:

> a transformative and integrative public-sector led, and socio-spatial process through which visions/frames of reference, justification for coherent actions, and means for implementation are produced that shape and frame what a place is and what it might become.

This is a targeted process, focusing on a limited number of key issues likely to shape the future trajectory of a metropolitan region, and also a normative process, underpinned by notions of what ought to be – the 'issues that really matter' (Albrechts, 2011, p. 82). Implementation also requires careful consideration, encompassing strategies to engage multiple actors, shorter-term action plans and explicit budget commitments.

In the European context such strategic spatial plans came increasingly to be described as 'relational' in the early twenty-first century, drawing in particular on the popularity amongst geographers of views of space which gave rise to new conceptions of cities and regions as:

nodes that gather flow and juxtapose diversity, as places of overlapping but not necessarily locally connected relational networks, as perforated entities with connections that stretch far back in time and space. (Amin, 2004, p. 34)

The eminent British planning theorist Patsy Healey (2007) explained the shift towards a relational view of strategic spatial planning as follows:

In the confident mid-twentieth century, an urban area was understood as a coherent entity, with a concrete physical pattern expressing a simple relation between economic and social dynamics on an environmental surface. Such an entity could be managed by strong spatial plans backed by powers of public ownership of land and engagement in development activity. This conception has given way to the contemporary recognition of the complexity of the relations that co-exist and transect in urban areas and the range of governance processes which affect how these relations evolve. (Healey, 2007, p. 266)

This complexity, according to Healey (2007, p. 267), required a new form of spatial strategy which was less a rigid plan and more a frame of reference:

Strategies exist as revisable, fluid conceptions continually interacting with unfolding experiences and understandings, but yet holding in attention some orienting sensibility. Such a notion of evolving strategy, continually in formulation, is a necessary complement to the recognition of the relational multiplicity of the lived experiences of contemporary urban worlds.

McCosker and Searle have suggested recently that, while relational thinking has certainly influenced recent Australian metropolitan plans, most retain elements of a traditional blueprint form. They ascribe this to:

an institutional context in which state governments had sole constitutional responsibility for urban planning and development and a historical context whereby they operated or had close regulatory control over major urban infrastructure. (McCosker and Searle, 2017, p. 671)

In other words, there is a clear path dependency between this historical context and the characteristics of the crop of metropolitan planning strategies prepared in the early twenty-first century. But the style and nature of these strategies have also, inevitably, been modified in recent decades by broader forces of globalization and neoliberalism, leading to hybrid metropolitan plans which combine global practices with distinctly Australian cultural and spatial elements, and which reflect changes in the relationship between public agencies and private developers in the building and management of Australian cities.

The Framework for the Book

The Australian Metropolis: A Planning History (Hamnett and Freestone, 2000) was a first attempt to provide a single-volume introduction to the historical development of metropolitan planning in Australia. It traced the evolution of metropolitan planning from the first colonial settlements to the late 1990s, by which time most state governments were pursuing strategies intended to make their capital city-regions more sustainable, particularly through encouraging more compact urban forms and reduced car dependency. This growing environmental awareness was seen as underpinning some renewed popular and political support for public planning, but at odds with broader currents of 'market-triumphalism', preoccupied with deregulation, market-based solutions to public policy issues and the growth and global competiveness of Australia's cities.

The first of a biennial series of conferences on the 'State of Australian Cities' was held in 2003 and these have contributed significantly to a growing body of academic urban research which has allowed the complexity of Australian cities to be better understood. A number of commentators have also focused specifically on metropolitan planning issues and the chapters which follow draw from their theoretical, thematic and comparative research (see, amongst others, Gleeson and Low, 2000; Gleeson *et al.*, 2004, 2010; Forster, 2006; Dodson, 2009; Searle and Bunker, 2010; Abbott, 2011; Davidson and Arman, 2014). The issues identified in *The Australian Metropolis* at the end of the twentieth century have not disappeared and some have intensified. There are also new agendas – economic, social, technological, and environmental – which are reshaping Australian cities in the twenty-first century. These include some evidence of a willingness to experiment with new forms of metropolitan governance and a revived, if spasmodic, interest in cities on the part of the Commonwealth government, tending to emphasize the contribution of well-planned and efficient cities to national productivity (Productivity Commission, 2011; Commonwealth of Australia, 2016).

This new book looks at what has happened to Australian metropolitan planning in the years since *The Australian Metropolis* was published.[1] As with the original work, the book comprises invited chapters from expert contributors. But rather than covering large periods of time synoptically and sequentially, here the brief was to focus more intensively on the recent history of specific cities. Each chapter covers some common ground, but they were not written to a strict template. Each thus reflects the style and interests of its authors and their perceptions of the particular factors of significance in shaping their city and its plans.

This introductory chapter is followed by a historical chapter which both consolidates the major findings from *The Australian Metropolis* and draws on recent planning history literature to provide a common historical prolegomenon. Thereafter, five chapters describe and analyze the metropolitan strategic planning experiences since 2000 of Australia's major cities – Melbourne, Sydney, Adelaide, Perth and the urban region of South-East Queensland, centred on Brisbane. A further chapter deals with the recent history of Canberra, included as the national capital and in deference to its place in planning history. The smaller state and territory capitals of Hobart and Darwin are not discussed in detail but their experiences have elements in common with those of the major cities. The book ends with an essay on the metropolitan condition reflecting on the recent history recounted and the future prospects of the Australian metropolis.

The Changing Nature of Australian Society and its Cities

Australia's Economy in the Twenty-First Century

The Australian Metropolis reflected on some fundamental changes to Australian society which became apparent in the closing decades of the twentieth century. The changing economic environment was central. In his influential text *The End of Certainty*, the journalist Paul Kelly described how the Hawke-Keating Labor national governments of the 1980s oversaw the dismantling of 'the old protected Fortress Australia' (1992, p. 13) and opened up the Australian economy to the world. This led to an increased emphasis on what was described as 'economic rationalism' (Pusey, 1992) and to demands for greater efficiency and competitiveness, to be obtained by privatizing or 'outsourcing' traditionally public responsibilities, with a consequential reduction in the size of the public service. Gleeson and Low (2000, p. 35) noted that Kelly also described not only what we now recognize as an inexorable progression to neoliberalism but a parallel transition from 'a relatively stable, homogeneous society towards a more volatile, more sophisticated, and certainly more diverse social formation'. While they questioned how homogeneous Australian society actually was in earlier times, Gleeson and Low concurred with Kelly's conclusions about the pace of social change in the late twentieth century, which fostered 'new senses of diversity and insecurity in the popular imagination' (2000, p. 36).

In the twenty-first century Australia's economic fortunes have become increasingly dependent on Asian trading partners as the world has entered the 'Asian century'. The opening decade saw strong and sustained economic growth. This slowed after the Global Financial Crisis of 2007–2008, although Australia weathered this better than most developed countries. This was partly as a consequence of a brief return to Keynesian policies, but also principally thanks to a serendipitous resource boom triggered by rising levels of industrial activity and consumption amongst Australia's largest trading partners, particularly China. The resource boom inevitably came to an end, with iron ore prices falling from US\$160 a tonne in 2011 to less than US\$40 a tonne in 2015, although commodity prices have recovered somewhat since then. The national economy continues to grow slowly, buoyed by increased public investment, growth in the 'knowledge economy' and by a strong agricultural sector.

Population Growth, Change and Distribution

The national population in June 2015 of a little over 24 million (ABS, 2017) is projected to double by 2075 (ABS, 2013). The rate of population growth remains high relative to that of most other Organisation for Economic Co-operation and Development countries (OECD, 2016). At the time of the 2011 census – the most recent census for which data are available – over 85 per cent of Australians lived in urban areas (ABS, 2014). At June 2015, an estimated 15.9 million people, around two-thirds of Australia's population, lived in the greater capital city areas which together accounted for 82 per cent of national population growth between June 2015 and June 2016 (ABS, 2017).

The national population is ageing – between 1996 and 2016 the proportion of Australia's population aged 65 years and older increased from 12 per cent to 15.3 per cent and the proportion of people aged 85 years and over almost doubled from 1.1 per cent of the total population in 1996 to 2.0 per cent in 2016 (ABS, 2016).

The proportion of the population born overseas reached 28 per cent or 6.6 million people in 2015 (ABS, 2015). For most of its history Australia's migrant population came largely from Europe, but the last two decades have seen a major shift, with a greater number of migrants now coming from Asia, especially India and China. Immigration is increasingly geared to the needs of the labour market. Australia is a highly multicultural 'cosmopolitan democracy' (see Maginn and Hamnett, 2016), but it is changing 'from a settler immigration country to one where guest workers are arriving in large and increasing numbers' (Collins, 2013). In 2015–2016 there were just under 190,000 new permanent migrants of whom about two-thirds came as 'skilled migrants' with the balance primarily having some family relationship to an Australian citizen or permanent resident (Department of Immigration and Border Protection, 2016). Temporary migrants now outnumber permanent migrants and are dominated by international students, of whom there were more than 300,000 in 2015–2016. There were also some 85,000 workers on short-term employment (or 457) visas and a further group numbering about 17,500 entered Australia under the humanitarian programme (i.e. as refugees) in 2015–2016 (Phillips and Simon-Davies, 2017). Net overseas migration was the major component of total national population growth for the year ended June 2016, accounting for 53.9 per cent (ABS, 2016).

Australia's indigenous population also increasingly resides in major cities, with about half of the indigenous populations of South Australia and Victoria found, respectively, in Adelaide and Melbourne (Wensing and Porter, 2016).

Australia's distinctive pattern of urban settlement, evolving at the interface of colonial economic development and environmental constraints favouring the eastern and southern seaboards, was etched early to drive the path-dependent geography still evident today (see, for example, McCarty, 1974; Maher, 1985). In 1901, when Australia's six separate colonies established a federation, more than

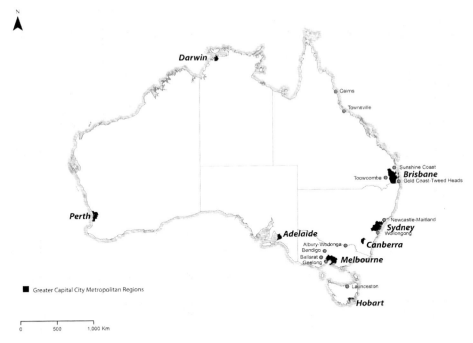

Figure 1.1. Greater capital city metropolitan regions. (*Source*: adapted from ABS, 2011; 2017; and see also http://stat.abs.gov.au/itt/r.jsp?ABSMaps)

half of the population lived in centres of 2,500 or more (Logan *et al.*, 1981). This degree of urbanization was higher than that of any comparable country at the time and it has increased since. It pointed to 'metropolitan primacy' as the normal state for the Australian urban system (BITRE, 2014).

Urban hotspots in rural and regional Australia are driven largely by resource development (Tonts *et al.*, 2016), 'sea-change' and 'tree-change' retirement and relocation (Gurran *et al.*, 2005; Osbaldiston, 2012), and tourism (Mullins, 2003), but the overall non-metropolitan trajectory is one of 'shrinking cities' (Martinez-Fernandez *et al.*, 2016), especially for smaller and remote country towns.

In 2016 Greater Sydney was Australia's largest city and its population reached 5 million in the course of the year. Greater Perth has been the fastest growing capital city for most of the twenty-first century, increasing its population from 1.45 million in 2001 to more than 2 million in 2016, but Melbourne was the fastest growing city in 2015–2016, increasing its population by 2.4 per cent to over 4.6 million people. Adelaide was a larger city than Perth in the early 1980s but it is now significantly smaller, with slightly more than 1.3 million people in 2016, and it has the slowest population growth rate of mainland capital cities, increasing by only 0.7 per cent in 2015–2016. Canberra grew by 1.3 per cent over the same period to a population slightly below 400,000. The greater capital city areas continue to grow more quickly than the national average and the urban clusters around Sydney, Melbourne, Brisbane and Perth will together grow from 12.8 million in 2011 to

Table 1.1. Population growth of Greater Capital City Statistical Areas 2001–2016.

	2001 ERP	2011 ERP	% change 2001–2011	2016 ERP	% change 2011–2016	% change 2015–2016
Greater Sydney	4,128,347	4,605,992	11.6	5,005,358	8.6	1.7
Greater Melbourne	3,521,939	4,169,103	18.4	4,641,636	11.3	2.4
Greater Brisbane	1,714,320	2,146,577	25.2	2,349,699	9.5	1.8
Greater Adelaide	1,154,742	1,262,940	9.4	1,326,354	5.0	0.7
Greater Perth	1,452,058	1,832,114	26.2	2,066,564	12.8	1.3
ACT	319,317	367,752	15.2	396,294	7.8	1.3
Greater Darwin	106,842	129,062	20.8	143,629	11.3	0.8
Greater Hobart	198,296	216,276	9.1	222,802	3.0	0.8

Source: Derived from ABS (2017) *Regional Population Growth, Australia, 2015–16: Estimated Resident Population (ERP), Greater Capital City Statistical Areas*; ABS 2011 census data; and earlier releases of ABS Cat. 3218.0 data.

18.6 million by 2031, thereby accounting for almost three-quarters of Australia's total population growth over that period (Coleman, 2017). By the middle of the twenty-first century both Sydney and Melbourne are projected to have populations of around 8 million (ABS, 2013).

A recent article by George Megalogenis goes beyond simple population metrics to propose a spatial categorization of different parts of Australia based on economic and demographic trends. This provides a broad but useful context for the discussion of the development of particular states and cities. Megalogenis suggests that, as a result of recent economic and social trends, Australia now comprises three distinct economic and cultural zones:

> The people most comfortable with globalization in the Asian century live in the south-east corner: New South Wales, Victoria and the ACT. These states (and territory) generally pay their own way in the federation. (Megalogenis 2016/17, pp. 13–14)

The other two zones comprise the mining states of Queensland and Western Australia which 'track the extremes of our national income, collecting the greatest windfall in the boom and suffering the hardest landing in the bust'; and the 'outsider belt' of Tasmania, South Australia and the Northern Territory, the places most dependent on government welfare.

Change within Metropolitan Regions

While aggregate descriptions of demographic and economic trends at the national and metropolitan level provide important context, there are also significant changes occurring within metropolitan regions. The effects of long-established policies of urban consolidation are becoming increasingly evident in a shift towards higher-density development in all major cities, particularly in the inner suburbs. The pressure to redevelop existing urban areas at higher densities has led to the displacement of existing uses as 'upzoning' encourages urban renewal to push up property prices (Bunker, 2015*a*, p. 19).

The change in urban densities in Australia's largest cities has been accompanied by an increase in the number of semi-detached and apartment dwellings. The number of detached dwellings is declining as a proportion of all dwellings, while the number of medium- and higher-density dwellings is increasing, especially in the inner parts of the larger cities (SGS Economics and Planning, 2013). In Sydney semi-detached and apartment dwellings made up 56 per cent of all new dwellings built between 2001 and 2011. In Melbourne higher-density housing made up only 24 per cent of the housing stock of the city in 2001 but by 2011 it accounted for 29 per cent (Commonwealth of Australia, 2015).

These recent changes to the housing stock are significant although, after more than a century of housing development focused mainly on the construction of detached housing, it will take decades to bring about truly transformative shifts in the mix of housing types right across each city. Detached housing continues to grow strongly in many metropolitan fringe locations and, in 2009, new freestanding houses in Australia had a median floor area of 240 square metres, making them amongst the largest in the world (Kellett, 2016, p. 149). Despite the move towards higher densities in and around the urban cores, Australia's major cities thus remain essentially suburban in character and recent research has estimated that more than three-quarters of the population of the largest cities continue to live in suburbs (Gordon *et al.*, 2015).

Nearly 70 per cent of Australian households own or are purchasing their homes but home ownership is harder to achieve for younger Australians than was the case for earlier generations. Housing is particularly unaffordable in the inner parts of the two largest cities of Sydney and Melbourne, leading to continuing pressure to increase the supply of housing land, to drive up housing densities and to reform planning systems which, under neoliberal governance, are held to be constraints on housing supply and on economic development more generally.

Most cities have gradually assumed more polycentric forms, albeit with secondary suburban activity centres and employment zones complementing rather than challenging traditional Central Business Districts (CBDs). Only Parramatta in Sydney approaches the scale of a genuine second CBD.

A major issue is that of inequity within the major cities. In 2008 McGuirk (2008, p. 255) observed that 'Australia's large cities have begun to exhibit development trends and social tendencies symptomatic of intensified social stratification and of straining social cohesion'. More recently, Randolph and Tice (2016) have demonstrated that urban inequality continues to rise and have traced the 'suburbanization of disadvantage' in Australia's major cities. While patterns of disadvantage are complex, they perpetuate a long-standing concern in Australian urban policy with the unequal life chances of people in inner and outer suburbs.

New jobs in the knowledge economy are replacing traditional manufacturing jobs to some extent but tend to be located in inner areas, leaving reduced employment opportunities in outer suburbs (Bunker *et al.*, 2017), while out-commuting rates from outer suburbs and travel distances to work have increased in recent years (Fagan and O'Neill, 2015). Overall, Dodson (2016*b*) has concluded that:

> After three decades of market-driven urbanisation, our cities have become engines of social inequality. The rich have been lifted, inflating housing markets and capturing sites with the best government services and infrastructure and near to high-paid jobs. The poor are displaced to cheaper distant sites where employment, infrastructure and services are lean.

Public transport is readily accessible in inner suburbs but this tends not to be the case in middle and outer suburbs, where commuting distances are also inevitably longer and where cross-suburban services are generally lacking. The middle and outer suburbs of the major cities are where 'the labour force is less skilled, unemployment is greatest, housing stresses are most acute and dependence on automobiles for travel is most entrenched' (Dodson, 2016*a*, p. 26).

Part of the logic of the push for more compact cities is to make public transport accessible to more people in dense transport corridors, although the late Paul Mees argued persuasively that low-density cities could still have excellent public transport without forcing up urban densities (Mees, 2000; 2010). Burke (2016) has also pointed to the potential of the extensive but underused rail networks found in most larger Australian cities, although he observes that the failure to pursue these and other alternative ways of increasing public transport's share of journeys has had much to do with the power of the constituency of land developers, freight companies, car manufacturers, 'big oil', road agencies and infrastructure providers which has long supported road construction. Investment in urban public transport was not helped during the period of the Abbott Liberal–National Coalition government (2013–2015) by a Prime Minister who believed that:

> there just aren't enough people wanting to go from a particular place to a particular destination at a particular time to justify any vehicle larger than a car, and cars need roads. (Abbott, 2009, p. 174)

Malcolm Turnbull, who replaced Abbott as Prime Minister in 2015, has more conventional views on the respective roles of private and public transport, pledging Commonwealth support for a light rail extension on the Gold Coast in his first week in office. The emphasis under his leadership appears to be on a higher level of private sector involvement in the provision of urban infrastructure including the development of funding arrangements which, to date, have been relatively little used in Australia – notably 'value capture', the taxing of the increased property values derived from major infrastructure investment to recoup part of the capital outlay (Burke, 2016; Department of Infrastructure and Regional Development, 2016).

Climate Change and Sustainability

Evidence that Australia's large, car-dependent metropolitan regions are unsustainable continues to mount. Higher temperatures, a decline in rainfall in major settled areas and the threat of sea level rise are already posing important challenges to coastal towns and cities (Kellett, 2016). Climate change was defined by former Prime Minister Kevin Rudd in 2007 as 'the great moral challenge of our generation' (Rudd, 2007), but it slipped down the agenda of national political priorities thereafter, especially between 2013 and 2015, as did policies to encourage a shift from fossil fuels to renewable energy.

Australia is rich in gas, coal, uranium, hydro-electric power and various forms of renewable energy, with some states likely to achieve as much as half of their electricity from renewable sources in the next few years. Yet it appears at present that national energy policy is incoherent and stranded in an ideological and Commonwealth-state impasse. Meanwhile, evidence continues to grow of the vulnerability of Australian cities to climate-related events and other 'natural' disasters (Kellett, 2016).

Metropolitan Governance

Responsibility for the planning of Australia's metropolitan areas remains primarily with state governments. These governments continue to have the advantage of responsibility and resourcing for many key planning policies relating to physical infrastructure, transport, elements of housing policy, urban renewal and the assessment of significant projects, amongst others. Effective implementation, however, has long been constrained by the silo-like organization of state agencies and by adversarial relationships between different levels of government (Stilwell and Troy, 2000).

The Australian Metropolis described the various brief episodes of engagement with cities by the Commonwealth government to the end of the twentieth century – the postwar reconstruction era of the 1940s, the ambitious aspirations of the Whitlam Government between 1972 and 1975 and the Hawke and Keating governments' Building Better Cities Program between 1991 and 1996. The election of the Rudd Labor government in 2007 brought a renewed Commonwealth interest in urban questions and led to the establishment of two principal urban policy streams – a Commonwealth infrastructure programme and the development of a national urban policy (Burton and Dodson, 2014). The latter was complemented by reform initiatives from the Council of Australian Governments (COAG), which sought to establish national principles for best practice metropolitan planning and to encourage metropolitan plans which conformed with those principles (COAG, 2009; COAG Reform Council, 2012).

The COAG Reform Council noted the need for some 'reconsideration of Australia's settlement pattern' (2012, p. 2), although little of this has occurred, despite the urgings of some academic commentators (see, in particular, Weller and Bolleter, 2013). Indeed, with the election of the Abbott government in 2013, urban issues largely disappeared from the national agenda, but in 2015 the Turnbull government appointed a Minister for Cities, the first such appointment ever on the conservative side of Australian politics (albeit soon downgraded to 'Assistant' status following a ministerial reshuffle early in 2016). Since then slow progress has been made on an urban agenda under the rubric of 'Smart Cities'. Key elements of this agenda include the twin propositions that Australia's growth as a knowledge based economy, and the prosperity that this may offer, depends on the orderly growth of the major cities and the regions surrounding them; and that 'smart investment that enables partnerships between governments and the private sector will deliver better infrastructure sooner, and within budget constraints' (Commonwealth of Australia, 2016, p. 3). The first significant initiative in 2017 was a A\$50 million 'Smart Cities and Suburbs' programme to fund projects utilizing innovative, technology-based approaches to improve urban liveability.

Turnbull's new urban agenda also includes an adaptation of the UK government's approach to 'City Deals' – collaborative ventures between local councils, state governments and the Commonwealth to identify local economic development projects which then become the subject of a 'deal' to secure the necessary funding (Burton, 2016). There is not yet much to see as a result of these new urban initiatives, but clearly they do not involve any direct return to the social justice concerns that inspired Commonwealth urban policy at earlier times. Rather, the emphasis seems to rest squarely on the assumption that the building of more highways, airports, rail lines and digital networks will improve people's employment prospects and thus the quality of their lives.

A recurring theme in recent Australian urban scholarship has been that of a 'governance deficit' between the contemporary challenges facing Australian cities and the planning arrangements and policies of various levels of government (Gleeson *et al.*, 2010, 2012; Tomlinson, 2017). As a consequence, metropolitan planning is undertaken in a fragmented way by a range of state and local agencies. It is also increasingly influenced by the large, private sector interests that now own and operate key elements of urban infrastructure. For much of the period examined in this book there were no responsible forums or authorities capable of guiding urban development in metropolitan regions in a way that brings together and transcends the conflicting priorities of state, local and Commonwealth governments. In recent times, however, there have been tentative steps towards better collaborative arrangements between different levels of government, primarily through COAG. The establishment of a Greater Sydney Commission in 2015 to better guide and coordinate strategic property, transport and housing development at a regional level in that city may mark the beginning of a new era in metropolitan governance.

Metropolitan Plans in the Early Twenty-First Century

In addressing old and new forces and manifestations of change and disruption, every mainland state capital city has been through several iterations of metropolitan plan-making since 2000 (table 1.2). Metropolitan plans are being revised or replaced more frequently, often as the consequence of a change of state government as much as the need to respond to emergent urban challenges.

The Metropolitan Plans and their Characteristics

What general characteristics can be identified from studying Australian metropolitan plans of the early twenty-first century? Several observers have picked up on certain common aspirations including Forster (2006) who identified a 'consensus' around three main objectives in the earliest part of the period under review, namely: 'containment', 'consolidation' and 'centres'.

The most common form of plan retains elements of earlier traditional, detailed spatial blueprints, reflective of the dominance of state governments in planning, their monopoly of most physical infrastructure, their longstanding orientation towards greenfield growth and the predominantly physical means of implementation available to them (Searle and Bunker, 2010; McCosker and Searle, 2017). But there is also clear evidence in more recent plans of the incorporation of relational elements – arcs, nodes, networks and flows of people and goods – leading to more hybrid metropolitan strategies which are indicative, aspirational and layered rather than didactically prescriptive, while still retaining, to varying degrees, firm housing and employment targets (Searle, 2013).

Plan-making processes now also routinely extend beyond government to involve stakeholders and the wider citizenry in the framing of strategies, although few have had the ambition seen in the serious but short-lived attempt of Perth's *Network City* strategy (2004) to adopt a more communicative and deliberative style of metropolitan planning discourse. It is more common, however, for certain stakeholders – especially those in the property development industry – to enjoy higher levels of access to government.

Recent metropolitan plans have also made extensive use of a small number of major national planning consultancies in their preparation, reflecting both the growth of these consultancies and also the 'hollowing out' of planning capacity at state government level after a quarter of a century or so of attempts to reduce the size of the public service.

The plans grow ever-ambitiously. There has been a move towards schemes for extended metropolitan regions – 'Greater Adelaide', 'Greater Sydney', Perth and Peel – often encompassing larger peri-urban fringe areas in consideration of

Table 1.2. Principal metropolitan planning documents 2000–2017 (at May 2017).

Year	City	Plan	Responsible Agency
2002	Melbourne	Melbourne 2030	Victorian Department of Infrastructure
2003	Adelaide	Planning Strategy for Metropolitan Adelaide	Premier of South Australia
2004	Canberra	Canberra Plan	Australian Capital Territory (ACT) Planning and Land Authority
	Perth	Network City	Western Australian Planning Commission (WAPC)
2005	Sydney	Sydney – City of Cities	New South Wales (NSW) Department of Planning
	Brisbane/South East Queensland (SEQ)	SEQ Regional Plan 2005–2026	Queensland Office of Urban Management
2006	Adelaide	Planning Strategy for Metropolitan Adelaide	Government of South Australia
2008	Canberra	Territory Plan	ACT Government
		Canberra Plan: Towards Our Second Century	ACT Government
	Melbourne	Melbourne 2030 – A Planning Update	Victorian Department of Planning and Community Development
2009	Brisbane/SEQ	SEQ Regional Plan 2009–2031	Queensland Department of Infrastructure and Planning
2010	Sydney	Metropolitan Plan for Sydney 2036	NSW Department of Planning
	Adelaide	30 Year Plan for Greater Adelaide	South Australian Department of Planning and Local Government
	Perth	Directions 2031 and Beyond	WAPC
2012	Canberra	Planning Strategy: Planning for a sustainable city	ACT Government: Environment and Sustainable Development Directorate
2014	Sydney	A Plan for Growing Sydney	NSW Department of Planning and Environment
	Melbourne	Plan Melbourne	Victorian Department of Transport, Planning and Local Infrastructure
	Canberra	City Plan	ACT Government
2015	Perth	Draft Perth and Peel @ 3.5 million	WAPC
2016	Brisbane/SEQ	Draft SEQRP: Shaping SEQ	Queensland Department of Infrastructure, Local Government and Planning
	Adelaide	30 Year Plan for Greater Adelaide Update (Draft)	South Australian Department of Planning, Transport and Infrastructure
	Sydney	Towards our Greater Sydney 2056 (Draft)	Greater Sydney Commission
2017	Melbourne	Plan Melbourne 2017–2050	Victorian Department of Environment, Land, Water and Planning

the future growth of the major cities. There have also been experiments with the setting of urban growth boundaries to limit spread and protect environmental and agricultural zones, but with mixed outcomes (Buxton and Taylor, 2009).

The timescale has also extended, with most plans now having 30-year time horizons. In reviewing the metropolitan plans to have appeared since 2000, however, an obvious paradox appears between their detailed long-term housing and population targets, and the frequency with which they have been revised, resonating with Healey's reference, quoted earlier, to a trend towards 'evolving strategy, continually in formulation'. Shorter-term intermediate targets would seem more appropriate in most cases, with longer-term targets, where they are retained, being necessarily more indicative.

Plans also continue to aspire to an ambitious and seamless reconciliation of the 'triple bottom line' of economic, social and environmental sustainability goals, but with an increased emphasis on facilitating economic development through new growth sectors such as finance and property, knowledge industries, communications, producer services and tourism. Employment targets are referred to in most strategies but it is not always clear how these are to be achieved. Notwithstanding planners' traditional desire to see a balance between work and living, the impression remains of a set of growth strategies driven primarily by residential development proposals with few specific policies to stimulate employment in particular locations.

Also observable have been the importation of notions of smart growth, new urbanism, polycentricity and transit-oriented development to flavour the ideas and the language of recent metropolitan plans. The central notion of the compact city remains underpinned by such notions, leading to policies based on mixed-use (re) development in activity centres and along transport corridors. Improvements to public transport and other alternative modes to the private car are seen as necessary conditions for bringing about increased residential densities.

Evidence in most states points to the particular influence of the property industry in encouraging state governments to release additional land at the urban fringe, justified on the basis that a shortage of greenfield land availability is the key factor in making housing more affordable and that opportunities for straightforward brownfield land redevelopment are now declining (Newton *et al.*, 2012*)*. Lobbying from the property industry has also been influential in increasing or removing height limits in central cities.

There has been a substantial amount of investment in infrastructure projects generally, leading to the suggestion that metropolitan spatial plans themselves have become less significant in shaping the growth of major cities than independent infrastructure plans and major projects (Dodson, 2009). While state governments have been the traditional providers of metropolitan transport and 'pipes-and-wires' infrastructure, and retain that oversight, delivery is increasingly sourced through privatized agencies and private–public partnerships.

There is some patchy evidence in the most recent plans of an awareness, based on a growing body of urban research, of the differential trends and patterns of growth within cities – in particular, the divide in access to opportunities and experiences between inner suburbs (more affluent, the focus of jobs in the knowledge economy and more likely to be favoured by substantial urban design interventions) and the outer suburbs (affected by the decline in manufacturing employment, poor public transport and high levels of car dependency). The actual impact of this research on more finely grained policies is harder to discern, however (Kelly and Donegan, 2015). The suburbanization of disadvantage is not a major policy focus of recent metropolitan plans and some recent observers have suggested that they:

> simply ignore much of suburbia, in effect, identifying these areas, where the majority of the urban population live, as a new urban *terra nullius* over which planners appear to have relinquished responsibility and interest. (Pinnegar *et al.*, 2015, p. 280)

Awareness of vulnerability to climate change is reflected in a greater emphasis on 'resilience' and in some detailed strategies on water management, conservation of native vegetation, coastal protection and also agricultural land. However, most responses to climate change in metropolitan plans remain based primarily on higher densities and reduced car use as well as on generalized commitments to more sustainable and resilient cities of the sort with which it would be difficult to disagree.

Metropolitan Plans, Planning Reform and Neoliberalism

Mention was made earlier of the profound changes to the Australian economy and governance which occurred from about the 1980s under what has come to be known internationally as 'neoliberalism' – an ideology which, at root:

> proposes that human wellbeing can best be advanced by the maximization of entrepreneurial freedoms within an institutional framework characterized by private property rights, individual liberty, free markets and free trade. (Harvey, 2006, p. 145)

The recent metropolitan strategic plans for Australian cities have been prepared within a context of ongoing reforms to state planning systems to make them more market-responsive. Planning reform in Australia typically forms part of the broader shift towards neoliberal urban governance (Gleeson and Low, 2000; Sager, 2011), characterized by reduced state involvement, deregulation, an increased emphasis on market mechanisms and a push for more efficient bureaucratic processes to facilitate investment. Reforms to planning systems in most states have included the imposition of simplified and standardized planning provisions across local council areas in pursuit of less 'red tape'; the reduction or removal of third party rights of appeal, intended, in particular, to make it more difficult for local communities to resist higher-density developments; the transfer of significant development control powers from local to state governments; and a much-reduced role for local elected representatives in the assessment of development proposals, with responsibility for approving all but the most minor developments increasingly given to state governments or to expert professional bodies (Buxton and Groenhart, 2013, p. 3).

The reform of local government has also been pursued in most states. Victorian local councils were restructured in the 1990s to provide a smaller number of larger authorities and a similar process is currently underway in Sydney. Queensland has a tradition of large, powerful local governments (McCosker and Searle, 2017) whereas the smallest metropolitan council in Adelaide has fewer than 10,000 people.

While certain broad tendencies are obvious, the precise form that planning reforms have taken has varied from state to state and from time to time according to factors such as changes to government, the historical pattern of powers and responsibilities and local economic circumstances (Gurran and Phibbs, 2014). This is not surprising. Allmendinger and Haughton (2013, p. 8) have pointed out that:

> the term neoliberalism is widely and sometimes misleadingly used as shorthand for what are in reality fast evolving, multi-faceted and spatially variable practices and policies to support a market-enabling approach.

In similar vein, Miller and Orchard (2014, p.7) have described neoliberalism as 'a dynamic, complex, multifaceted, even contradictory set of ideas', while McGuirk (2005, p. 60) has referred to 'hybrid neoliberalisms' (see also Bunker *et al.*, 2017). Thus, from time to time the neoliberal agenda might be advanced not by winding back planning controls but by more and more nuanced state-driven *dirigiste* planning policies (Peck *et al.*, 2009). For example, the privatization of Australia's airports since the late 1990s, leading to significant employment nodes in most metropolitan areas, has been accompanied by ongoing modifications to legislation and regulations (Freestone, 2011). Meanwhile, major land developers tend to be firm supporters of government intervention when it reduces investment uncertainty.

Allmendinger and Haughton (2013, p. 10) further suggest that:

> the introduction of policies such as climate change into planning objectives and tools could be understood as neoliberal setbacks, but a closer examination would reveal other possibilities and dimensions including the need for planning to demonstrate continued legitimacy.

The need to seek legitimacy by addressing public concerns about issues such as social exclusion or sustainable development leads to the advocacy in most metropolitan plans of a seamless integration of economic, social and environmental policies. There are tensions, however, between the competing notions of planning which underlie different strands of the plans – for example, planning as a facilitator of markets and economic growth; planning as a communicative activity and as a forum for dialogue; and planning as a process for achieving certain public ends, such as sustainability or affordable housing. These tensions are typically not resolved simply by including mutually-conflicting ideas within the pages of a single strategic planning document.

The Achievements of Metropolitan Plans

A broad scan of the outcomes of metropolitan plans over the period studied leads to the following observations about their achievements (see also COAG Reform Council, 2012; Bunker, 2014; Hamnett and Maginn, 2016; Hamnett and Freestone, 2016).

First, a much wider variety of dwellings is now being constructed in a range of locations. Building of medium-density development has increased everywhere and high-rise apartment living is now increasingly evident in the central and inner parts of major cities. New vertiginous precincts present their own challenges in social, environmental and design terms.

Second, most cities have fallen short of their ambitious targets for infill development, in part because of the continuing release of land for development at the urban fringe within generous and regularly revised urban growth boundaries. Recent plans do show some evidence of a quickening of the pace of infill development, however, leading in turn to ever higher targets for densification and renewal.

Third, and despite a major focus on housing supply and the release of developable land, metropolitan plans have been relatively ineffective in relation to housing affordability. This reflects to a significant extent the unwillingness of successive Commonwealth governments to adopt housing policies which seek to intervene in Australia's 'deeply speculative housing property market' (Troy, 2017, p. 1). To quote the late Hugh Stretton: 'Whether for market demand or for human need, we have a serious failure of supply and no current program, public or private, to correct it' (Stretton, 2005, p. 123).

Fourth, investment in public transport has been generally inadequate to support the aspirations for transit-oriented development. Where increases in public transport ridership have been noted, these tend to be primarily in journeys to the CBD or within the better served inner suburbs (the areas also where most increases in walking and cycling are observed). The failure to provide a sufficient amount of accessible and well-managed public transport has been a conspicuous obstacle to the achievement of more compact urban form to date in most major cities. Significant investments in new rail and tram projects have been made or announced recently in some cities, but these remain vulnerable to short-term changes in political direction at both state and Commonwealth levels.

Fifth, there is considerable investment, particularly in inner-city brownfield locations, which is usually guided by state government economic development directives through special planning arrangements sitting outside, only lightly connected to or otherwise needing to be retrofitted to metropolitan strategies. The revitalization and continual upscaling of the Barangaroo precinct as a waterfront extension to Sydney's CBD under the auspices of a light-handed special 'delivery authority' has been particularly controversial.

Finally, there is evidence that, while the policy of concentrating mixed uses and activities in a hierarchy of activity centres has been effective in a few major locations, employment in middle and outer suburbs remains widely dispersed. A recent study of employment patterns in Western Sydney found that, despite the objectives of metropolitan strategies since the 1980s, levels of regionalization and self-sufficiency in the Greater Western Sydney labour market have fallen and out-commuting rates and travel distances to work have increased (Fagan and O'Neill, 2015). Poor access to employment has also raised unemployment levels, led some workers to withdraw from the labour market and generally exacerbated labour market inequalities.

Conclusion

This last point leads into a more general observation. Overall, despite the gains that all metropolitan planning strategies can point to across targets such as increased job-creating development, densification, open space, promotion of active transport, conservation and urban design standards, there remains a demonstrable gap between plans and reality. Forster observed in 2006 that current metropolitan planning strategies suggest 'an inflexible, over-neat vision for the future that is at odds with the picture of increasing geographical complexity that emerges from recent research on the changing internal structure of our major cities' (Forster, 2006, p. 180). Randolph (2013, p. 131) has commented more recently that metropolitan planning still remains 'bedevilled by a lack of understanding of how the cities being planned actually work'.

There is a growing body of academic urban research which provides rich and nuanced understanding of this complexity. Much evidence of plan performance derives from this research. Yet new documents are generally released without explicit reporting of any monitoring or evaluation of previous plans conducted by state planning agencies. The disconnect between academic research and plan-making, despite a widely-professed enthusiasm for 'evidence based' policies, relates to its inaccessibility to practitioners, its lack of detailed immediacy for applied interventions, theoretical drift, a lack of alignment between research need and timelines for delivering results, and a competitive marketplace for policy ideas increasingly dominated by planning and management consultants (Troy, 2013; Bunker, 2015b; Taylor and Hurley, 2015). There is still support, in short, for Forster's proposition of:

... the existence of parallel urban universes: one occupied by metropolitan planning authorities and their containment – consolidation – centres consensus; the other by the realities of the increasingly complex, dispersed, residentially differentiated suburban metropolitan areas most Australians live in. (Forster, 2006, p.180)

The notion of 'parallel universes' is a theme picked up in a concluding essay to this volume by Brendan Gleeson which reflects on the 'metropolitan condition' in contemporary Australia and on the future prospects for Australia's capital city regions. Gleeson suggests that, a decade or so after Forster wrote these words, Australian cities have made little progress, under weak metropolitan planning arrangements, towards the long-held aspirations of metropolitan plans for more sustainable resource use, social justice, an innovative, more inclusive economy and a more compact urban form. Rather, under neoliberal governance regimes, they have been shaped primarily by national immigration, tax and finance policies, by disruptive technological innovations, by cultural shifts and by increasingly unrestrained market power.

Gleeson discerns a renewed political interest in managing Australian cities as concerns mount about their dysfunctional elements. He notes recent experiments such as the establishment of the Greater Sydney Commission, but his somewhat bleak prognosis is that these are unlikely to lead to a rebirth of the sort of public planning that characterized the second half of the twentieth century. Rather, as an extension of the privatization of urban infrastructure, services and capabilities which has occurred in recent years, Gleeson foresees the emergence of stronger metropolitan governance from the fusing of private resources with government power in a new form of corporatism.

This book canvasses the many drivers of growth, change and dysfunction that future metropolitan planning of whatever complexion will need to address. Despite the unusual structure of the Australian urban system, many of these challenges are comparable to those faced by metropolitan spatial planning internationally. Australian cities offer a relatively high standard of living, but for this to be maintained and enhanced, metropolitan policy-making will have to increase its capacity and effectiveness in managing the ongoing dynamics and problematics of the metropolitan condition.

References

ABS (Australian Bureau of Statistics) (2011) *Australian Statistical Geography Standard (ASGS): Volume 1 – Main Structure and Greater Capital City Statistical Areas*. Cat 1270.0.55.001. July. Canberra: ABS. Available at: http://www.abs.gov.au/AUSSTATS/abs@.nsf/allprimarymainfeatures/9593E 06A9325683BCA257FED001561EA?opendocument.

ABS (2013) *Population Projections 2012–2101*. Cat 3222.0. Canberra: ABS. Available at: http://www. abs.gov.au/AUSSTATS/abs@.nsf/mf/3222.0.

ABS (2014) *Australian Historical Population Statistics*. Cat 3105.0.65.001. Canberra: ABS. Available at: http://www.abs.gov.au/ausstats/abs@.nsf/PrimaryMainFeatures/3105.0.65.001.

ABS (2015) Overseas Born Aussies hit a 120 Year Peak. Media release 29 January. Canberra: ABS.

Available at: http://www.abs.gov.au/AUSSTATS/abs@.nsf/Previousproducts/3412.0Media%20 Release12013-14?opendocument&tabname=Summary&prodno=3412.0&issue=2013-14&num=&view=.

ABS (2016) *Australian Demographic Statistics, June 2016.* Cat 3101.0. Canberra: ABS. Available at: http://www.abs.gov.au/ausstats/abs@.nsf/mf/3101.0.

ABS (2017) *Regional Population Growth, Australia, 2015-16.* Cat 3218.0. Canberra: ABS. Available at: http://www.abs.gov.au/AUSSTATS/abs@.nsf/mf/3218.0.

Abbott, A. (2009) *Battlelines.* Melbourne: Melbourne University Press.

Abbott, J. (2011) Regions of cities: metropolitan governance and planning in Australia, in Xu, J. and Yeh, A. (eds.) *Governance and Planning of Mega-City Regions: An International Comparative Perspective.* London: Routledge, pp. 72–190.

Albrechts, L. (2006) Shifts in strategic spatial planning? Some evidence from Europe and Australia. *Environment and Planning A*, **38**(6), pp. 1149–1170.

Albrechts, L. (2011) Strategic planning and regional governance in Europe: recent trends and policy responses, in Xu, J. and Yeh, A. (eds.) *Governance and Planning of Mega-City Regions: An International Comparative Perspective.* London: Routledge, pp. 75–98.

Albrechts, L. (2017) Strategic planning as a catalyst for transformative practices, in Haselsberger, B. (ed.) *Encounters in Planning Thought.* London: Routledge, pp. 184–201.

Albrechts, L., Balducci, A. and Hillier, J. (2017) (eds.) *Situated Practices of Strategic Planning.* London: Routledge.

Allmendinger, P. and Haughton, G. (2013) The evolution and trajectories of English spatial governance: 'neoliberal' episodes in planning. *Planning Practice and Research*, **28**(1), pp. 6–26.

Amin, A. (2004) Regions unbound: towards a new politics of place. *Geografiska Annaler*, Series B, **86**(1), pp. 33–44.

BITRE (2014) *The Evolution of Australian Towns.* Report 136, Canberra: Bureau of Infrastructure, Transport and Regional Economics, Department of Infrastructure and Regional Development.

Bunker, R. (2014) How is the compact city faring in Australia? *Planning Practice and Research*, **29**(5), pp. 449–460.

Bunker, R. (2015a) The changing political economy of the compact city and higher density urban renewal in Sydney. Planning in a Market Economy: ARC Discovery Project Working Paper No. 1. Sydney: City Futures Research Centre, Faculty of Built Environment, University of NSW. Available at: https://www.be.unsw.edu.au/sites/default/files/upload/pdf/cityfutures/publications/ othercfresearch/PIME%20Sydney%20Policy%20WP%20Final%201-12-15.pdf.

Bunker, R. (2015b) Linking urban research with planning practice. *Urban Policy and Research*, **33**(3), pp. 362–369.

Bunker, R. and Searle, G. (2009) Theory and practice in metropolitan strategy: situating recent Australian planning. *Urban Policy and Research*, **27**(2), pp. 101–116.

Bunker, R., Crommelin, L., Troy, L., Easthope, H., Pinnegar, S. and Randolph, B. (2017) Managing the transition to a more compact city in Australia. *International Planning Studies*, pp. 1–16. Published online 17 March. Available at: http://www.tandfonline.com/doi/full/10.1080/13563 475.2017.1298435.

Burke, M. (2016) Problems and prospects for public transport planning in Australian cities. *Built Environment*, **42**(1), pp. 37–54.

Burton, P. (2016) City deals: nine reasons this imported model of urban development demands due diligence. *The Conversation.* 2 April. Available at: https://theconversation.com/city-deals-nine-reasons-this-imported-model-of-urban-development-demands-due-diligence-57040.

Burton, P. and Dodson, J. (2014) Australian cities: in pursuit of a national urban policy, in Miller, C. and Orchard, L. (eds.) *Australian Public Policy: Progressive Ideas in the Neo-Liberal Ascendancy.* Bristol: Policy Press, pp. 245–262.

Buxton, M. and Groenhart, L. (2013) System and Strategy: Recent Trends in Governance and Planning Systems in Australia. Paper presented to the State of Australian Cities Conference, November, Sydney. Available at: http://apo.org.au/node/59879.

Buxton, M. and Taylor, E. (2009) Urban Land Supply, Governance and the Pricing of Land. Paper presented to the State of Australian Cities Conference, November, Perth. Available at: http:// apo.org.au/node/60101.

Coleman, S. (2017) *Australia: State of the Environment 2016 – Built Environment*. Independent report to the Australian Government Minister for the Environment and Energy. Canberra: Australian Government Department of the Environment and Energy. Available at: https://soe. environment.gov.au/theme/built-environment.

COAG (2009) *National Objective and Criteria for Future Strategic Planning of Capital Cities*. Council of Australian Governments Meeting, 7 December. Available at: https://www.coag.gov.au/meeting-outcomes/coag-meeting-communiqu%C3%A9-7-december-2009.

COAG Reform Council (2012) *Review of Capital City Strategic Planning Systems*. Report to the Council of Australian Governments. Sydney: COAG Reform Council.

Collins, J. (2013) The changing face of Australian immigration. *The Conversation*, 8 June. Available at: https://theconversation.com/the-changing-face-of-australian-immigration-14984.

Commonwealth of Australia (2015) *State of Australian Cities 2014–2015: Progress in Australian Regions*. Canberra: Department of Infrastructure and Regional Development.

Commonwealth of Australia (2016) *Smart Cities Plan*. Canberra: Department of Prime Minister and Cabinet.

Davidson, K. and Arman, M. (2014) Planning for sustainability: an assessment of recent metropolitan planning strategies and urban policy in Australia. *Australian Planner*, **51**(4), pp. 296–306.

Department of Immigration and Border Protection (2016) *2015–2016 Migration Programme Report*. Programme Year to 30 June 2016. Canberra: Australian Government. Available at: https://www. border.gov.au/ReportsandPublications/Documents/statistics/2015-16-migration-programme-report.pdf.

Department of Infrastructure and Regional Development (2016) *Using Value Capture to Help Deliver Major Land Transport Infrastructure: Roles for the Australian Government*. Discussion Paper. Canberra: Commonwealth of Australia. Available at: http://investment.infrastructure.gov.au/ whatis/Value-Capture-Discussion-Paper.pdf.

Dodson, J. (2009) The 'infrastructure turn' in Australian metropolitan spatial planning. *International Planning Studies*, **14**(2), pp. 109–123.

Dodson, J. (2016*a*) Suburbia in Australian urban policy. *Built Environment*, **42**(1), pp. 23–36.

Dodson, J. (2016*b*) Ideas for Australia: City v4.0, a new model of urban growth and governance for Australia. *The Conversation*. Available at: https://theconversation.com/ideas-for-australia-city-v4-0-a-new-model-of-urban-growth-and-governance-for-australia-56372.

Fagan, R. and O'Neill, P. (2015) *Work, Places and People in Western Sydney: Changing Suburban Labour Markets 2001–2014*. University of Western Sydney: Centre for Western Sydney.

Forster, C. (2006) The challenge of change: Australian cities and urban planning in the new millennium. *Geographical Research*, **44**(2), pp. 173–182.

Freestone, R. (2011) Managing neoliberal urban spaces: commercial property development at Australian airports. *Geographical Research*, **49**(2), pp. 115–131.

Gleeson, B. and Low, N. (2000) *Australian Urban Planning: New Challenges, New Agendas*. Sydney: Allen and Unwin.

Gleeson, B., Darbas, T. and Lawson, S. (2004) Governance, sustainability and recent Australian metropolitan strategies: a socio-theoretic analysis. *Urban Policy and Research*, **22**(4), pp. 345–366.

Gleeson, B., Dodson, J. and Spiller, M. (2010) Metropolitan Governance for the Australian City: The Case for Reform. *Issues Paper 12*. Brisbane: Griffith University Urban Research Program.

Gleeson, B., Dodson, J. and Spiller, M. (2012) Governance, metropolitan planning and city-building: the case for reform, in Tomlinson, R. (ed.) *Australia's Unintended Cities: The Impact of Housing on Urban Development*. Melbourne: CSIRO Publishing, pp. 117–134.

Gordon, D., Maginn, P.J., Biermann, S., Sisson, A., Huston, I. and Moniruzzaman, M. (2015) *Estimating the Size of Australia's Suburban Population*. Perth: University of Western Australia/ PATREC. Available at: http://www.patrec.uwa.edu.au/__data/assets/pdf_file/0005/2808410/ OCT-2015-PATREC-PERSPECTIVES.pdf.

Gurran, N., Squires, C. and Blakely, E. (2005) *Meeting the Sea Change Challenge: Sea Change Communities in Coastal Australia*. Report for the National Sea Change Task Force. Sydney: University of Sydney/Planning Research Centre.

Gurran, N. and Phibbs, P. (2014) Evidence-free zone? Examining claims about planning performance and reform in New South Wales. *Australian Planner*, **13**(4), pp. 381–407.

Hall, P. (2011) Looking backward, looking forward: the city region of the mid-21st century, in Neuman, M. and Hull, A. (eds.) *The Futures of the City Region*. London: Routledge/Regional Studies Association.

Hamnett, S. and Freestone, R. (2000) (eds.) *The Australian Metropolis: A Planning History*. Sydney: Allen and Unwin.

Hamnett, S. and Freestone, R. (2016) The Australian Metropolis 2000–2015. *Proceedings of the 17th International Planning History Society Conference*, Delft, The Netherlands, 17–21 July. Available at: http://journals.library.tudelft.nl/index.php/iphs/article/view/1324.

Hamnett, S. and Maginn, P.J. (2016) Australian cities in the 21st century: cities and beyond. *Built Environment*, **42**(1), pp. 5–22.

Harvey, D. (2006) Neoliberalism as creative destruction. *Geografiska Annaler*, **88B**(2), pp. 145–158.

Healey, P. (2007) *Urban Complexity and Spatial Strategies: Towards a Relational Planning for Our Times*. London: Routledge.

Hillier, J. (2007) *Stretching Beyond the Horizon: A Multiplanar Theory of Spatial Planning and Governance*. Farnham: Ashgate.

Katz, B. and Bradley, J. (2013) *The Metropolitan Revolution: How Cities and Metros Are Fixing Our Broken Politics and Fragile Economy*. New York: Brookings Institution Press.

Kellett, J. (2016) Australian cities and climate change. *Built Environment*, **42**(1), pp. 145–157.

Kelly, J-F. and Donegan, P. (2015) *City Limits: Why Australia's Cities are Broken and How We Can Fix Them*. Melbourne: Melbourne University Press/Grattan Institute.

Kelly, P. (1992) *The End of Certainty: The Story of the 1980s.* Sydney: Allen and Unwin.

Lang, T. and Török, I. (2017) Metropolitan region policies in the European Union: following national, European or neoliberal agendas? *International Planning Studies*, **22**(1), pp. 1–13. Published on-line at DOI: 10.1080/13563475.2017.1310652

Laquian, A. (2005) *Beyond Metropolis: The Planning and Governance of Asia's Mega-Urban Regions*. Washington DC: Woodrow Wilson Center Press.

Logan, M.I., Whitelaw, J.S. and McKay, J. (1981) *Urbanization: The Australian Experience*. Melbourne: Shillington House.

McCarty, J. (1974) Australian capital cities in the 19th century, in Schedvin, C.B. and McCarty, J. (eds.) *Urbanization in Australia: The 19th Century*. Sydney: Sydney University Press, pp. 11–39.

McCosker, A. and Searle, G. (2017) Towards a classification of world metropolitan spatial strategies: a comparative analysis of ten plans. *Town Planning Review*, **87**(6), pp. 655–680.

McGuirk, P. (2005) Neoliberalist planning? Re-thinking and re-casting Sydney's metropolitan planning. *Geographical Research*, **43**(1), pp. 59–70.

McGuirk, P. (2008) Building the capacity to govern the Australian metropolis. *Built Environment*, **34**(3), pp. 255–272.

Maginn, P.J. and Hamnett, S. (2016) Multiculturalism and metropolitan Australia: demographic change and implications for strategic planning. *Built Environment*, **42**(1), pp. 120–144.

Maher, C. (1985) The changing character of Australian urban growth. *Built Environment*, **11**(2), pp. 69–82.

Martinez-Fernandez, C., Weyman, T., Fol, S., Audirac, I., Cunningham-Sabot, E., Wiechmann, T. and Yahagi, H. (2016) Shrinking cities in Australia, Japan, Europe and the USA: from a global process to local policy responses. *Progress in Planning*, **105**, pp. 1–48.

Mees, P. (2000) *A Very Public Solution: Transport in the Dispersed City*. Melbourne: Melbourne University Press.

Mees, P. (2010) *Transport for Suburbia: Beyond the Automobile Age*. London: Earthscan.

Megalogenis, G. (2016/17) Australia divided. *The Monthly*, December 2016/January 2017, pp. 12–15.

Miller, C. and Orchard, L. (eds.) (2014) *Australian Public Policy: Progressive Ideas in the Neo-liberal Ascendancy*. Bristol: Policy Press.

Mullins, P. (2003) The evolution of Australian tourism urbanization, in Hoffman, L.M., Fainstein, S.S. and Judd, D.R. (eds.) *Cities and Visitors: Regulating People, Markets, and City Space*. Oxford: Blackwell, pp. 126–142.

Murphy, P. (2012) The Metropolis, in Thompson, S. and Maginn, P.J. (eds.) *Planning Australia: An Overview of Urban and Regional Planning,* 2nd ed. Melbourne: Cambridge University Press, pp. 155–179.

Newton, P., Newman, P., Glackin, S. and Trubka, R. (2012) Greening the greyfields: unlocking the redevelopment potential of the middle suburbs in Australian cities. *International Journal of Social, Behavioral, Educational, Economic, Business and Industrial Engineering*, **6**(11), pp. 2870–2899.

OECD (2016) *OECD Factbook 2015–2016: Economic, Environmental and Social Statistics*. Paris: OECD. Available at: http://dx.doi.org/10.1787/factbook-2015-en.

Osbaldiston, N. (2012) *Seeking Authenticity in Place, Culture, and the Self: The Great Urban Escape*. Basingstoke: Palgrave Macmillan.

Peck, J., Theodore, N. and Brenner, N. (2009) Postneoliberalism and its malcontents. *Antipode*, **41**(1), pp. 94–116.

Phillips, J. and Simon-Davis, J. (2017) *Migration to Australia: A Quick Guide to the Statistics*. Parliamentary Library Research Paper Series (updated 18 January). Canberra: Department of Parliamentary Services, Parliament of Australia.

Pinnegar, S., Randolph, B. and Freestone, R. (2015) Incremental urbanism: characteristics and implications of residential renewal through owner-driven demolition and rebuilding. *Town Planning Review*, **86**(3), pp. 279–301.

Productivity Commission (2011) *Performance Benchmarking of Australian Business Regulation: Planning, Zoning and Development Assessments*. Research Report. Melbourne: Commonwealth of Australia.

Pusey, M. (1992) What's wrong with economic rationalism? in Horne, D. (ed.) *The Trouble with Economic Rationalism*. Newham Vic: Scribe, pp. 63–69.

Randolph, B. (2013) Wither urban research? Yes, you read it right first time! *Urban Policy and Research*, **31**(2), pp. 130–133.

Randolph, B. (2015) Metropolitan Governance and Planning. Address to the Future of Cities Roundtable, Melbourne School of Design, 23 October. Available at: http://blogs.unsw.edu.au/cityfutures/blog/2015/10/metro-governance-and-planning/.

Randolph, B. and Tice, A. (2016) Relocating disadvantage in five Australian cities: socio-spatial polarisation under neo-liberalism. *Urban Policy and Research*. Published on-line at http://dx.doi.org/10.1080/08111146.2016.1221337.

Roberts, P., Thomas, K. and Williams, G. (1998) (eds.) *Metropolitan Planning in Britain: A Comparative Study*. London: Jessica Kingsley.

Ross, C. (2009) *Megaregions: Planning for Global Competitiveness*. Washington DC: Island Press.

Rosan, C. (2016) *Governing the Fragmented Metropolis: Planning for Regional Sustainability*. Philadelphia, PA: University of Pennsylvania Press.

Rudd, K. (2007) Rudd says climate change is the great moral challenge of our generation. Speech to the National Climate Change Summit, 31 March. Available at: http://australianpolitics.com/2007/08/06/rudd-says-climate-change-is-great-moral-challenge.html.

Sager, T. (2011) Neo-liberal urban planning policies: a literature survey 1990–2010. *Progress in Planning*, **76**(4), pp.147–199.

Sassen, S. (2011) Novel spatial formats: megaregions and global cities, in Xu, J. and Yeh, A. (eds.) *Governance and Planning of Mega-City Regions: An international comparative perspective*. London: Routledge, pp. 101–126.

Searle, G. (2013) 'Relational' planning and recent Sydney metropolitan and city strategies: practice review. *Urban Policy and Research*, **31**(3), pp. 367–378.

Searle, G. and Bunker, R. (2010) Metropolitan strategic planning: an Australian paradigm? *Planning Theory*, **9**(3), pp.163–180.

SGS Economics and Planning (2013) *Infrastructure Investment and Housing Supply*. Canberra: National Housing Supply Council.

Spiller, M. (2014) Social justice and the centralisation of governance in the Australian metropolis: a case study of Melbourne. *Urban Policy and Research*, **32**(3), pp. 361–380.

Stilwell, F. and Troy, P. (2000) Multilevel governance and urban development in Australia. *Urban Studies*, **37**(5/6), pp. 909–930.

Stretton, H. (1974) *Housing and Government* (1974 Boyer Lectures). Sydney: Australian Broadcasting Corporation.

Stretton, H. (2005) *Australia Fair*. Sydney: UNSW Press.

Taylor, E.J. and Hurley, J. (2015) 'Not a lot of people read the stuff': Australian urban research in planning practice. *Urban Policy and Research*, **34**(2), pp. 116–131.

Tomlinson, R. (2017) An argument for metropolitan government in Australia. *Cities*, **63**, pp. 249–253.

Tonts, M., Haslam McKenzie, F. and Plummer, P. (2016) The resource 'super-cycle' and Australia's remote cities. *Built Environment*, **42**(1), pp. 174–188.

Troy, L. (2017) The politics of urban renewal in Sydney's residential apartment market. *Urban Studies*, pp.1–17. Published online on 15 March. Available at: http://journals.sagepub.com/doi/abs/10.1177/0042098017695459.

Troy, P. (2013) Australian urban research and planning. *Urban Policy and Research*, **31**(2), pp. 134–149.

Weller, R. and Bolleter, J. (2013) *Made in Australia: The Future of Australian Cities*. Perth: UWA Press.

Wensing, E. and Porter, L. (2016) Unsettling planning's paradigms: towards a just accommodation of indigenous rights and interests in Australian urban planning? *Australian Planner*, **53**(2), pp. 91–102.

Xu, J. and Yeh, A. (2011) (eds.) *Governance and Planning of Mega-City Regions: An International Comparative Perspective*. London: Routledge.

Note

1.   The editors wish to acknowledge the assistance of Hilary Hamnett in the preparation of the figures in the book; the financial support of the Faculty of Built Environment, UNSW Sydney; Margaret Park for preparing the index; copyright holders for permission to reproduce images and the many others whose assistance is acknowledged in various chapters; and Ann Rudkin, the series editor, for her prompt and rigorous comments on drafts and for her constant encouragement.

Chapter 2

Beginnings: The Evolution of Metropolitan Planning to the Late Twentieth Century

Robert Freestone and *Christine Garnaut*

The future builds upon the past, even when the connections are fractured and disrupted by the dynamism of change. The first post World War Two metropolitan plans built on an earlier generation of plans and provided 'an ideological and institutional substrate' that helped shape 'the ambitions and methodologies' of later strategies (Gleeson *et al.*, 2004, p. 351). Indeed, the long prelude of planning advocacy and experimentation through the nineteenth and early twentieth centuries produced most of the building blocks underpinning the more institutionalized model of planning that followed.

The *Australian Metropolis* (Hamnett and Freestone, 2000) charted an evolution of planning theory and practice to the late 1990s against an evolving backdrop of metropolitan growth and change. This chapter consolidates some of the essential findings from that book and draws on more recent research to provide a prelude to this book's focus on progress and developments in the early twenty-first century. What emerges is a deeper appreciation of a succession of official metropolitan visions and innovations and path dependencies back to the nineteenth century that have sought to influence Australian metropolitan life for the better and which constitute the early chapters of a never-ending story.

The Nineteenth Century

A key intent of Britain's colonization policy was to establish a principal town in each of its imperial outposts. Australia's capital cities developed from those origins. Their coastal location was the direct result of maritime exploration and established a national template for urban settlement still evident today. Their development as administrative, trade and cultural hubs through the nineteenth century laid the foundation for latter day metropolitan primacy (Rose, 1966). The scale of urban development in the Australian colonies was modest and British planning conventions influenced approaches to the laying out of settlements. The initial focus was on gridiron townships that adopted the contained character of Lord Shaftesbury's 'Grand Modell' (Home, 2013). Adelaide, with its rigorous grid of symmetrically aligned streets, squares and encircling ring of parklands, is recognized as an exemplar of this paradigm. However, the discipline inherent in the grid did not carry over into the way that the biggest cities grew. Generally, the suburbs were the product of unplanned, *laissez-faire* driven expansion producing first an inner ring of high-density living which came to be associated with the slum menace and then an outer ring of scattered and uncoordinated low-density suburbs anticipating later problems with urban sprawl. Private speculators led the charge and there was limited government control over building regulations or the orderly provision of infrastructure and public facilities. These circumstances did not change markedly into the early twentieth century.

What did change was the standing of several of the capital cities. Population growth, fuelled substantially by the gold rushes in the eastern colonies from the 1850s, the evolution of the capital cities as centres of trade, and the rise of import-substituting local manufacturing, meant that by the 1880s both Sydney and Melbourne assumed the title of 'metropolis' (Proudfoot, 2000). The population

Figure 2.1. Addressing the problems of 'Marvellous Smellbourne': proposed order of works for a metropolitan sewerage scheme, c1889. (*Source*: Public Records Office of Victoria, VPRS 8609/P20 Historical Records Collection, Unit 332, p. 2.)

and spatial expansion of the cities forced colonial authorities to consider the larger issues associated with servicing and administering the metropolis including water supply, sewage disposal, and public transit. The preferred model was the establishment of specialized state agencies. British precedent influenced pragmatic responses like the formation in 1891 of the Melbourne Metropolitan Board of Works (MMBW) modelled on a similar agency established in London 30 years earlier (figure 2.1). Its attention to water and sewerage led to a significant decline in mortality and morbidity rates within Melbourne's population over the next decade (Buxton *et al.*, 2016).

Some urban reformers looked farther into the future. In his book *Sanitary Reform of Towns and Cities* (1857), Dr William Bland, a member of the Legislative Council of New South Wales, envisioned greater Sydney surrounded by a hierarchy of parks and reserves (Proudfoot, 2000). His emphasis was on improving urban sanitation through chains of open spaces that would provide 'a system of air-channels, for conducting the currents of air now purified, as far as possible … throughout the entire city' (Bland, 1857, p. 20). In his address on 'The Laying Out of Towns' delivered to the Australasian Association for the Advancement of Science in 1890, architect John Sulman endorsed 'the intersecting radial and circumferential lines of a spider's web' in preference to gridiron planning (Freestone, 2000*a*, p. 28). Considering city expansion, Sulman stated that suburbs 'should not be extended too far without a break, and if the admirable example of Adelaide could be followed by introducing a belt of parklands, the gain to the health of the town or city would be great' (reproduced in Sulman, 1921, p. 215). Here Sulman presciently not only anticipated the Garden City model of Ebenezer Howard but also Howard's specific reference to Adelaide to illustrate the concept of multi-centred urban form (Howard, 1902). Both schemes were antipodean echoes of the 1820s proposal of British landscape gardener John Claudius Loudon for alternating rings of buildings and parks for London that he saw being worked out in a greenfield regional setting, as would be required for a new federal capital city in Australia (Loudon, 1829).

The 1900s and 1910s

Much later, the federal capital project did indeed provide a major stimulus to local thinking about city planning as a comprehensive rather than an *ad hoc* process. The 'Congress of Engineers, Architects, Surveyors, and Members of Allied Professions' held in Melbourne in May 1901 to consider 'Questions relating to the Laying Out and Building of the Federal Capital, and matters of professional interest generally' was a landmark event in integrating hitherto piecemeal suggestions into a more complete and prioritized set of understandings for locating, planning and building a *de novo* urban environment (Freestone and Nichols, 2011). The winning scheme for the federal capital competition of 1911–1912, submitted by Chicago-based architects Walter Burley Griffin (1876–1937) and Marion Mahony Griffin (1871–1961), brilliantly demonstrated how that goal could be achieved.

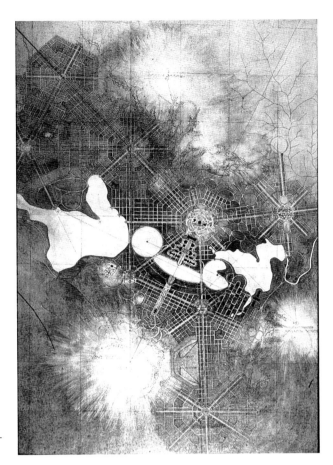

Figure 2.2. A spatial plan for suburban growth: the Griffins' 'City and Environs' competition plan for the federal capital, 1911. (*Source*: Commonwealth of Australia Federal Capital Competition, city and environs, ca.1911, National Library of Australia, NLA-pic-vn3821852-o-v-1)

The Griffins' plan referenced a diversity of disciplinary and cultural influences and ideas. It drew upon world's best practice, notably Burnham and Bennett's seminal *Plan of Chicago* (1909), the orderly approach to city extension planning applied in Germany, and the City Beautiful and Garden City Movements. Its treatment of long-term growth at a metropolitan scale was a distinguishing feature (figure 2.2) with the vision of a 'suburban metropolis structured around a triangulated series of specialized sub-centres and three times as large as the town of 25,000 population required for the competition' (Freestone, 2000a, p. 40).

The first decades of the twentieth century witnessed a new dawn of awareness about the physical and social conditions in Australian cities and led to suggestions and responses to ameliorate them. Initiatives were driven by professional bodies, community organizations like town planning associations, and progressive politicians looking beyond predominantly small-scale and project-focused endeavours towards wider statutory and strategic reforms at the metropolitan level. The Royal Commission for the Improvement of the City of Sydney and Its Suburbs (1908–1909) records this transition (figure 2.3). Although preoccupied with restructuring the central city as a commercial and maritime centre, there

30 • PLANNING METROPOLITAN AUSTRALIA

Figure 2.3. Anticipating transport infrastructure needs: proposals for enhancing Sydney's main roads and railway networks, 1909. (*Source*: Royal Commission for the Improvement of the City of Sydney and Its Suburbs, NSW Parliamentary Papers, 1908–09)

were also bigger ideas about metropolitan transit, a new harbour crossing and the distribution of open spaces (Freestone, 2006, 2007).

The influence of the Garden City Movement was felt mainly in small-scale suburban schemes which not only advanced the causes of enlightened neighbourhood planning but also provided a source for thinking about the city at the larger scale, particularly in relation to the provision and distribution of open space, green belts, and satellite centres (Freestone, 1989; Garnaut, 2000). While partial schemes along these lines emerged for various Australian cities – a greenbelt around Perth, a parkland girdle for Melbourne and an agricultural belt framing Brisbane, for example – the most complete forward-looking vision at metropolitan scale was a 1917 plan for 'Adelaide and Suburbs' by town planning missionary turned state government official Charles Reade (Reade, 1919). His 'innovative scheme' integrated 'a host of novel ideas, notably an outer ring of parklands as a corridor for a parkway belt to help bring some order to the then "outer" suburbs' (Freestone, 2010, p. 140). Although 'well ahead of its time' it was 'largely ignored' (Garnaut, 2008, p. 120).

So, despite the promulgation of such ideas, real progress was negligible and critics lamented their slow uptake. In an August 1918 lecture titled *The Metropolitan Problems of Sydney* delivered to the National Debating Club, politician John

Fitzgerald described Sydney's situation as 'an uncoordinated metropolitan muddle' (quoted in Freestone and Park, 2009, p. 28). Reade characterized the Australian metropolis as 'a metropolitan city without a metropolitan plan' (Reade, 1919, p. 6). An allied source of thinking was addressing the inefficient fragmentation of suburban local government through council amalgamations to facilitate sub-regional planning. This was the 'greater city' movement, set to make by far its most significant impact in Brisbane through the federation of twenty local authorities into one single authority under the *City of Brisbane Act 1924* (Minnery, 2004; Baker, 2012).

The 1920s

National town planning conferences held in Adelaide in 1917 and in Brisbane in 1918 had addressed a range of philosophical and practical topics, foregrounding ideals in relation to 'the organisation, coordination and regulation' of cities (Hutchings, 2000, p. 65). The decade following the conferences challenged 'planning advocates to demonstrate how comprehensive town planning could be used to guide metropolitan growth' (*Ibid.*, p.70). Planned suburbanization came to be regarded as the panacea for the problems of the Australian city. Sulman (1921) canvassed alternate urban forms which graphically captured the advanced thinking emerging from Western Europe and North America through competitions and commissioned plans.

The 1920s was the heyday for emergence of a more scientifically grounded, expert-driven and functional planning, heavily influenced by developments in the United States and more directly anticipating the modern style of planning post World War One. A feature of the American approach was the establishment of city planning commissions comprised of members drawn from government, business and professional circles, and authorized to draw up comprehensive city plans. Several initiatives along these lines were taken in Australia but differed in their mandates as orientated to 'civic–bureaucratic' rather than 'civic–commercial' interests; plan-making rather than plan-implementation; and, most distinctively, metropolitan as opposed to central city issues (Freestone, 2000*b*).

Melbourne's Metropolitan Town Planning Commission was established by an Act of Parliament in 1922. It comprised nine members led by Frank Stapley and undertook various surveys and studies and prepared reports and interim plans, informed by submissions from the Town Planning Association of Victoria (May and Reidy, 2009) and from members of the public on subjects including 'waterways, skywalks and street traffic' (Nichols, 2004, p. 50). The climactic *Plan of General Development* (1929) under the technical leadership of Frederick Cook emphasized transportation, land-use zoning and open space needs for a metropolitan population of 2 million (figure 2.4). It was 'Australia's first comprehensive metropolitan plan' (Hutchings, 2000, p. 71), its representational style reminiscent of the seminal Regional Plan for New York released the same

Figure 2.4. Zoning plan for commercial, residential and industrial land in interwar Melbourne. (*Source*: Metropolitan Town Planning Commission, *Plan of General Development,* Melbourne: Government Printer, 1929; Image courtesy of Department of Environment, Land, Water and Planning, Victoria)

year. Channelling the fears of restrictions on property rights and increased public expenditure as the Great Depression commenced, the Victorian Parliament did not support legislation to establish a Commission-style authority (Freestone and Grubb, 1998). City development was thus left largely 'to the whim of individuals, speculators, and development companies' (Buxton *et al.*, 2016, p. 15).

Inspired by Melbourne, Perth also established a Metropolitan Town Planning Commission in 1927 under the chairmanship of Harold Boas who travelled overseas to examine approaches to town planning in Europe, the United States and Canada (Newman, 2012). The Commission's remit was 'to advise the Government on a general plan for the metropolis, costs of associated public works, administration, transport, zoning, parks, distribution of warehouses and shops, and all of the other complex detail of day-to-day urban planning' (Hutchings, 2000,

p. 73). Its final report, issued in 1930, canvassed the same issues as Melbourne's with an accent on parklands as 'central to the report's vision' (Newman, 2012, p. 208). Although never comprehensively implemented, the work of the Commission laid the ground for the passage of town planning legislation in Western Australia (Freestone, 2010).

Sydney and Brisbane took different directions. In 1922 a Sydney Regional Plan Convention was formed as an adaptation of the organization that instigated the Regional Plan for New York. The loose-knit Convention held together by Norman Weekes 'brought together the rich, the influential and the technically expert' with the aim of formulating the basis of a comprehensive regional plan to be completed by the state government (Hutchings, 2000, p. 71). Initial survey work would assist identification of zones for different land uses and new traffic arteries to relieve city traffic congestion (James, 2008), but the Convention gained no traction with the state government and had disbanded by the end of 1925. That same year in Brisbane the newly formed City Council commenced its own civic survey 'as the basis for a future zoning scheme that would – along with civic improvement projects, improved traffic systems and local projects for embellishment and beautification of the public domain – provide the basis for a "grand design" for the next fifty years' (Minnery, 2004, p. 6). Despite lobbying from the Queensland Town Planning Association, the Brisbane effort also petered out (McConville, 2009).

The 1930s

The Great Depression put paid to the prospect of permanent planning commissions or other mechanisms for implementing metropolitan strategies, plans or policies. The widespread prevalence of poverty, substandard living conditions and inadequate public health provisions meant that a spotlight was shone on housing. The subject was a major focus for state governments and led to legislation to establish public housing authorities, commencing with the South Australian Housing Trust in 1936. Although not a priority, the idea of metropolitan-scale planning was not removed entirely from practitioner and political agendas. In Sydney at the beginning of the decade William McKell, Local Government Minister in the New South Wales Labor Government, engaged Weekes to assist him in drafting a bill for a Greater Sydney Council equipped with planning powers to prepare a metropolitan-wide plan (Auster, 1987; James, 2008). The bill lapsed but again prepared the way for more decisive action in the mid-1940s.

By then metropolitan-scale thinking had re-emerged on government and professional agendas assisted by growing knowledge of advances in regional planning abroad, including the greenbelt towns in the United States and a bolder conceptualization of town and country planning in the United Kingdom. Responding to international developments, in Sydney, town planning advocates like A.J. Brown returned to the garden city idea to shape the form and manage the

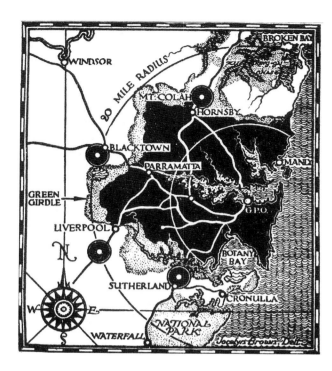

Figure 2.5. 'Green Girdle and Satellites for Sydney': setting 'desirable limits to uninterrupted building development in the metropolitan area'. (Source: Sydney Morning Herald, 4 September 1937; drawing by Jocelyn Brown)

size of the expanding metropolis (figure 2.5). World War Two dampened prospects for practical progress, but a receptive environment for exploring new ideas carried forward under the banner of post-war reconstruction.

The 1940s

The revival of idealism evident from the late 1930s was sustained into the post-war reconstruction period at the same time as 'the political saliency of planning rose to new heights ... and major metropolitan strategic plans appeared in many countries' (Ward, 2002, p. 10). The idea of planning as 'an all-encompassing concept was fundamental to international debates on the need for a new world order of peace and equality', and in Australia this was 'reflected in the mid-century shift towards more government control of the urban development process' (Howe, 2000, p. 80). The Australian Government, which had been largely quiet on city issues since its formation, apart from the special case of the national capital, was suddenly keen to accommodate planning as a progressive force into its agenda, albeit primarily through supporting state governments. This promoted a greater 'integration of economic and social policy with housing and planning strategies' than previously evident (Howe, 2000, p. 80).

In 1942 the Australian Government established the Department of Post-War Reconstruction that in turn sponsored the Commonwealth Housing Commission (CHC) to enquire into projected housing needs across the country. The Commission made recommendations not only in regard to national housing requirements and the design of houses and residential layouts but also for embedding them in rational community plans and metropolitan strategies. State housing agencies established in the 1930s began to take on the character of quasi-metropolitan planning agencies as their remit expanded to the development of metropolitan sites to house growing capital city populations. But there was growing concern at the prospect of uncoordinated sprawl. Planning advocates called for more top-down vision married to regulatory powers (Gregory, 2009; Reidy and May, 2009), and in several states new special-purpose state agencies were established, like Victoria's Town and Country Planning Board (TCPB).

As the 1940s progressed, ideas from overseas about how to manage city and population growth again influenced professional thinking (Figure 2.6). Common topics in the planning literature and in professional and public discourse were inner city renewal, spatial restructuring around distinct zones, ring roads, green belts, satellite cities and new towns (Howe, 2000). Particularly inspirational were Patrick Abercrombie's *County of London Plan* (1943) and *Greater London Plan* (1944). Brisbane and Sydney took the lead and prepared actual plans influenced by these exemplars.

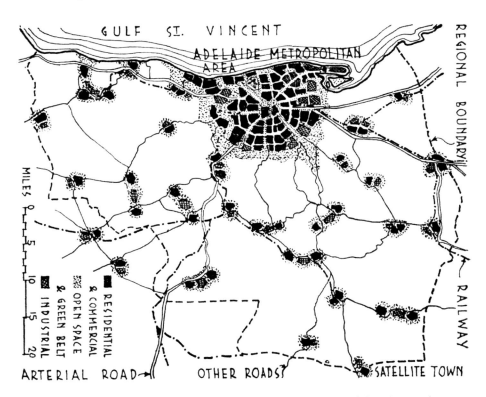

Figure 2.6. The future Adelaide region: 'Metropolitan Area with suggested outer green-belt, and Satellite Towns with main transport routes'. (*Source*: Benko and Lloyd, 1949; image courtesy of WEA Adult Learning)

Between 1944 and 1949 Ronald McInnis, who had drawn up a pioneering statutory plan for Mackay in the early 1930s, and his successor Frank Costello, produced a large-scale plan for the city of Brisbane. It comprised 'a compact and zoned city, encircled by a green belt, subdivided into neighbourhoods, with a hierarchical framework of open space and centred on a rebuilt city core' (Freestone and Low Choy, 2013, p. 58). Satellite towns and villages were intended to be located beyond the green belt. Although land was purchased for open space purposes the plan was not implemented, due partly to the difficulty of obtaining consensus between the state government and the city council on planning controls (Minnery, 2006; Freestone and Low Choy, 2013).

In Sydney the *New South Wales Local Government (Town and Country Planning) Amendment Act 1945* spawned the Cumberland County Council, a new type of authority reporting to the state government but led by elected councillors representing local government, with the task of preparing a comprehensive metropolitan plan by 1948, subsequently given statutory force 3 years later. The Council's three main goals were:

◆ coordination of land uses to foster a spatial arrangement maximizing convenience and separating incompatible activities;

◆ consolidation of development to address a backlog in service provision; and

◆ conservation of natural and historical assets (Winston, 1957, p. 39).

The planning ideas responsive to these suggestions integrated many concepts already in currency in Australia and abroad: a green belt regarded as an urban growth boundary (Howe, 2000); zoning and separation of land uses; reservation of land for open space and highways; urban renewal; district centres, and foreshore protection (figure 2.7).

Peter Harrison (1972, p. 68) lauded the County of Cumberland Planning Scheme as 'the most definitive expression of public policy on the form and content of an Australian metropolitan area ever attempted'. But it had its fair share of detractors as it irreversibly shifted the rhetoric of planning from an almost utopian ideal to a harsher language of regulation and controls (Freestone and James, 2015). There were also inherent managerial problems including a significant underestimation of the rate of population growth that, by the early 1960s, spelled the death knell for the centrepiece green belt concept (Toon and Falk, 2003). However, at the same time the Scheme produced major gains in the reservation of land for strategic purposes. For example, through the application of zoning provisions, between 1945 and 1962 the suburban distribution, and hence accessibility, of both jobs and open space increased significantly (Alexander, 1981). Near to the abolition of the Cumberland County Council in 1963, requirements were introduced for councils to pre-plan new land release areas and for developers to make financial contributions to the reticulation of water and sewerage in new subdivisions.

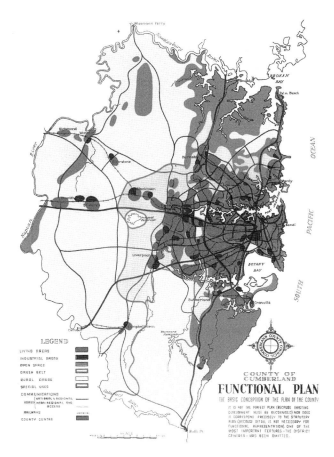

Figure 2.7. Town and country planning, Australian style: Sydney's first metropolitan strategy, 1948. (Source: Cumberland County Council, 1948; image courtesy of Lachlan Abercrombie)

The 1950s

The 1950s heralded the beginning of the 'long boom', a sustained period of growing material prosperity for most Australians in an era also remembered for its political conservatism and social homogeneity. The growth rate of all capital cities increased by 40–50 per cent per annum between 1947 and 1954, fuelled by the Commonwealth's post-war immigration programme which was 'poorly coordinated with states and local government in relation to planning and housing' (Howe, 2000, p. 88). The challenge for metropolitan planning was to cope with high growth rates and, within various institutional frameworks, to oversee the roll-out of comprehensive local planning schemes based largely on monofunctional land-use zoning (Alexander, 2000). Neither scale accommodated much in the way of community input. Facilitation of orderly outward expansion and decentralization of jobs on the one hand and renewal of inner suburbs and central cities on the other were common objectives in metropolitan plans.

While Adelaide, Brisbane and Hobart commenced plan-making, Melbourne and Perth completed major schemes in tandem, as in the 1920s. Sydney's Cumberland County Scheme spurred Melbourne into action with the MMBW completing

Figure 2.8. Exhibition of the Melbourne and Metropolitan Board of Works Planning Scheme 1954 at the Public Library of Victoria, November 1953. (*Source*: Public Records Office of Victoria, VPRS8663 P1 Unit20, Photograph, TP 54-43)

its task by 1954 and launched with due ceremony (figure 2.8). Chief among the major problems uncovered through civic surveys were low-density sprawl; decline in the liveability of the inner city; the need for industrial area planning; congestion in and around the CBD; broader constraints on the movements of people and goods; lack of sites for community facilities; lack of recreation areas; and concern with protection from the effects of aerial warfare. Six key principles were enunciated: (*i*) limitation of the urban area; (*ii*) zoning of specific areas for various community purposes; (*iii*) decentralization within the urban area of industry and commerce; (*iv*) provision for an adequate road communication system; (*v*) reservation of adequate areas for all community needs; and (*vi*) preservation of existing opportunities for civic improvement (Freestone *et al.*, 2016). There was resistance to British-style satellite towns and the state government would not revisit these again until the late 1960s. Instead, demand-driven development on the urban fringe was willingly accommodated along with the spread of American-style retail malls disconnected from the train and tram transport networks. Howe (2000) depicted a conservative plan reflecting an 'engineer culture' while Buxton *et al.* (2016, p. 21) declared it a flawed and unresponsive technical exercise that was a 'lost opportunity' for Melbourne.

In Perth the 315-page report and atlas prepared by Gordon Stephenson and Alastair Hepburn was 'by any standard, a remarkable work' (Gregory, 2012, p. 308). It comprised eleven chapters dealing with historical development, the region and the state, people, employment, land use, open space and recreation, communication (roads, railways and ports) and other public utilities, development standards, the central areas, additional proposals dealing mainly with different districts, and implementation. The plan envisaged a relatively compact metropolis with one major centre, complemented by community districts connected by highways and railways and encircled by rural land, forest reserves, natural vegetation and the ocean (*Ibid.*). Stephenson, a highly respected 'pracademic' schooled in the British tradition but with strong global connections, included many detailed design suggestions for various Perth hotspots (Newman, 2012). It was a highly competent if restrained document that fell short of, say, the innovative Greater London Plan that Stephenson worked on with Abercrombie. But it was a fitting successor to the Town Planning Commission report of 1930 and was the key precursor to the Metropolitan Region Scheme in 1963, a metropolitan-wide mapping of statutory land-use zones (Adams, 2010).

The 1960s

Metropolitan dominance became an even more entrenched feature of Australian population distribution in the 1960s. This decade was characterized by growth and a shift away from the first generation of metropolitan blueprints towards more flexible strategic plans underpinned by social science-style research in contrast to the older architectonic values that came to the fore in the 1940s. Contemporary-sounding problems were becoming more evident – land supply, affordable housing, infrastructure provision, rising rates of car ownership, and environmental degradation. It was a climate in which 'growth was expected to continue unabated and major societal change was not anticipated … market forces were not challenged' and the planning task was 'to guide or coordinate development and ensure government infrastructure investment met the requirements of growth' (Cardew, 1998, p. 93).

The turn to a more adaptable planning methodology was marked by the rise of structure planning with virtually unlimited growth projected. Spatial strategies were dominated by corridors conceived as spines for integrated networks, notably roads and public transport (Morison, 2000). This approach was a global phenomenon with its historical roots in iconic strategies like Steen Eiler Rasmussen's 'finger plan' for Copenhagen (1947) and endorsed prominently by Hugh Stretton in his path-breaking *Ideas for Australian Cities* (1970).

In general, corridor planning from the 1960s and early 1970s was influential in setting the general direction and form of metropolitan growth over subsequent decades. The first new look metropolitan plan capturing this turn was the *Report on the Metropolitan Area of Adelaide* in 1962 prepared under the leadership of State Town Planner, Stuart Hart. The plan envisaged a number of metropolitan districts of 80,000–150,000 people with their own centres orientated in a linear fashion on the Adelaide plains (figure 2.9). It was a catalyst for wider informed debate

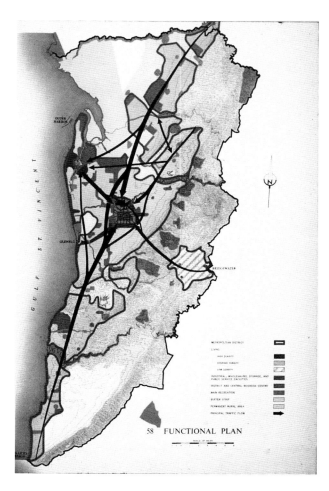

Figure 2.9. Functional Plan for Adelaide, 1962: 'in diagrammatic form the future location of the main living, working and recreation areas, and the main lines of communication'. (*Source*: Town Planning Committee, 1962, p. 130)

on metropolitan land-use and transport planning captured by formation of a Town and Country Planning Association in 1964 (Garnaut and Round, 2009), but was subsequently 'authorized' into the Metropolitan Development Plan in 1967 (Hutchings, 2011). In that context, Elizabeth, a standalone new town from the 1950s, was re-imagined as a metropolitan district. The Town and Country Planning Board of Victoria also speculated on linear cities, dramatically extending Melbourne to the east and south. And the State Planning Authority of NSW backed the corridor extensions of the *Sydney Region Outline Plan* (1968) with strategic land acquisitions for town centres and other key areas, signposting a more entrepreneurial approach to implementation. The Metropolitan Regional Planning Authority in Perth adopted a similar model in 1970 with over 600 square kilometres of land projected for future development within four urban corridors (Adams, 2010, p. 38).

The zenith of the corridor approach was in Canberra where the National Capital Development Commission needed to plan for a city growing inexorably beyond the limitations of Griffin's Canberra with an ordered pattern of discrete urban districts, previewed in *The Future Canberra* (1964). This was taken further in *Tomorrow's Canberra* (1970) with even larger-scale districts linked along multi-centred corridors not unlike the 'social city' conception of Ebenezer Howard and justified by transport-land-use modelling undertaken by American consultant Alan Voorhees and Associates. New suburban towns of 80,000–100,000 people were envisaged, organized around strong multi-purpose centres, linked by a public transport system on its own right-of-way along the corridors which were to be flanked by freeways. Named the Y Plan, this approach was implemented progressively and faithfully to the early 2000s until overtaken by new imperatives of infill development for a more compact and contained urban form.

The 1970s

The decade of the 1970s was one 'of marked change in economic, political and social conditions from the previous twenty years of post-war growth' (Huxley, 2000, p. 131). In Australia it signalled an end to the long boom as rising oil prices threatened the hegemony of motorized private transport and as the global economy shifted away from a traditional focus on manufacturing. Unemployment, demographic change and social unrest followed, building on the civil disputation occasioned by the Vietnam War. Critiques of environmental damage gained momentum and demands grew for greater social and gender equality. The ideology of modernism was critically questioned, as were mainstream approaches to city planning and design (Hamilton, 2016). The election of the Whitlam Labor Government on an electoral platform including greater engagement in urban affairs was symptomatic of a time of change. The restlessness of the period was global and led to a breakdown of the dominant technocratic paradigm of urban planning and the search for alternative models (Yiftachel, 1989).

Four major urban issues confronted metropolitan planners from the early 1970s: 'economic downturn and changes in industrial and employment structure; slowed population growth and decreasing household size; environmental issues; and questions of participation in decision-making about local and regional development' (Huxley, 2000, p. 135). Corridor plans as singular responses to urban and more especially suburban growth were challenged by new concepts such as urban consolidation and revitalization. The era of large-scale analytical studies driven by state governments and recommending extensive metropolitan freeway networks as the primary solution to urban transportation problems also came to an end. Mainstream planning was increasingly contested by direct action over unpopular old-fashioned proposals such as slum clearance, high-rise social housing, freeway plans, threats to traditional 'high street' shopping strips, demolition of historic buildings, and loss of valued open spaces. Inner suburbs became battlegrounds of urban activism over issues of gentrification, redevelopment and conservation (Howe *et al.*, 2014). The green ban insurgency headquartered in Sydney captured many such controversies. 'Green bans' aimed

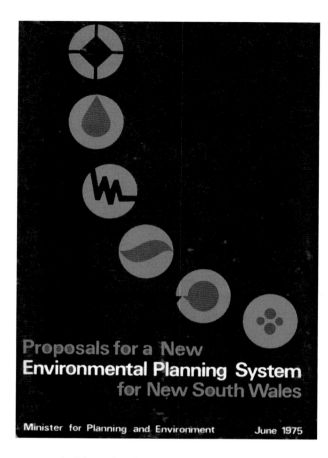

Figure 2.10. Towards a new planning system in New South Wales: environmental considerations were injected more explicitly into planning at all levels from the 1970s. (*Source*: Collection of Robert Freestone)

to put a hold on development to allow time for broader community consideration of proposed projects (Colman, 2016).

The 1970s was a period of administrative innovation with new ministries, commissions and departments searching for better horizontal and vertical integration of decision-making (figure 2.10): 'almost every state embarked on major attempts at institutional and administrative reorganization of its planning and urban infrastructure agencies' (Huxley, 2000, p. 138). A disillusionment with metropolitan plans set in. Harrison (1974, p. 137) reached the unsettling conclusion that, while they may have provided some guidance and coordination to infrastructure authorities, there was 'little to suggest that planning has made any significant difference to the patterns of urban growth and change over the postwar period'. In an environment of review, critique and fundamental rethinking, including a turn towards a more responsive 'urban management' paradigm, the production of new plans virtually dried up.

The 1980s

Bunker (2009*a*) characterizes metropolitan plans in Australia in the period up until about 1980 as shaped by common concerns: long-range and comprehensive planning; a predilection for detailed specifications as to spatial arrangement of land uses, centres, corridors and other activities; belief in suburban development; coordinating public infrastructure but relying on the market to drive growth; complementarity of state directives and local controls; and an absence of Commonwealth interest, with the significant exception of the Department of Urban and Regional Development years of 1972–1975. However, with new drivers from the 1980s there were 'fundamental changes in these circumstances' (*Ibid*., p. 5) including the macro-forces of globalization and neo-liberalism; a turn to the flexibility and short-termism of urban managerialism; the demise of the welfare state commitment to public infrastructure provision; and critiques of the inefficiency, costliness and soullessness of low-density suburban cities in favour of compact cities, turning the conventional pro-suburb historical wisdom of the town planning movement on its head.

By the 1980s, metropolitan planning was not simply at the crossroads, it was 'in the doldrums' (Lennon, 2000, p. 149). Hutchings (2011, p. 13) refers to it as a 'period of introspection'. However, the mood shifted. Economic development surged as an objective of planning as 'state governments become adventurous in their attempts to build the economic base of their cities and regions' (Lennon, 2000, p. 153). The importance of justifying capital investment within more certain long-term scenarios as an offset to short-term flexibility was increasingly understood (Neutze, 1988). Internationally, the Brundtland report of 1987 signalled a compelling and dynamic new rationale for planning around the mission of sustainability.

The 1980s can be cast as a period of transition from metropolitan plans that turned away from wholesale endorsement of growth on the urban fringe towards plans that facilitated higher density development in built-up areas, often through a repertoire of deregulation, fast tracking, privatization and private-public partnerships. Urban consolidation emerged in this decade as the 'leading idea with regard to metropolitan form' driven substantially by 'the desire of state governments, subject increasingly to tight monetary controls, to reduce their expenditure on infrastructure' (Lennon, 2000, p. 154). While later plans were less equivocal in their strong pursuit of consolidation, many of the plans of the 1980s sought an appropriate balance between centralization and decentralization. Strategies increasingly favoured 'concentrated' over 'dispersed' urban form but nonetheless with ample capacity for extension, as was the case for both Melbourne's 1981 (figure 2.11) and Sydney's 1988 metropolitan strategies.

The 1990s

By the early 1990s the transition was complete and, as 'reactive, short-range thinking' made way for 'proactive, long-range planning' (Lennon, 2000, p. 164), the dominant motif of the decade became strategic planning' (Hamnett, 2000, p. 182). This was not before time because, by the 1990s, 'Australia's cities …

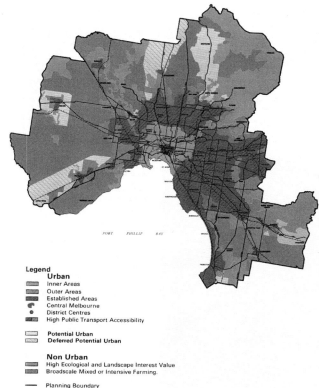

Figure 2.11. Melbourne's Strategic Framework Plan: aiming 'to encourage and facilitate opportunities for diversity in dwelling density, type and tenure'. (*Source:* Melbourne and Metropolitan Board of Works, 1981; image courtesy of Melbourne Water)

face[d] some daunting problems' (*Ibid.*, p. 168), notably coping with the fallout of economic restructuring, ageing of the population, social inequality, natural resource management, public finance, and the revival of inner-city populations.

The conceptualization of metropolitan plans as increasingly strategic and 'relational' (Bunker, 2009b) rather than absolutely precise land-use instruments injected them with arguably more rhetorical emphasis (Gleeson *et al.*, 2004, p. 345). Substantively, the prevailing trend was towards integration of broad economic, social and environmental objectives (Hamnett, 2000). A 'sustainability imperative' emerged (Gleeson *et al.*, 2004, p. 350). Recurring themes, to be writ larger in the twenty-first century, could be ticked off: for example, the pursuit of more compact and polycentric cities, mixed-use development, jobs and growth, public transport, affordable housing, heritage, conservation and biodiversity, infrastructure, and equity (figure 2.12). The dominant approach to implementation became 'whole of government', with inter-agency cooperation but led from the top by state premiers. Despite a short-lived 'better cities' programme in the early 1990s, supporting innovative urban development projects nominated by state and territory governments involving infrastructure, services and improved coordination processes (Gerner, 2002), the interest of the Australian Government in cities continued to waver.

Politically, neo-liberalism held sway with a 'diminishing role for government

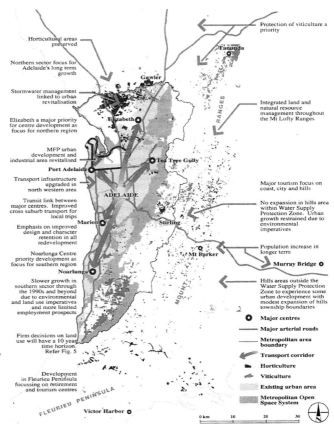

Figure 2.12. Dealing with complexity and interdependence: visions for Adelaide, 1992. (*Source*: Planning Review, 1992; image courtesy of the Department of Planning, Transport and Infrastructure, South Australia)

in the regulation of urban form and development' (Hamnett, 2000, p. 169). Entrepreneurialism was valued as enhancing city competitiveness. Waves of 'microeconomic' planning reform worked to try to free-up, simplify and standardize development assessment frameworks.

Despite the apparent commonalities of purpose across various jurisdictions, different approaches and preoccupations manifested themselves in several cities. In Sydney it was global city themes; in Canberra, adjusting to slow growth; and in Brisbane, a regional approach embracing the Sunshine and Gold Coasts. Planning in some cities remained mired in controversy as light-handed regulation facilitating development dominated in government (Lewis, 1999). Potential conflicts in practice were also evident, particularly across the goals of environmental and economic development planning. As the turn of another century approached, two major challenges loomed (Hamnett, 2000). The first was for cities to be at once both productive and sustainable. The second was an apparent gulf between the 'optimistic and inclusive visions of official metropolitan plans' and 'dystopian views of the current and future Australian metropolis' (*Ibid.*, p. 184). At the close of the 1990s, the challenges ahead for metropolitan planning typically remained formidable.

Conclusion

This retrospective of metropolitan planning to the end of the twentieth century suggests several overarching phases reflecting cycles of planning fashion refracted through local conditions. Adapting and extending the epochal change identified by Gleeson *et al.* (2004), we are able to distinguish five main eras expressing different assemblages of institutional settings, professional preoccupations, and global trends: the city functional – 1920s; town and country planning – 1930s–1950s; structure planning – 1960s–1970s; environmental planning – 1980s; and integrated planning – 1990s. The rate and number of metropolitan strategies has accelerated over time in response to disruptive economic, social, and environmental change.

Across this sequence several exercises stand out as particularly innovative for their times. We would nominate at least four: Melbourne's *Plan of General Development* (1929) as the first fully rounded modern statement; the *County of Cumberland Planning Scheme* (1948) as the zenith of the post-war blueprint in the British town and country planning mould; the Canberra Y Plan (1969) in capturing the nexus between the dominant linear city thinking and analytical research (structure planning meets systems planning); and the *2020 Vision* for Metropolitan Adelaide (1992) which offered a balanced strategic vision underpinned by extensive public consultation and pointed the way forward for later plans.

The extent to which the Australian quest for metropolitan strategies was distinctive globally is worthy of reflection. We would suggest that, in the first half of the century, distinctively Australian elements included the metropolitan focus of the pre-war town planning commissions, instilling a synoptic strand into professional practice at birth; the synthesis and adaptation of ideas from overseas, particularly British and American in the foundational years; and the orientation to particular issues then registering nationally, notably controlling subdivision and providing for transport needs. In the second half of the century we defer to Bunker's (2009*b*) identification of a distinctive style of Australian metropolitan planning organized around 'set-piece representations', managing suburban expansion, and orchestrating state instrumentalities to deliver the required infrastructure. New issues that still resonate today were registered in the last two decades: economic competitiveness, sustainability, privatization, and urban renewal.

Despite the diverse environments to which these plans responded, a convergence of aspirations and rhetoric is evident. The 'core difference' between strategies has been their governance and capacity for implementation (Gleeson *et al.*, 2004). There have been many and recurring historical impediments to full realization still familiar today, including flawed assumptions and methodologies; soft political will; changes of government and short-term electoral cycles; the debt aversion of government; subverting long-term rationality for short-term impact; lack of cross-institutional coordination; the subversive power of development interests; and community insurgencies. More often than not, plans have been shelved without comprehensively critical evaluations of performance; their time has simply passed

(McLoughlin, 1992). Significant disjunctures between spatial visions and actual needs and outcomes lay the seeds for new plans – a theme continued into the early twenty-first century as evident in the chapters that follow.

References

Adams, T. (2010) Taming an urban frontier? Urban expansion and metropolitan spatial plans in Perth 1970–2005, in Alexander, I., Greive, S. and Hedgcock, D. (eds.) *Planning Perspectives from Western Australia: A Reader in Theory and Practice*. Fremantle: Fremantle Press, pp. 33–47.

Alexander, I. (1981) Post-war metropolitan planning: goals and realities, in Troy, P.N. (ed.) *Equity in the City*. Sydney: Allen and Unwin, pp. 145–171.

Alexander, I. (2000) The post-war city, in Hamnett, S. and Freestone, R. (eds.) *The Australian Metropolis: A Planning History*. Sydney: Allen and Unwin, pp. 98–112.

Auster, M. (1987) Origins of the Australian regional and metropolitan planning movement, 1900–1940. *Journal of Australian Studies*, **11**(21), pp. 29–39.

Baker, M. (2012) *Visions, Dreams and Plans: Selected Aspects of the History of Town Planning in Queensland*. Brisbane: Mark Baker Town Planning Consultant Ltd.

Benko, A. and Lloyd, T.R.V. (1949) *Replanning Our Towns and Countryside*. Adelaide: Workers Educational Association.

Bland, W. (1857) *Sanitary Reform of Towns and Cities*. Sydney: J. Cox.

Bunker, R. (2009*a*) Paradigm Lost or Paradigm Regained? – Current Australian Metropolitan Strategies. Paper to the 4th Biennial State of Australian Cities Conference, University of Western Australia, Perth. Available at: http://apo.org.au/node/60096.

Bunker, R. (2009*b*) Situating Australian metropolitan planning. *International Planning Studies*, **14**(3), pp. 233–252.

Buxton, M., Goodman, R. and Moloney, S. (2016) *Planning Melbourne: Lessons for a Sustainable City*. Melbourne: CSIRO Publishing.

Cardew, R. (1998) Corridors of planning: recollections of the Sydney Region Outline Plan Preparation, in Freestone, R. (ed.), *The Twentieth Century Urban Planning Experience: Proceedings of the 8th International Planning History Society Conference and 4th Australian Planning/Urban History Conference*. Sydney: UNSW, pp. 89–94.

Colman, J. (2016) *The House that Jack Built: Jack Mundey, Green Bans Hero*. Sydney: NewSouth Publishing.

Cumberland County Council (1948) *The Planning Scheme for the County of Cumberland, New South Wales*. Sydney: Cumberland County Council.

Freestone, R. (1989) *Model Communities: The Garden City Movement in Australia*. Melbourne: Nelson.

Freestone, R. (2000*a*) From city improvement to the City Beautiful, in Hamnett, S. and Freestone, R. (eds.) *The Australian Metropolis: A Planning History*. Sydney: Allen and Unwin, pp. 27–45.

Freestone, R. (2000*b*) Master plans and planning commissions in the 1920s: the Australian experience. *Planning Perspectives*, **15**(3), pp. 301–322.

Freestone, R. (2006) Royal Commissions, planning reform and Sydney improvement 1908–1909. *Planning Perspectives*, **21**(3), pp. 213–231.

Freestone, R. (2007) *Designing Australia's Cities*. Sydney: UNSW Press.

Freestone, R. (ed.) (2009) *Cities, Citizens and Environmental Reform: Histories of Australian Town Planning Associations*. Sydney: Sydney University Press.

Freestone, R. (2010) *Urban Nation: Australia's Planning Heritage*. Melbourne: CSIRO Publishing.

Freestone, R. and Grubb, M. (1998) The Melbourne Metropolitan Town Planning Commission, 1922–30. *Journal of Australian Studies*, **22**(57), pp. 128–144.

Freestone, R. and Park, M. (2009) Spreading the good news about town planning in Sydney 1913–1934, in Freestone, R. (ed.) *Cities, Citizens and Environmental Reform: Histories of Australian Town Planning Associations*. Sydney: Sydney University Press, pp. 27–63.

Freestone, R. and Nichols, D. (2011) The Australian Federal Capital Congress, Melbourne, May 1901. *Planning Perspectives*, **26**(3), pp. 373–401.

Freestone, R. and Low Choy, D. (2013) Enriching the community: the life and times of Frank Costello (1903–1987). *Australian Planner*, **50**(1), pp. 55-67.

Freestone, R. and James, P. (2015) Exhibition to implementation: introducing democratic planning for Metropolitan Sydney 1948–51. *Urban Policy and Research*, **33**(1), pp. 1–16.

Freestone, R., Amati, M. and Mills, P. (2016) The renaissance of post-war metropolitan planning in Melbourne, Australia 1949–1954, in Hein, C. (ed.) *International Planning History Society Proceedings*, Vol. 1. Delft: TU Delft, pp. 311–317.

Garnaut, G. (2000) Towards metropolitan organisation: town planning and the Garden City idea, in Hamnett, S. and Freestone, R. (eds.) *The Australian Metropolis: A Planning History*. Sydney: Allen and Unwin, pp. 46–64.

Garnaut, C. (2008) The Adelaide Parklands and the endurance of the green belt idea in South Australia, in Amati, M. (ed.) *Urban Greenbelts in the Twenty-First Century*. Farnham: Ashgate, pp. 107–128.

Garnaut, C. and Round, K. (2009) 'The kaleidoscope of town planning': planning advocacy in post-war South Australia, in Freestone, R. (ed.) *Cities, Citizens and Environmental Reform: Histories of Australian Town Planning Associations*. Sydney: Sydney University Press, pp. 203–234.

Gerner, R.P. (2002) Urban Design and the Better Cities Program: The Influence of Urban Design on the Outcomes of the Program. PhD thesis, University of Sydney.

Gleeson, B., Darbas, T. and Lawson, S. (2004) Governance, sustainability and recent Australian metropolitan strategies: a socio-economic analysis. *Urban Policy and Research*, **22**(4), pp. 345–366.

Gregory, J. (2009) Visions of the city: town planning and community activism in postwar Perth, in Freestone, R. (ed.) *Cities, Citizens and Environmental Reform: Histories of Australian Town Planning Associations*. Sydney: Sydney University Press, pp. 235–259.

Gregory, J. (2012) Stephenson and metropolitan planning in Perth. *Town Planning Review*, **83**(3), pp. 297–317.

Hamilton, C. (2016) *What Do We Want! The Story of Protest in Australia*. Canberra: National Library of Australia Publishing.

Hamnett, S. (2000) The late 1990s: competitive versus sustainable cities, in Hamnett, S. and Freestone, R. (eds.) *The Australian Metropolis: A Planning History*. Sydney: Allen and Unwin, pp. 168–188.

Hamnett, S. and Freestone, R. (eds.) (2000) *The Australian Metropolis: A Planning History*. Sydney: Allen and Unwin.

Harrison, P. (1972) Planning the metropolis: a case study, in Parker, R.S. and Troy, P.N. (eds.) *The Politics of Urban Growth*. Canberra: ANU Press, pp. 61–99.

Harrison, P. (1974) Urban planning, in Forward, R. (ed.) *Public Policy in Australia*. Melbourne: Cheshire, pp. 127–156.

Home, R. (2013) *Of Planting and Planning: The Making of British Colonial Cities*, 2nd ed. London: Routledge.

Howard, E. (1902) *Garden Cities of Tomorrow*. London: Swan Sonnenschein.

Howe, R. (2000) A new paradigm: planning and reconstruction in the 1940s in Hamnett, S. and Freestone, R. (eds.) *The Australian Metropolis: A Planning History*. Sydney: Allen and Unwin, pp. 80–97.

Howe, R., Nichols, D. and Davison, G. (2014) *Trendyville: The Battle for Australia's Inner Cities*. Melbourne: Monash University Publishing.

Hutchings, A. (2000) From theory to practice: the inter-war years, in Hamnett, S. and Freestone, R. (eds.) *The Australian Metropolis: A Planning History*. Sydney: Allen and Unwin, pp. 65–79.

Hutchings, A. (2011) Process, Policy and Product: Urban and Regional Planning in South Australia 1967–2009. PhD thesis,University of South Australia, Adelaide.

Huxley, M. (2000) Administrative coordination, urban management and strategic planning in the 1970s, in Hamnett, S. and Freestone, R. (eds.) *The Australian Metropolis: A Planning History*. Sydney: Allen and Unwin pp. 131–148.

James, P. (2008) Reading Sydney regional planning through the life of Norman Weekes, in Finch, L. (ed.) *Seachange: New and Renewed Urban Landscapes*. Proceedings of the 9th Australasian Urban History/Planning History Conference, Caloundra.

Lennon, M. (2000) The revival of metropolitan planning, in Hamnett, S. and Freestone, R. (eds.) *The Australian Metropolis: A Planning History*. Sydney: Allen and Unwin, pp. 149–167.

Lewis, M. (1999) *Suburban Backlash: The Battle for Melbourne, the World's Most Livable City*. Melbourne: Bloomings Books.

Loudon, J.C. (1829) Hints on breathing places for the metropolis, and for country towns and villages, on fixed principles. *Gardener's Magazine*, **5**, pp. 686–690.

McConville, C. (2009) Queensland's popular movement in planning 1914–30: socialism, regularity and profit, in Freestone, R. (ed.) *Cities, Citizens and Environmental Reform: Histories of Australian Town Planning Associations*. Sydney: Sydney University Press, pp. 64–90.

McLoughlin, J.B. (1992) *Shaping Melbourne's Future: Town Planning, the State and Civil Society*. Melbourne: Cambridge University Press.

May, A. and Reidy, S. (2009) Town planning crusaders: urban reform in Melbourne during the progressive era, in Freestone, R. (ed.) *Cities, Citizens and Environmental Reform: Histories of Australian Town Planning Associations*. Sydney: Sydney University Press, pp. 91–119.

Melbourne and Metropolitan Board of Works (1981) *Metropolitan Strategy Implementation*. Melbourne: MMBW.

Minnery, J.R. (2004) The Wonderful Possibilities of the Future: Town Planning in Greater Brisbane. Paper presented to the 11th International Planning History Society Conference, 'Planning Models and the Culture of Cities', Barcelona, Spain. Available at: http://www.etsav.upc.es/personals/iphs2004/eng/en-pap.htm.

Minnery, J. (2006) The past matters in Metropolitan Regional Planning: A case study of South East Queensland, in Miller, C.L. and Roche, M.M. (eds.) *Past Matters: Proceedings of the 8th Australasian Urban History/Planning History Conference*. Wellington, NZ: Massey University, pp. 349–358.

Morison, I. (2000) The corridor city: planning for growth in the 1960s, in Hamnett, S. and Freestone, R. (eds.) *The Australian Metropolis: A Planning History*. Sydney: Allen and Unwin, pp. 113–130.

Neutze, M. (1988) Planning as urban management: a critical assessment, in *Metropolitan Planning in Australia: Urban Management*. Urban Research Unit Working paper No 6. Canberra: Australian National University.

Newman, D. (2012) Harold Boas: the 1930 Metropolitan Town Planning Commission and the 1959 Metropolitan Region Scheme, in Gaynor, A., Gralton, E., Gregory, J. and McQuade, S. (eds.) *Transformations, Booms, Busts and Other Catastrophes. Proceedings of the 11th Australasian Urban History/Planning History Conference*. Perth: University of Western Australia, pp. 206–216.

Nichols, D. (2004) Merely the man in the street: community consultation in the planning of 1920s Melbourne. *Australian Planner*, **41**(3), pp. 49–55.

Planning Review (1992) *2020 Vision – Planning Strategy for Metropolitan Adelaide*. Adelaide: Department of Environment and Planning.

Proudfoot, H. (2000) Founding cities in nineteenth century Australia in Hamnett, S. and Freestone, R. (eds.) *The Australian Metropolis: A Planning History*. Sydney: Allen and Unwin, pp.11–26.

Reade, C. (1919) Report on Planning and Development of Towns and Cities in South Australia, *South Australian Parliamentary Papers*, No. 63.

Reidy, S. and May, A. (2009) Dreams come true? Town planning ideals and realities in postwar Melbourne, in Freestone, R. (ed.) *Cities, Citizens and Environmental Reform: Histories of Australian Town Planning Associations*. Sydney: Sydney University Press. pp. 342–372.

Rose. A.J. (1966) Dissent from down under: metropolitan primacy as normal state. *Pacific Viewpoint*, **7**(1), pp. 1–27.

Stimson, R. (1992) A place in the sun? Policies, planning and leadership for the Brisbane Region. *Urban Futures*, **2**(2), pp. 51–67.

Stretton, H. (1970) *Ideas for Australian Cities*. Melbourne: Georgian House.

Sulman, J. (1921) *An Introduction to the Study of Town Planning in Australia*. Sydney: NSW Government Printer.

Toon, J. and Falk, J. (2003) (eds.) *Sydney: Planning or Politics. Town Planning for Sydney Region since 1945*. Sydney: Planning Research Centre, University of Sydney.

Town Planning Committee (1962) *Report on the Metropolitan Area of Adelaide*. Adelaide: Government of South Australia.

Ward, S. (2002) *Planning the Twentieth Century City: The Advanced Capitalist World*. Chichester: John Wiley & Sons.

Winston, D. (1957) *Sydney's Great Experiment: The Progress of the Cumberland County Plan*. Sydney: Angus and Robertson.

Yiftachel, O. (1989) Towards a new typology of urban planning theories. *Environment and Planning B*, **16**(1), pp. 23–39.

Chapter 3

Melbourne:
Growing Pains for the
Liveable City

Robin Goodman

Population growth has been the overriding characteristic of Melbourne during the first 16 years of the twenty-first century. This is cause for both celebration and concern. In many respects this is a boom time for the city. Civic pride and interstate rivalry abound, with gleeful estimates of when Melbourne might overtake Sydney and become Australia's largest metropolis (Alison, 2016). In recent years Melbourne has attracted accolades for the character of its inner city, its laneways adorned with street art, its 'foodie' culture and its general liveability (Carmody and Dow, 2016; Wright, 2016).

At the same time obvious community concern exists about the rapid rate of change to the built environment accompanying continued expansion (see, for example, GERA, 2014; DADA, 2015). Noticeable symptoms of growth pressures are overcrowded public transport and traffic congestion, escalating housing prices and the rapid appearance of inner-city apartment towers, prompting concern and a review of design standards. Population increases strain existing infrastructure and services, and create demand for new facilities such as childcare, hospitals and schools. Responding to and managing this growth runs through all recent planning strategies and underlies their need for regular revision.

This chapter reviews the major strategic plans produced for Melbourne since 2000, discussing their overall direction, style and means of implementation. It begins with an overview of the city in the early twenty-first century, the pressures experienced and drivers for change. It then looks at significant changes to the planning system, and investigations into its efficiency and need for reform. A wide range of stakeholders spent considerable time and effort to produce ambitious plans for Melbourne but, in the end, they had rather less effect than intended. The impacts of these plans, where they can be demonstrated, are evaluated and their efficacy is discussed.

The relationship between strategy and implementation is therefore a dominant theme, as it is in many planning analyses and debates in Australia and elsewhere. Local and state governments typically have strategic and statutory planning in separate departments. This disjuncture is undermining planning's ability to achieve its purposes and to have a significant impact on an otherwise market-driven environment at both local and metropolitan scale.

Demographic and Social Changes in Melbourne since 2000

Melbourne has been growing rapidly, particularly in the decade to 2015, and in 2014–2015 had both the largest and fastest population increase of all Australian capital cities (ABS, 2016). It is predicted to overtake Sydney as the largest city by 2061 (DIRD, 2015, p. 27). Melbourne's population grew by 647,200 people in the 10 years from June 2001 to June 2011, from 3.5 million to 4.14 million. Its annual growth rates for the years ending June 2014 and 2015 were 2.2 per cent and 2.1 per cent respectively. A small portion of this is net internal migration (4,143 in 2014), but most comes from immigration and natural increase.

The city's population has increased in cultural diversity as it has grown. At the 2011 census only 63.3 per cent of its population was Australian-born. More Melbourne residents had both parents born overseas (46 per cent) than born in Australia (42 per cent) (ABS, 2017a). The respective figures for the nation as a whole were 34 per cent and 54 per cent. One-third of Melbourne residents in 2012

Figure 3.1. Metropolitan Melbourne Urban Footprint. (*Source*: ABS (2011) *Australian Statistical Geography Standard (ASGS): Volume 4 – Significant Urban Areas, Urban Centres and Localities*)

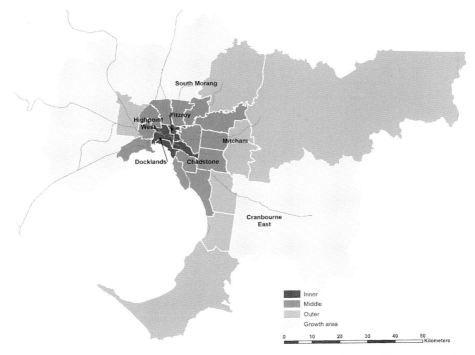

Figure 3.2. Metropolitan Melbourne: inner, middle, outer and growth areas. (*Source*: Based on ABS (2012) *Australian Statistical Geography Standard (ASGS): Volume 3 – Non ABS Structures. Local Government Areas*)

spoke a language other than English at home (ABS, 2017*a*). This multiculturalism, which has contributed greatly to the city's cultural character, has wide and general community acceptance, despite the sporadic appearance of tensions over planning permits for mosques (Lucas, 2014; Dow, 2016).

Melbourne has a very large geographic footprint, spreading out around Port Phillip Bay in a lopsided form skewed to the south-east, although significant growth in the northern and western suburbs is starting to rebalance it. Since formal planning for Melbourne began in the post-war era, urban expansion has been directed along growth corridors following radial transport lines out from the centre, with the undeveloped areas in between, known as 'green wedges', set aside for non-urban purposes. Planning documents commonly divide the metropolitan area into inner, middle, outer and growth areas (see figure 3.2). Very little new housing on the fringe is built outside designated growth areas. Traditionally the growth areas have supplied the bulk of new housing and in recent years they have rapidly expanded due to the population surge. Cranbourne East, 57 kilometres to the south-east of the CBD, and South Morang, 40 kilometres to the north, were two of Australia's fastest growing suburban areas in 2014–2015, each with over 4,000 new residents (ABS, 2016). However, significant growth has also occurred in the inner suburbs, with central Melbourne increasing by 2,600 people in 2014–2015 and adjacent areas such as Docklands also fast-growing.

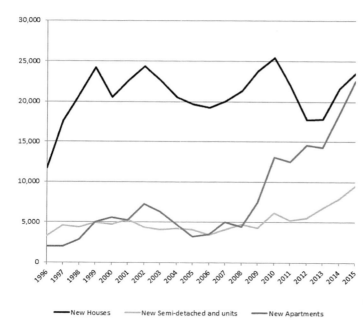

Figure 3.3. Annual number of building approvals by dwelling type. (Source: ABS (2016) *Building Approvals Australia, October 2016*)

At the 2012 census the vast majority of Melbournians, 73 per cent, lived in detached houses with 15 per cent in apartments and 12 per cent in semi-detached terraces or town houses. However, there has been a considerable increase in the number of apartments approved for construction since 2008 (see figure 3.3) so the proportion of people living in apartments is likely to increase (DELWP, 2015*a*; Letts, 2016; ABS, 2017*b*). In 2015, more apartments than houses were approved for construction across metropolitan Melbourne (DELWP, 2015*a*, p. 3). A strong differentiation in new housing supply exists between new apartments, the majority of which are small in size with one or two bedrooms, located in the central city and inner suburbs (Schlesinger, 2016); and the most common form of housing in the growth areas – large detached houses with four or more bedrooms (Goodman *et al.*, 2010).

While housing supply has increased in recent years, house prices have continued to rise, causing a housing affordability crisis second only to Sydney. The median house price across Melbourne more than doubled between 2000 and 2011, going from A$190,000 to A$500,000, an increase of 163 per cent. Over the same period, average wages increased by only 57 per cent, from A$42,500 to A$66,500 (DTPLI, 2012). Debates on the cause of these house price hikes have continued, with the development industry and some commentators blaming planning restrictions for a lack of supply, while others note that negative gearing (a taxation arrangement which allows losses on investment in rental housing to be a deduction on income tax payable) and other fiscal measures have encouraged investors to compete with homebuyers (Grattan, 2016; Daley *et al.*, 2016). In addition, foreign investment in Melbourne's housing market has reached significant proportions, recently exceeding 30 per cent of total sales of residential property during 2016 (Scutt, 2016).

House price rises have not been uniform across the metropolitan area and this has exacerbated the growing differentiation between inner and outer areas. Currently, only the outer areas of Melbourne are affordable for homebuyers on moderate to low incomes. Analyses by the Victorian Government have shown changes over time in the income needed to afford housing in different parts of Melbourne (DTPLI, 2014a). In 1994, a household on an average income could afford to buy a residence 10 kilometres from the CBD, but by 2000 this distance had increased to 24 kilometres and by 2009 to 40 kilometres (DTPLI, 2014a, p. 65).

The inner and outer areas of Melbourne are divided by more than just house prices. Demographic patterns show a clear and repeated spatial pattern across a range of variables (DTPLI, 2015). Concentrations of higher-income, tertiary-educated, professionally-employed households are clearly displayed in the inner and middle suburbs, while recent immigrants, lower-income households and those with lower levels of education primarily live in outer urban areas, and most particularly the designated urban growth areas.

These demographic patterns suggest that more affordable outer areas are sites of relative disadvantage. They are frequently at great distances from the largest concentrations of jobs and services. Spiller (2014a) compared the number of jobs within a reasonable drive or public transport ride from inner and outer Melbourne suburbs. This research showed that, with a half hour car commute, a typical outer suburban resident could access just 16 per cent of total metropolitan jobs by car while an inner suburban resident could reach 41 per cent, a finding supported by Kelly *et al.* (2014, p. 24). For those without access to a car, Spiller found that only 0.2 per cent of total metropolitan jobs could be reached by public transport from fringe suburbs within three-quarters of an hour compared to 33 per cent for inner areas (Spiller, 2014a, p. 364). The great outward spread of Melbourne over recent decades, combined with growing congestion and inadequate transport services, is clearly exacerbating geographic disadvantage. Spiller concludes that 'the suburban fringe generation of today has relatively few choices compared to their counterparts of 20 or 40 years ago' (Spiller, 2014a, p. 365).

While the suburban growth areas have the worst access to jobs, some of the newly densified inner areas are also lacking some vital services. The great population growth in the Docklands urban renewal area has highlighted shortages of child care centres, health services and particularly schools. This area is estimated to need an extra 4,800 primary school places and 2,000 secondary school places by 2031 (Capire Consulting Group, 2016, p. 3), demonstrating the problems created by allowing housing provision to run ahead of coordinated services.

Plans, Strategies and Planning Reform

The Australian Labor Party (ALP) dominated Victorian state politics in the first decade and a half of the twenty-first century. The previous period of Liberal-

National Party Coalition Government, led by Jeff Kennett in the 1990s, saw a radical overhaul of local government and the planning regulatory system. The programme of local government reforms included council amalgamations that reduced 210 municipalities down to seventy-eight and the introduction of compulsory competitive tendering. The Victoria Planning Provisions (VPPs) were introduced in 1996 to replace all previous planning schemes. They increased state-level control with a set of standardized land-use zones from which local governments could select but not alter. This neoliberal-inspired reform era emphasized development facilitation and metropolitan expansion, often characterizing planning as excessively bureaucratic and restrictive (Buxton, *et al.*, 2016). There was little in the way of new metropolitan strategic planning.

The Kennett Government was defeated at the state election in October 1999 by the ALP led by Steve Bracks. The ALP remained in office for 11 years, with John Brumby taking over as leader in 2007 after Labor won a third term in office. The Bracks/Brumby Governments saw a return to interest in strategic planning, introducing a major new metropolitan strategy in 2002, *Melbourne 2030*, and an update to that policy in 2008, *Melbourne@5Million*. Alongside this strategic planning agenda were several investigations into further regulatory reform. These produced a number of reports and discussion papers but little major change to legislation or procedure (Ruming and Goodman, 2016).

In December 2010 a new Liberal-National Coalition Government led by Ted Baillieu was elected. It had two leaders and lasted only one term, with a change of leadership to Denis Napthine in 2013. During this time significant changes to statutory controls occurred with the introduction of new residential and commercial zones (discussed below). A new metropolitan strategy, *Plan Melbourne*, was also introduced in 2014. The Baillieu/Napthine Government was defeated by a new ALP leader, Daniel Andrews, in 2014, in a campaign with the decision on whether to build a freeway – the East-West Link – at its centre. The Andrews Government immediately commenced a revision of *Plan Melbourne*, initially known as *Plan Melbourne Refresh*, to put its stamp on metropolitan planning. Each of these metropolitan strategies since 2001 is discussed in turn below.

Melbourne 2030

Melbourne 2030 was the first significant metropolitan strategy in more than a decade. It was substantial in scope, ambition and appearance, and unlike any previous Victorian Government planning policy. The printed document was glossy and pictorial in style, illustrated with over 450 photographs presenting the many desirable aspects of life in Melbourne. It was both a testament to the best existing aspects of the city and an aspirational statement about its future. What it lacked in clarity it made up for in breadth and complexity. The overall thrust of *Melbourne 2030* was to provide for the forecast population growth by encouraging urban consolidation and reducing the city's outward spread. The presentations given on the new strategy at the time of its release invariably began with the words 'in the next 30 years Melbourne will grow by up to one million people' (DOI, 2002a). It was a policy aimed at a more sustainable urban form while addressing the central concern of growth management (DOI, 2002a).

The strategy was focused around nine key directions. Each was supported by a number of policies and associated 'initiatives'. The nine directions were mainly uncontroversial aspirational goals such as 'better management of metropolitan growth', 'a more prosperous city' and 'a great place to be'. The exception to this was 'a more compact city', the implications of which prompted considerable debate (Birrell *et al.*, 2005; Hogg, 2007). Compactness was to be delivered by the re-direction of a greater proportion of new housing away from outward expansion and into the existing areas, particularly focused around nominated activity centres. Outward incremental spread was to be halted through the imposition of a legislated Urban Growth Boundary (UGB) which appeared overnight on planning scheme maps around the edge of the existing urban area and growth area land at the launch of the new strategy in October 2002. This decisive action was intended to finally protect Melbourne's green wedges from the incremental erosion of undeveloped land experienced over the previous decade (Buxton and Goodman, 2003).

A key element of *Melbourne 2030* was the recognition of a role for activity centres as appropriate foci for new commercial, retail and office development, and also for new and higher density housing (see figure 3.4). This was not new to metropolitan

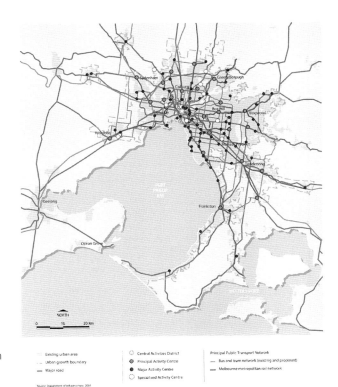

Figure 3.4. Melbourne 2030: Network of Activity Centres. (*Source*: Based on Activity Centre Network in DOI, 2002a, p. 50)

planning for Melbourne as it had been adopted under a District Centre Policy introduced in 1981. This policy of restricting large retail and office developments to fourteen designated centres had been difficult to maintain during the 1980s, however, and the Kennett Government gradually weakened and then abandoned it (Goodman and Moloney, 2004). The new iteration under *Melbourne 2030* identified a hierarchy of five different categories of centres, from the central city to neighbourhood centres. It named 114 centres comprising twenty-five principal, seventy-nine major and ten specialized centres and described an additional 900 neighbourhood centres throughout the metropolitan area (DOI, 2002*b*, p. 31). The list of principal and major centres included some located far from train stations and, surprisingly, included large car-based shopping malls such as Chadstone and Highpoint West (DOI, 2002*a*). The list was too extensive to provide focus for new development or infrastructure and appeared merely descriptive (Goodman and Moloney, 2004; Goodman, 2011). The aim was to increase the proportion of new housing in these activity centres from the 2002 level of 24 per cent to 41 per cent, with the proportion of new housing on the urban fringe in growth corridors to decrease from 39 per cent to 31 per cent. By 2030 fringe development was intended to account for only 22 per cent of all new households (DOI, 2002*c*, p. 5).

Melbourne 2030 was initially launched as a draft with many implementation details still to be developed. Many of the initiatives were, in reality, suggestions for further studies and policy development before action could be taken. From its release, however, the development industry picked up the general direction to increase density within existing areas and began to submit proposals for approval to councils, before the government had worked through the details of implementation or had developed guidelines. Resident action groups, such as Save Our Suburbs, began to oppose developments in their neighbourhoods. Some high-profile cases of high-rise developments in Fitzroy and Mitcham ended up in planning appeals before the Victorian Civil and Administrative Appeals Tribunal (VCAT) (Hogg, 2007). In the absence of detailed local plans, VCAT made rulings based on its interpretation of priorities within the broad policy directions in *Melbourne 2030* (Barber *et al.*, 2003). The plan gave little indication as to what ought to take precedence between sometimes competing aims of housing diversity, location, affordability and quality urban design (Kroen and Goodman, 2012).

Melbourne 2030 generated both public and academic debate, initially around its process, then its potential implications and later around failure to deliver on what it had promised (Mees, 2003; Goodman and Moloney, 2004; Birrell *et al.,* 2005; Goodman and Coote, 2007; Dodson, 2009). Five years after its release an Expert Panel conducted an audit of progress and reviewed public submissions (Audit Expert Group, 2008). Its report found that key policies of *Melbourne 2030* had not been sufficiently implemented. It showed that the proportion of new greenfield development had continued to increase and concluded that 'on-the-ground' implementation was insufficient in several key areas, including the redirection of residential growth to established areas, increased development in and around activity centres, and the commitment to public transport investments (Audit Expert Group, 2008). The report attributed this lack of progress on implementation in part to the tendency to focus on further studies and planning rather than on actual built form outcomes. It also pointed out the lack of clarity around responsibility for implementation, inadequate provision of resources and insufficient support from all stakeholders, particularly the community.

Melbourne@5Million

In 2008, in response to new population forecasts, the Victorian Government released *Melbourne@5Million* (DPCD, 2008). This was described as an update and was considered complementary to *Melbourne 2030*. It was considerably shorter (at 33 pages) and less flamboyant in style. The update brought an outward expansion of the urban growth boundary intended to accommodate higher population predictions (DPCD, 2008, p.18). The target for the location of future housing in growth areas was 47 per cent – a significant retreat from the more ambitious target in *Melbourne 2030* of only 31 per cent (DPCD, 2008, p. 5). It also included a

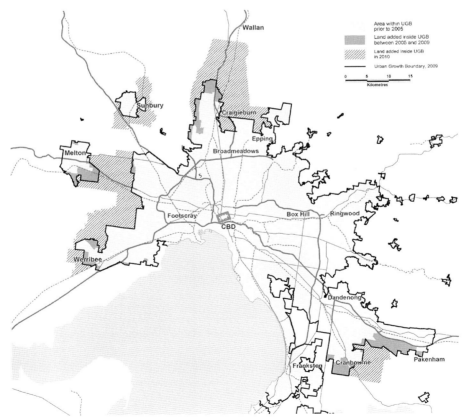

Figure 3.5. *Melbourne@5milliion*: Urban Growth Boundary Map. (*Source*: Based on DPCD, 2008)

further elaboration of the activity centre hierarchy with a new additional category of designated centres to be known as Central Activities Districts (CADs). These would provide the focus for investment and activity, which the audit had indicated was lacking, and would move Melbourne decisively towards a more polycentric shape. CADs were intended to grow in scale and significance over time to reduce the dominance of the CBD as the location for higher order jobs, commercial and retail activities and civic and cultural services. Concerns about long commuting times and traffic congestion were behind the concept of decentralizing jobs to the CADs and along transport corridors (DPCD, 2008, pp. 7–8).

The expansion of the Urban Growth Boundary, originally designated to provide certainty and a permanent boundary to the urban area, was its third outward movement in 8 years – in 2003, 2005 and 2010. The first of these expansions could be justified as making reasonable adjustments in relation to submissions regarding its original position. However, subsequent outward expansions were claimed as necessary to maintain land supply for a further 15–25 years, with the largest of these in 2010 in response to upwardly revised population estimates (DPCD, 2008). This move was attributed by some to the failure to increase density and redirect growth away from the fringe with the consequence that land reserves were being rapidly consumed (Buxton, 2008). This lack of implementation, which over time became more apparent, can be blamed in part on the failure to make specific links in the strategy to the statutory planning system which might have been expected to implement it. As previously noted, many of the actions involved further planning and/or proposals for reform, that potentially could have led to specific regulatory changes but seldom did. Instead the language inserted within the Victorian Planning Provisions was advisory rather than directive, allowing differing interpretations and scope for deviation.

Plan Melbourne

The incoming Liberal-National Coalition Government, elected in December 2010, initiated a process to develop a new metropolitan strategy. A six person Ministerial Advisory Committee (MAC), chaired by planning consultant Roz Hansen, was established in March 2012 to oversee the process and provide input to the Minister, Matthew Guy, and his department. It produced a discussion paper, *Melbourne Let's Talk about the Future*, in October 2012, which set out many of the main themes for consultation and feedback. These survived community consultation and appeared in the final version of *Plan Melbourne*. They are described below. Despite a long period of preparation and consultation, criticisms remained about the degree to which community input was taken into account (Wood, 2013). A draft version of the *Plan Melbourne* strategy was released in October 2013 and the final version in 2014 (DTPLI, 2014a). Just before this final release, Hansen and all but one of the other members resigned from the MAC, speaking publicly about their dissatisfaction with the process, the government's commitment to the $6–8 billion East–West Freeway project and several other elements of the draft strategy (Dow, 2013).

While the process of devising *Plan Melbourne* became controversial, the document itself drew far less reaction than had *Melbourne 2030* a decade earlier. This might have been partly because so much of its content was signalled in the discussion paper and at consultation meetings, but most likely because the plan did not suggest any radical changes or represent a significant departure in planning practice. The new plan addressed the issue of increasing population growth to an extended horizon of 2050. It noted that if current population trends continued then the city might add an extra 3.4 million people, taking it to 7.7 million by 2050, requiring an extra 1.6 million dwellings (DTPLI, 2014a, p. 5). It also included regional cities in the planning for future population growth, outlining a need for improved transport connections for people and freight and a greater level of regional planning coordination across the state. However, it acknowledged that Melbourne's growth rate would be far more rapid than those of the regional cities (see figure 3.6).

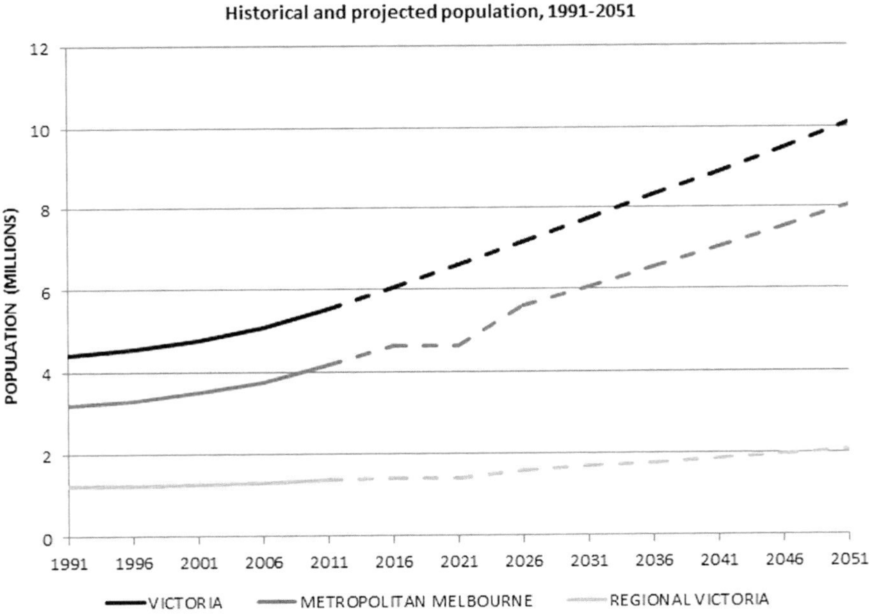

Figure 3.6. Historic and projected population change. (*Source:* Derived from ABS, 2016) and DELWP, 2016c)

Like *Melbourne 2030* before it, which had nine key directions, *Plan Melbourne* was based around nine principles which covered the descriptors of a good city such as 'distinctive', 'globally connected', 'competitive', 'resilient' and 'strong'. These resonated with themes found in most other Australian capital city plans (Goodman *et al.*, 2013). *Plan Melbourne* also included goals of polycentricity in an attempt to bring jobs and activities closer to people's homes, although this was really little more than an extension of the policy of focusing growth on activity centres. *Plan Melbourne* placed greater emphasis on infrastructure initiatives and their integration with land-use planning, and on employment and the location of jobs, than did its predecessors. It broke the metropolitan area into five sub-regions and promised coordinated planning with relevant authorities for each area and a pipeline of infrastructure investments and urban renewal projects.

It also introduced the notion of a '20-minute city'. The plan defined this as 'access to local shops, schools, parks, jobs and a range of community services within a 20-minute trip' (DTPLI, 2014a, p. 11), and also as giving people 'access to the goods and services they need for daily life within 20 minutes of where they live, travelling by foot, bicycle or public transport (DTPLI, 2014a, p. 117). Ambiguities around whether jobs and certain modes of transport were included made the prescription vague. The notion that Melbourne should be a city of local neighbourhoods also attracted criticism for ignoring the essential urban nature of cities, where some higher order activities could not be spread throughout suburbs (Davies, 2012).

The 2014 plan offered a new naming and classification of activity centres. It ignored the criticism of the previous policy that there were too many named centres to be strategically useful, and included all the principal and major centres from the

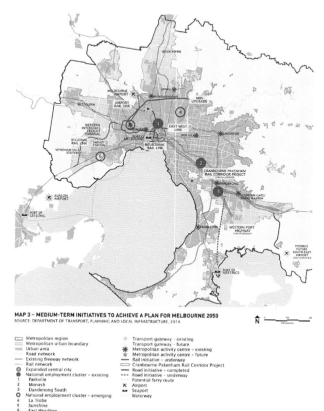

Figure 3.7. *Plan Melbourne* Activity Centres. (*Source:* DTPLI, 2014a, p. 12)

previous plans, with three now renamed as National Employment Clusters (two of which, Monash and Parkville were previously Specialised Activity Centres) and nine Metropolitan Activity Centres, previously called Principal Activity Centres. It also identified 'state-significant' industrial precincts, health and education precincts, transport gateways and sites for urban renewal (DTPLI, 2014*a*, p. 27). Once again, this very long list appeared merely descriptive.

Plan Melbourne reinforced a commitment to the permanence of the growth boundary in its current position but had unambitious goals for redirecting new housing away from growth areas. It nominated a target of 38 per cent housing in growth areas (compared with the *Melbourne 2030* target of 31 per cent and the *Melbourne@5Million* target of 47 per cent) and 61 per cent in established areas, with approximately one-third of this intended for the central city and surrounds (DTPLI, 2014*a*, p. 62). It introduced a new Metropolitan Planning Authority (MPA), which was formed out of the existing Growth Areas Authority (GAA) and retained the same Chief Executive Officer. The GAA had been established in 2006 to oversee the planning of new greenfield suburbs in collaboration with, and sometimes instead of, local government. This gave the state government a greater role in planning for these areas where it considered local government was not up to the task. This initially created some confusion and conflict over responsibilities and roles. The MPA continued the precinct planning work of the GAA while taking on an urban renewal planning role in the inner and middle suburbs. The concept of a metropolitan planning authority has received some support for its coordinating role, particularly in greenfield planning (Wear, 2016), but the lack of accountability through the absence of elected representation from the regional groupings of local governments has been noted (Spiller, 2014*b*; 2016).

Plan Melbourne Refresh

Another change of government in December 2014, back to the ALP, saw the new planning minister, Richard Wynne, re-form the MAC in March 2015 with its previous Chair, to revise *Plan Melbourne*. The reconvened committee was asked to focus particularly on housing, climate change, energy efficiency and public transport as 'these are core planks of any robust modern metropolitan strategy that were absent from the previous document' (Wynne, 2015*a*, p. 4). The MAC's report in June 2015 fed into a subsequent discussion paper (MAC, 2015; DELWP, 2015*b*).

The most significant changes to *Plan Melbourne*, which the MAC envisaged, were around housing supply and location, and climate change. Others provided further clarification on transport and infrastructure priorities, and on neighbourhood planning. The MAC recommended that *Plan Melbourne Refresh* recommit to a permanent UGB and to decreasing the proportion of new housing in growth areas, suggesting that a preferred ratio of 70:30 for established and growth areas be implemented by 2050 (although noting that this was already being achieved in 2015). It also suggested that growth area densities should increase from 12–15 dwellings per net hectare to an average of 25 with an increased focus on housing diversity and mixed-use development. Diversity or its lack would be identified through the development of a Residential Mix Diversity Index which could determine each sub-region's need for additional types of housing. Housing affordability could be addressed by setting targets for each subregion and the MAC also proposed 'new planning provisions, such as inclusionary zoning and/or floor space ratio bonuses' and 'mandated requirements in some instances, in the planning system to provide more social and affordable housing close to jobs and services' (MAC, 2015, p. ii).

The MAC indicated that the consequences of climate change had been downgraded in *Plan Melbourne* and required further emphasis. It included a number of specific recommendations to address the likely impacts of climate change including the implementation of a greening programme for buildings, roads and open spaces to cool the city, applying an 'infrastructure resilience assessment test' to proposed new capital works and implementing a biodiversity strategy. Some of these would utilize planning regulations, for example, using a planning scheme overlay to protect long-term agricultural production areas (MAC, 2015, p. iv). This suggested a desire not to repeat previous implementation failures. The MAC also stressed the need for the revised plan to be unambiguous, readable and understandable for a wide audience, noting that it should be 'a clear,

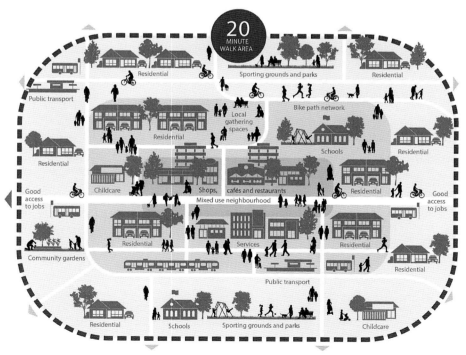

Figure 3.8. Plan Melbourne Refresh, the 20 minute neighbourhood. (*Source*: DELWP, 2015b, p. 22)

crisp document' (MAC, 2015, p. v). The 20-minute city concept was revised to mean 'the ability to meet your everyday non-work needs locally, primarily within a 20 minute walk' (MAC, 2015, pp. 15–16). This focus on walking and the removal of employment from the definition acknowledged that many people want, or have, to work in higher order employment areas.

In August 2016 the Metropolitan Planning Authority (MPA) was renamed the Victorian Planning Authority (VPA) and given an additional role in planning for regional towns and cities. It does not replace councils, or the relevant state government agency (currently the Department of Environment, Land, Water and Planning – DELWP), but offers both coordination and 'the provision of expert advice and assistance to councils about planning processes, rezoning, planning applications and community consultation to ensure high-quality development can occur in a timely fashion' (VPA, 2016, p. 2).

The refreshed version of *Plan Melbourne,* known as *Plan Melbourne 2017– 2050* (DELWP, 2017*a*), was finally released on 11 March 2017. It contained few surprises. With regard to housing supply it presented two differing scenarios for the location of new housing without clearly endorsing one over the other. The first had a ratio of 65:35 for established and growth areas and the second, described as aspirational despite having been achieved by 2014, has a ratio of 70:30. The revised plan endorsed the goal of increasing the supply of social and affordable housing but was light on specifics. In the tradition of previous strategies, it undertook to develop further policies and processes rather than immediately introduce them. It promised reforms to the planning system which will:

> include new planning provisions or tools to deliver social and affordable housing. These reforms will explore inclusionary zoning and mechanisms to capture and share value created through planning controls. (DELWP, 2017*a*, p. 56)

The 20 minute city concept within *Plan Melbourne 2017–2050* focused on non-work trips, as the MAC report had recommended, but has included a wider variety of means of transport in the definition, potentially making neighbourhoods larger. 'The 20-minute neighbourhood is all about "living locally" – giving people the ability to meet most of their everyday needs within a 20-minute walk, cycle or local public transport trip of their home' (DELWP, 2017*a*, p. 98). The revised plan also requires climate change risks to be considered in future infrastructure planning and sets a target of 25 per cent of electricity to be generated from renewable sources by 2010 and 40 per cent by 2025 (DELWP, 2017*a*, p. 108, 113).

Changes to the Planning System

Regardless of the concepts or ambitions within the latest metropolitan strategy, the system of planning regulation arguably has a greater influence on built form outcomes. A number of commentators have noted that, across Australian states, strategic planning ambitions have become broader, while the means to implement them have diminished due to the primacy of neoliberal thought on deregulation (Buxton and Groenhart, 2013; Goodman *et al.*, 2013; Rowley, 2017). The determination to remove red tape has run across governments of both political persuasions in Victoria since the beginning of this century.

As previously noted, an entirely new statutory planning system, the Victoria Planning Provisions (VPPs), was introduced in the late 1990s by the Kennett Coalition Government. When the Bracks Government was elected in 1999, no appetite existed for major system overhaul, much to the relief of many local government planners who were still getting used to the VPPs. However, the goal of a simplified and speedier planning system remained and several reports suggested ways to reduce bureaucratic delays, particularly with regard to development applications in residential zones. The Bracks Government considered revising the state enabling legislation, the Planning and Environment Act 1987, with the release of a discussion paper in 2009, but no major changes ensued (Ruming and Goodman, 2016).

The desire to replace the Act was revived again in 2011 when the legislative base of planning was included for investigation in the Victorian Planning System Ministerial Advisory Committee's (VPSMAC) review of the 'operation and effectiveness of the machinery of the planning system' (VPSMAC, 2011, p. 2). These investigations into possible revision or replacement of the Act did not result in any significant changes, however, and more attention was given to changes to zones and to means of making faster decisions. A discussion paper released on the zone changes suggested that 'these reformed zones will enable the planning system to act as an economic lever' (DPCD, 2012, p. 2).

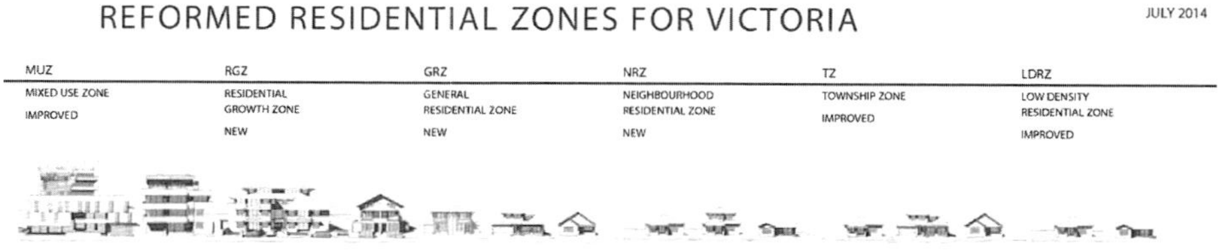

REFORMED RESIDENTIAL ZONES FOR VICTORIA   JULY 2014

MUZ	RGZ	GRZ	NRZ	TZ	LDRZ
MIXED USE ZONE	RESIDENTIAL	GENERAL	NEIGHBOURHOOD	TOWNSHIP ZONE	LOW DENSITY
IMPROVED	GROWTH ZONE	RESIDENTIAL ZONE	RESIDENTIAL ZONE	IMPROVED	RESIDENTIAL ZONE
	NEW	NEW	NEW		IMPROVED

Figure 3.9. Reformed Residential Zones Image. (Source: DTPLI, 2014*b*)

The new zones, which were released and partially implemented prior to the release of the first iteration of *Plan Melbourne*, constituted a major change in a number of areas. The reforms introduced three new residential zones – Neighbourhood Residential (NRG), General Residential (GRZ) and Residential Growth (RGZ) zones – allowing a clearer designation of the type of development appropriate for an area (see figure 3.9). The Neighbourhood Residential zones restricted growth and protected local character with an 8 metre height limit, the General Residential zone allowed some medium density and diversity and generally had a 9 metre height limit; and the Residential Growth zone encouraged medium density with a 13.5 metre height limit. Local governments had twelve months from July 2013 to apply the new zones. Some of the first adopting councils, such as the City of Glen Eira in the affluent eastern suburbs, applied the Neighbourhood Residential zone to 80 per cent of the municipality, with the General Residential zone applying to 19 per cent and the Residential Growth zone to just 1 per cent of residential land. This raised concerns that the new zoning would exacerbate Melbourne's housing affordability issues, effectively locking up the city's more desirable suburbs (Property Council of Australia, 2013; Kelly and Donegan, 2013). However, the General Residential zone, which allowed for some medium density development, has since been widely adopted (DELWP, 2016a, p. 24). In March 2017 the government brought in some modifications to the residential zones at the same time as releasing *Plan Melbourne 2017–2050*. These reforms, designed to address concerns about excessive restrictions on new housing, removed the default mandatory limit of two houses per lot from the NRZ and raised the height limit in the GRZ from 9 to 11 metres. The most publicized change, however, was to safeguard minimum garden areas – between 25 and 35 per cent depending on the block size (State of Victoria, 2017). A potential effect of this may be to make redevelopment of tight inner urban blocks, such as warehouse conversions, more difficult, directing further redevelopment into neighbourhoods with larger suburban blocks.

The new residential zones were not the only statutory changes from 2013 to cause concern. Changes to commercial and industrial zones allowed for a dispersal of retail and office development which, under successive earlier policies, had been encouraged to locate in activity centres. The Victorian Division of the Planning Institute of Australia highlighted that the zone reforms would 'pre-empt the introduction of the proposed Metropolitan Strategy and have potential to undermine key planning principles that have formed the basis of previous strategies' (PIA Victoria, 2012, p. 2).

Many investigations into, and reforms of, planning regulation ultimately tend to complicate the system and distract planners, rather than streamline their work. Despite this, the rhetoric of cutting red tape remains an unquestioned and essential part of any Victorian Government's agenda. The Liberal-National Coalition Government allocated this task to the newly-established Metropolitan Planning Authority in *Plan Melbourne* (DTPLI, 2014a, p. 171) and the incoming ALP Government in 2015 reiterated it (Wynne, 2015b). The development industry continues to lobby against any significant planning policy, attacking measures such as the UGB and targets to reduce the proportion of greenfield housing as constraining competition and exacerbating housing affordability through restriction of supply (UDIA, 2014; 2016).

Assessment of the Achievements of Metropolitan Plans and Planning Reforms

The previous overview of both strategic plans and interconnected planning system reform indicates the amount of effort and resources that have been dedicated to planning for Melbourne in the first sixteen years of this century. It represents a vast amount of human endeavour, political attention, state and local government activity, work for consultancies, attention from the development industry and grist for the mills of planning academics and students. It is, therefore, worth asking what has been achieved over this period.

As previously noted, a degree of convergence exists between the twenty-first century plans of Australian capital cities. This might be seen as policy transfer between planners and politicians, but they also face many of the same pressures and conundrums. Urban consolidation is the predominant theme of the two major strategic plans and their updates for Melbourne. There is not space here, nor available data, to provide serious assessment of achievements against all the specific goals in these strategies. However, the following brief discussion, focused on some of the most important aims, attempts to capture the progress made.

A number of policies and actions were intended to help achieve urban consolidation throughout the plans. First was the imposition of a definitive hard edge to the metropolitan area – the UGB introduced in 2002. The Victorian Parliament actually legislated this to make it more permanent. The boundary's placement allowed for future growth by including large amounts of non-urban land within the growth corridors set aside for future housing. The UGB moved three times, as previously noted, with the 2010 expansion adding an extra 43,000 hectares to Melbourne's urban area. These expansions clearly signalled to the development industry that the boundary, far from being firm, was in fact negotiable. This encouraged land speculation and undermined the credibility of planning as good public policy. *Plan Melbourne* and its refreshed version showed a renewed interest in maintaining the existing boundary without further expansion, but the past record does not inspire confidence.

Other aims related to urban consolidation in recent plans attempt to redirect growth away from the fringe and into existing areas, as well as to increase housing density. The various plan targets are discussed above, with the most recent a proportional split of 30 per cent of new housing in growth areas and 70 per cent in existing suburbs. The proportion on greenfield sites increased from 39 per cent in 2002 to an average of 48 per cent for the period 2001–2006/2007 (DPCD, 2007, p. 50). More recently, the proportion of new residential development in the six growth area municipalities has declined steadily – 36.5 per cent in 2011, 31.8 per cent in 2012, 30.7 per cent in 2013 and 30.1 per cent in 2014 (DELWP, 2016b). These figures are based on total new housing and include new houses built after demolition with no increase in number. They probably exaggerate the proportion of net gain in existing areas, therefore, while being accurate for greenfield areas. However, Melbourne's outer municipalities still top the list of Australia's fastest growing areas (ABS, 2016).

Coffee *et al.* (2016) have shown that Melbourne experienced density increases in inner, middle and outer areas over the period 1981–2011, although with some noticeable exceptions and different patterns over time. The density of new

Figure 3.10. Managing growth – houses on the urban fringe (Wyndham Vale, 2010). (*Photo*: Dianna Wells)

growth area subdivisions also grew from ten lots per hectare in 2001 to seventeen by 2016 (DOI, 2002c; DELWP, 2016b). Housing diversity has been a recurring theme in planning strategies. A 2010 AHURI (Australian Housing and Urban Research Institute) study showed very little change in housing diversity, with new apartments dominating the inner city and large detached houses on the fringe (Goodman *et al.*, 2010). In the period 2000 to 2007 detached housing constituted between 86 and 92 per cent of all new dwellings built in the growth areas (Goodman *et al.*, 2010, pp. 40–41). More recent figures show little change, with detached housing accounting for 90 per cent of new fringe dwellings in growth areas in 2011 and 87 per cent in 2014 (DELWP, 2016b). In contrast, apartments overwhelmingly dominate new dwelling supply in the four inner municipalities, hovering between 89 per cent and 94 per cent of total new supply in the years 2011–2014, with around 95 per cent of developments over four storeys (DELWP, 2016b). As noted earlier, the MAC report made policy recommendations for increasing housing diversity, starting with analysing housing diversity in any particular region and applying a diversity index. *Plan Melbourne 2017–2050* reiterates the need for diversity of housing types, particularly in growth areas, but lacks specific measures. Stronger tools, such as targets or mandated minimum levels of diversity for each major subdivision, bonuses or other incentives for achieving diversity, should be considered. Interestingly, this latest plan suggests increasing some lot sizes in growth areas to provide greater choice, along with providing smaller options such as town houses (DELWP, 2017a, p. 58). This suggests an end to the trend of decreasing average lot sizes in growth areas in order to increase density.

Figure 3.11. Apartment development in the inner city. (*Photo*: Kath Phelan)

The role of activity centres as locations for employment, commercial development and service provision is another consistent theme in planning strategies, with regular reformulation of lists and descriptions of different categories of centres. For all this naming and renaming, however, there has been no clear increase in housing or other forms of development within designated centres outside the inner-city areas experiencing the apartment boom. The AHURI study found that the overall amount of new housing built within one kilometre of a principal or major activity centre did not increase following the introduction of *Melbourne 2030* up until 2007, and may have slightly declined, although inner-city areas did experience a significant increase in new housing, particularly apartments, including in some activity centres (Goodman *et al.*, 2010, pp. 45–46). The study also found no increase in the proportion of new housing located within one kilometre of train stations across the metropolitan area, another stated goal of *Melbourne 2030*.

The lack of effect of strategic plans in this respect could be attributed to the absence of either incentive or compulsion to convince developers to alter their standard practices, particularly when it might be more difficult or costly for them to do so. Larger development sites near transport or within activity centres were harder to assemble than greenfield locations, which had the added advantage of little or no community resistance. Third party appeal rights are stronger in Victoria than in other Australian states, and avoiding areas where objections are likely to be strong saves time and money.

Progress towards the goal of increasing administrative efficiency in planning approvals is difficult to measure. The average time taken to determine applications for planning permits is recorded, with procedural implications for failing to meet statutory timeframes. However, this is a measure of throughput and timeliness, rather than effectiveness. Rowley (2017) is critical of the lack of state government monitoring and evaluation of the system's performance and a Victorian Auditor General's 2008 report highlighted the lack of data and analysis available to the government 'for evaluating the impact of the implementation of reforms and the operation of key statutory processes' (Victorian Auditor-General, 2008, p. 41).

The picture emerging here is that progress towards strategic goals, even those of improved system efficiency, varies a great deal and is sometimes hard to assess. A significant causality issue exists in all matters related to evaluating planning success. Urban development has multiple drivers and attributing a particular outcome to a specific strategic aim or policy is difficult. However, the slowing down of outward expansion and densification of the inner suburbs can at least be partly attributed to policy signalling to the market the type of development likely to be approved. The attraction of inner areas, which has encouraged development and pushed up housing prices, reflects many factors, including employment and demographic trends, gentrification and lifestyle changes. A greater test of policy effect occurs when market drivers are weaker, such as housing around activity centres and train stations away from the inner area, or diversification of housing types in any given location. In these areas there is no evidence that planning strategies have had any significant effect.

Lack of attention to implementation is often described as *Melbourne 2030*'s greatest failure. Commentators have generally attributed this to insufficient links between the strategy and the regulatory system which should implement it. Where changes were made to the VPPs to reflect the strategy, the language was frequently imprecise and advisory in tone. The aversion to strong and binding statements resulted in much of the policy being simply ignored. The authors of the first iteration of *Plan Melbourne* indicated that they were aware of this shortcoming. A separate 5-year implementation plan was released alongside *Plan Melbourne 2017–2050* in March 2017 containing 112 new actions divided into short-, medium- and long-term frameworks. Each of these has an identified lead agency or agencies and a range of implementation partners. The progress of plan implementation will be reviewed every 5 years beginning in 2022 and DELWP will undertake annual monitoring and reporting (DELWP, 2017*b*).

Conclusion

This review of metropolitan planning for Melbourne in the first 16 years of the twenty-first century shows recurring strategic themes responding to a time of great change for the city. But comparatively little evidence exists to show that successive governments of differing political persuasions have truly and decisively shaped the urban agenda. Instead they struggle to catch up with trends determined by growth imperatives or the actions of developers and investors. The success of metropolitan strategies depends on having effective means to implement both ambitious and more modest plans. A major tool for implementation is the planning regulatory system.

Strategic plans for Melbourne have not been sufficiently linked to planning regulations or other means of implementation. Planning reform has occurred independently of planning strategy, and has even preceded it. Specific changes to planning regulation in order to implement strategy should follow immediately after its adoption, but this has not always happened. The metropolitan strategic plans have also often not been linked seamlessly with other government strategies or with the spending priorities of critical areas such as transport, education and infrastructure provision. The newly created VPA is intended to coordinate planning between councils, local governments and service delivery agencies. The creation of its predecessor organizations brought greater state government control over local government planning, particularly in the growth areas. Its role has now expanded to all of Victoria and the value it will add to planning for all of the state's cities remains to be seen. There remains some potential for duplication of roles between the VPA, the state government planning department, and the local governments that administer the planning system. However, the analysis in this chapter has identified lack of implementation, rather than plan making, as a key problem. Addressing this requires courage on behalf of governments to take more decisive action and a degree of bipartisan agreement on critical issues around metropolitan planning and management.

References

ABS (Australian Bureau of Statistics) (2016) *Regional Population Growth, Australia, 2014–15*. Cat. 3218.0. Canberra: Australian Bureau of Statistics. Available at: http://www.abs.gov.au/AUSSTATS/abs@.nsf/Latestproducts/3218.0Media%20Release12014-15?opendocument&tabname=Summary&prodno=3218.0&issue=2014-15&num=&view.

ABS (2017*a*) Data from 2011 census, using Quick Stats. Available at: http://www.censusdata.abs.gov.au/census_services/getproduct/census/2011/quickstat/2GMEL?opendocumentandnavpos=220.

ABS (2017*b*) Data from 2011 census on building approvals, using Quick Stats. Available at: http://stat.abs.gov.au/Index.aspx?DataSetCode=BA_GCCSA.

Alison, G. (2016) Melbourne is Australia's fastest-growing city, with more than 1700 newcomers a week. *Herald-Sun*, 31 March. Available at: http://www.heraldsun.com.au/news/victoria/melbourne-is-australias-fastestgrowing-city-with-more-than-1700-newcomers-a-week/news-story/8b8f81c44d32cbbd818aedaf45f34f65.

Audit Expert Group (2008) *Melbourne 2030 Audit Expert Group Report*. Melbourne: Audit Expert Group.

Barber, P., Marsden, I., Moles, J., O'Farrell, P., Sibonis, B. and Testra, G. (2003) VCAT decisions. *Planning News*, **29**(5), pp. 16–19.

Birrell, B., O'Connor, K., Healy, E. and Rapson, V. (2005) *Melbourne 2030: Planning Rhetoric Versus Urban Reality*. Clayton: Monash University ePress.

Buxton, M. (2008) Why deniers can't be implementers – the Melbourne 2030 Audit and the Government response. *Planning News*, **34**(7) pp. 6–8.

Buxton, M. and Goodman, R. (2003) Protecting Melbourne's Green Belt. *Urban Policy and Research*, **21**(2), pp. 205–209.

Buxton, M. and Groenhart, L. (2013) System and strategy: recent trends in governance and planning systems in Australia, in Ruming, K., Randolph, B. and Gurran, N. (eds.) *Proceedings of State of Australian Cities Conference 2013: Refereed Proceedings*, Sydney, pp. 1–11. Available at: http://apo.org.au/node/59879.

Buxton, M., Goodman, R. and Moloney, S. (2016) *Planning Melbourne: Lessons for a Sustainable City*. Melbourne: CSIRO Publishing.

Capire Consulting Group (2016) *School Provision Review for Docklands - Stage One: Needs Analysis*. Department of Education and Training. Carlton, Vic: Capire Consulting Group Pty Ltd and Spatial Vision.

Carmody, B. and Dow, A. (2016) Top of the world: Melbourne crowned world's most liveable city, again. *The Age*, 18 August. Available at: http://www.theage.com.au/victoria/top-of-the-world-melbourne-crowned-worlds-most-liveable-city-again-20160817-gqv893.html.

Coffee, N., Lange, J. and Baker, E. (2016) Visualising 30 years of population density change in Australia's major capital cities. *Australian Geographer*, **47**(4), pp. 511–525. DOI: 10.1080/00049182.2016.1220901.

DADA (Darebin Appropriate Development Association) (2015) *Darebin Appropriate Development Association Charter* (May). Available at: http://www.darebinada.org/about-dada.

Daley, J., Hurley, J., Gurran, N., Goodman, R. and Rowley, S. (2016) Solutions beyond supply to the housing affordability problem. *The Conversation*, 24 October. Available at: http://theconversation.com/solutions-beyond-supply-to-the-housing-affordability-problem-67536.

Davies, A. (2012) The urbanist. *Crikey*, 3 December. Available at: http://blogs.crikey.com.au/the urbanist/2012/12/03/should-the-20-minute-city-be-the-key-objective-of-planning/.

DELWP (Department of Environment, Land, Water and Planning) (2015a) *Better Apartments Public Engagement Report*. Melbourne: State of Victoria Department of Environment, Land, Water and Planning.

DELWP (2015b) *Plan Melbourne Refresh Discussion Paper*. October 2015. Melbourne: State of Victoria Department of Environment, Land, Water and Planning.

DELWP (2016a) *Managing Residential Development Task Force – Overarching Report, Residential Zones State of Play Report*. 29 January. Melbourne: State of Victoria Department of Environment, Land, Water and Planning.

DELWP (2016b) Urban Development Program growth area statistics (unpublished).

DELWP (2016c) *Victoria in Future 2016: Population and Household Projections to 2051*. Melbourne: State of Victoria Department of Environment, Land, Water and Planning.

DELWP (2017a) *Plan Melbourne 2017–2050*. Melbourne: State of Victoria Department of Environment, Land, Water and Planning.

DELWP (2017b) *Plan Melbourne 2017–2050 Five-Year Implementation Program*. Melbourne: State of Victoria Department of Environment, Land, Water and Planning.

DIRD (Department of Infrastructure and Regional Development) (2015) *State of Australian Cities 2014–15: Progress in Australia's Regions*. Canberra: Commonwealth of Australia.

Dodson, J. (2009) The 'Infrastructure Turn' in Australian metropolitan spatial planning. *International Planning Studies*, **14**(2), pp. 109–123.

DOI (Department of Infrastructure) (2002a) *Melbourne 2030. Planning for Sustainable Growth*. Melbourne: DOI.

DOI (2002b) *Melbourne 2030. Planning for Sustainable Growth – Implementation Plan 4, Activity Centres*. Melbourne: DOI.

DOI (2002c) *Melbourne 2030. Planning for Sustainable Growth – Implementation Plan 2, Growth Areas*. Melbourne: DOI.

Dow, A. (2013) Doubts over planning strategy after key advisers quit. *The Age*, 12 December. Available at http://www.theage.com.au/victoria/doubts-over-planning-strategy-after-key-advisers-quit-2013 1212-2z8lz.html.

Dow, A. (2016) Casey Council mosque decision draws protest and hostility in Melbourne's south east. *The Age*, 15 October. Available at: http://www.theage.com.au/victoria/casey-council-mosque-decision-draws-protest-and-hostility-in-melbournes-south-east-20161015-gs31u4.html.

DPCD (Department of Planning and Community Development) (2007) *Melbourne 2030 Audit: Analysis of Progress and Findings from the 2006 Census*. Melbourne: DPCD.

DPCD (2008) *Melbourne 2030: A Planning Update – Melbourne @ 5 Million*. East Melbourne: DPCD.

DPCD (2012) *Reformed Zones for Victoria – A Discussion Paper on Reforming Victoria's Planning Zones*. Melbourne: Department of Planning and Community Development.

DTPLI (Department of Transport, Planning and Local Infrastructure) (2012) *Metropolitan Planning Strategy – Housing Fact Sheet*. Melbourne: Department of Transport, Planning and Local Infrastructure. Available at: http://www.planmelbourne.vic.gov.au/__data/assets/pdf_file/0011/130322/330_60_2-NEW-fact-sheets-Housing-11052012.pdf.

DTPLI (2014a) *Plan Melbourne Metropolitan Planning Strategy*. Melbourne: Department of Transport, Planning and Local Infrastructure.

DTPLI (2014b) *Reformed Residential Zones for Victoria Fact Sheet*. Melbourne: Department of Transport, Planning and Local Infrastructure. Available at: http://www.dtpli.vic.gov.au/__data/assets/pdf_file/0003/229854/Reformed-Residential-Zones-fact-sheet-1_07_2014.pdf.

DTPLI (2015) *Social Atlas of Melbourne Geelong and Regional Cities*. Available at: http://www.dtpli.vic.gov.au/data-and-research/population/census-2011/social-atlas.

GERA (Glen Eira Residents' Association Inc) (2014) *What is Inappropriate/Overdevelopment*? Glen Eira Residents Association, 28 October. Available at: https://geresidents.wordpress.com/tag/inappropriate-development/.

Goodman, R. (2011) Melbourne's activity centre policy: a post-mortem, in State of Australian Cities National Conference 2011, Melbourne, pp. 1–11. Available at: http://apo.org.au/node/59982.

Goodman, R., Buxton, M., Chhetri, P., Taylor, E. and Wood, G. (2010) *Planning and the Characteristics of Housing Supply in Melbourne*. AHURI Final Report No. 157. Melbourne: Australian Housing and Urban Research Institute.

Goodman, R. and Coote, M. (2007) Sustainable urban form and the shopping centre: an investigation of activity centres in Melbourne's growth areas. *Urban Policy and Research*, **25**(1), pp. 39–61.

Goodman, R., Maginn, P., Gurran, N. and Ruming, K. (2013) Simpler, faster, cheaper – Australia's urban aspirations and the planning reform agenda, in Ruming, K., Randolph, B. and Gurran, N. (eds.) Proceedings of State of Australian Cities Conference 2013: Refereed Proceedings, Sydney, pp. 1–17. Available at: http://apo.org.au/node/59883.

Goodman, R. and Moloney, S. (2004) Activity centre planning in Melbourne revisited. *Australian Planner*, **41**(2), pp. 47–54.

Grattan, M. (2016) Morrison targets state planning regulations as problem for housing affordability. *The Conversation*, 24 October. Available at: http://theconversation.com/morrison-targets-state-planning-regulations-as-problem-for-housing-affordability-67524.

Hogg, T. (2007) Mitcham Towers – a major M2030 development proposal finally bites the dust! *Save Our Suburbs Newsletter*. Available at: http://sos.asn.au/category/m2030/.

Kelly, J-F. and Donegan, P. (2013) *City Limits: Why Australia's Cities are Broken and How We Can Fix Them*. Melbourne: Grattan Institute.

Kelly, J-F., Donegan, P., Chisholm, C. and Oberklaid, M. (2014) *Mapping Australia's Economy: Cities as Engines of Prosperity*. Melbourne: Grattan Institute.

Kroen, A. and Goodman, R. (2012) Implementing metropolitan strategies: lessons from Melbourne. *International Planning Studies*, **17**(3) pp. 303–321.

Letts, S. (2016) Building approvals up on apartment surge: ABS. ABC News online. Available at: http://www.abc.net.au/news/2016-08-30/building-approvals-up-on-apartment-surge/7798198.

Lucas, C. (2014) Shiite mosque approved next to Assyrian Christian church, triggering tension. *The Age*, 14 July. Available at: http://www.theage.com.au/victoria/shiite-mosque-approved-next-to-assyrian-christian-church-triggering-tension-20140714-zt6wi.html.

MAC (Ministerial Advisory Committee) (2015) *Plan Melbourne Review 2015 Ministerial Advisory Committee Report*. Melbourne: State of Victoria Department of Environment, Land, Water and Planning.

Mees, P. (2003) Paterson's curse: the attempt to revive metropolitan planning in Melbourne. *Urban Policy and Research*, **21**(3), pp. 287–299.

PIA Victoria (2012) *Reformed Zones for Victoria*. Submission by the Planning Institute of Australia, Victoria Division. Available at: www.planning.org.au/documents/item/4394.

Property Council of Australia (2013) Glen Eira Plans a Sweet and Sour Future. *Propertyoz*, 5 August, p. 1. Available at: https://www.propertycouncil.com.au/Web/Content/Media_Release/VIC/2013/Glen_Eira_plans_a_sweet_and_sour_future.aspx.

Rowley, S. (2017) *The Victorian Planning System: Practice, Problems and Prospects*. Sydney: Federation Press.

Ruming, K. and Goodman, R. (2016) Planning system reform and economic development: unpacking policy rhetoric and trajectories in Victoria and New South Wales. *Built Environment*, **42**(1), pp. 72–89.

Schlesinger, L. (2016) Melbourne CBD apartments: tiny and expensive. *Australian Financial Review*, 6 June. Available at: http://www.afr.com/real-estate/melbourne-cbd-apartments-tiny-and-expensive-20160605-gpc44y.

Scutt, D (2016) Foreign investment in Australia's housing market is slowing. *Business Insider Australia*, 13 October. Available at: http://www.businessinsider.com.au/foreign-investment-in-australias-housing-market-is-slowing-2016-10.

Spiller, M. (2014*a*) Social justice and the centralisation of governance in the Australian Metropolis: a case study of Melbourne. *Urban Policy and Research*, **32**(3), pp. 361–380.

Spiller, M. (2014*b*) Nimble metropolitan governance for a dynamic metropolis, in Whitzman, C., Gleeson, B. and Sheko, A. (eds.) *Melbourne: What Next?* Research Monograph No. 1. Melbourne: Melbourne Sustainable Society Institute/The University of Melbourne.

Spiller, M. (2016) Taking the Metropolitan Planning Authority to the next level. Insights Bulletin, SGS Economics and Planning. Available at: https://www.sgsep.com.au/publications/taking-metropolitan-planning-authority-next-level.

State of Victoria (2017) *Plan Melbourne 2017–2050*. Press release 11 March. Available at: http://www.vic.gov.au/news/plan-melbourne-2017-2050.html.

UDIA (Urban Development Institute of Australia) (2014) *UDIA Submission to the Competition Policy Review*. Urban Development Institute of Australia. Available at: www.udia.com.au/LiteratureRetrieve.aspx?ID=167861.

UDIA (2016) *State of the Land*. Urban Development Institute of Australian National Land Supply Study. Available at: www.udia.com.au/_literature_210584/UDIA_2016_State_of_the_Land_Report.

Victorian Auditor-General (2008) *Victoria's Planning Framework for Land Use and Development*. Melbourne: Victorian Government Printer.

VPA (Victorian Planning Authority) (2016) *About Us*. Brochure. Available at: https://vpa.vic.gov.au/about/.

VPSMAC (Victorian Planning System Ministerial Advisory Committee) (2011) *Victorian Planning System Ministerial Advisory Committee Initial Report*. Melbourne: Department of Planning and Community Development.

Wear, A. (2016) Planning, funding and delivering social infrastructure in Australia's outer suburban growth areas. *Urban Policy and Research*, **34**(3), pp. 284–297 DOI: 10.1080/08111146.2015.1099523.

Wood, I. (2013) Plan Melbourne – a lost opportunity for community. *Planning News*, **39**(10), pp. 14–15.

Wright, P. (2016) Melbourne ranked world's most liveable city for sixth consecutive year by EIU. *ABC News*, 18 August. Available at: http://www.abc.net.au/news/2016-08-18/melbourne-ranked-worlds-most-liveable-city-for-sixth-year/7761642.

Wynne, R. (2015*a*) Minister for Planning Column. *Planning News*, (**41**)4, p. 4.

Wynne, R. (2015*b*) Infrastructure Contributions Overhauled. Media Release, 11 June. Melbourne: Victorian Minister for Planning.

Acknowledgements

The author wishes to warmly thank Kath Phelan for assistance with housing data and locating illustrations, and to Stephen Rowley for comments on the draft.

Chapter 4

Sydney: Growth, Globalization and Governance

Raymond Bunker, Robert Freestone and *Bill Randolph*

Since 2000 there have been profound changes in Australian society, technology, economic activity and attitudes towards sustainability and urbanism. In turn, metropolitan planning has become more complex, reflecting the increasingly diverse and dynamic cities that it seeks to shape, accompanied by state governments turning to the marketplace to deliver purposeful change. The entrenching of neoliberalist ideology has had significant impacts across the spectrum of public policy including the steering of urban development (Gleeson and Low, 2000; McGuirk, 2005). Yet far from governments retreating from intervention in metropolitan planning, they have constructed new spatial configurations, rebooted regulatory regimes and forged closer partnerships with business and the property industry. These mixed dynamics reflect path dependency and both creative and destructive processes (Peck and Tickell, 2002; Brenner and Theodore, 2002).

In Sydney, there has been a robust history of state control over urban development in which the institutions of planning have been sequentially refashioned to promote dominant urban objectives (McGuirk, 2005). In the past few decades, strategic plans have increasingly been focused on delivering more compact urban development outcomes – essentially by restraining growth on the urban fringe and encouraging intensified development within the urban footprint through multi-unit development (Bunker and Searle, 2009). The focus of development has shifted decisively towards urban renewal. Underpinned by a dominant commitment to economic development through job creation and awareness of integrating infrastructure provision and land use planning, compactness and urban renewal are now the main foci of city planning in Sydney.

Table 4.1 draws together some of these complex shifts and currents in a representation of the major elements of Sydney's planning since 2000. The driving philosophy or ideology is a changing mixture of neoliberalism, sustainability and compact city thinking. Economic growth, competitiveness and efficiency dominate

Table 4.1. A representation of Sydney's Planning 2000–2016.

Key elements	Elaboration
Urban change	Population growth; multiculturalism; socio-economic differentiation; spatial polarization; housing unaffordability; urban renewal; densification; infrastructure provision; congestion
Planning ideology	A shifting alliance of sustainability, the compact city and neoliberalism with the dominance of 'efficiency' considerations and economic competitiveness
Policies/plans/resource allocation	Strategic plans for metropolitan Sydney 2005, 2010, 2014; Subregional plans; Draft District Plans (2016); Local Environmental Plans; National Competition Policy; transport plans; infrastructure plans; budget subventions; use of and reform of the planning system; Infrastructure NSW
Implementation mechanisms	Public-private partnerships; development corporations, amalgamated councils, development assessment panels; Joint Regional Planning Panels; Greater Sydney Commission; state instrumentalities e.g. Ports Corporation, Transport for NSW; City Deals

this discourse and have appropriated and co-opted concepts of sustainability: a comment made in general about current urban policy in the OECD (Davidson and Gleeson, 2014). Similar sentiments underpin strategic planning in Sydney both under the Labor government to 2011 (Freestone and Williams, 2012; Freestone *et al.*, 2012) and since 2011 by the Coalition government of the Liberal and Country Party (Cui and Gurran, 2015). This evolving ideology has redirected traditional instruments of planning and introduced new players.

These preliminary observations establish the structure for this chapter. The next section outlines some of the most important characteristics of, and trends in, Sydney's population since 2000. A section follows on the three major metropolitan strategies guiding Sydney's growth and change through this period. Following this, other important actors and influences in Sydney's planning scene are discussed. We then offer an appraisal of Sydney's planning which deals with achievements and continuing issues. Amidst the constraints and ongoing challenges arising from this account, there are indications of a breakthrough in integrated governance more capable of delivering positive outcomes than in the past. A concluding section draws on the arguments in the chapter to reflect on future metropolitan planning.

A Changing Metropolis

Four key features can be highlighted (see also table 4.1). First, the overarching context is continuing growth in the population of Sydney. From 4.3 million in 2011, Sydney is expected to grow to 6.4 million by 2036 and then to 8 million by 2056. These are rapid rates of increase, averaging 85,000 people per year over the next 20 years. The increasing pressures from this projected population on housing, jobs and infrastructure are therefore considerable. The main driver of growth has been net overseas migration, leading also to an inexorably changing socio-cultural mix across the city. The new wave of migrants from South-East and East Asia is adding a further distinctive cultural flavour to Sydney's already highly diverse population.

Second, growth has been accompanied by an increasing socio-economic polarization which has reflected the general increase in income and wealth inequality in Australian society over the last 30 years (ACOSS, 2015; Leigh, 2013). The Gini coefficient is a simple measure of income inequality. A coefficient of 0 means that the total income in the area in question is distributed evenly across all persons while a coefficient of 1 means all income is captured by one person or household in the area depending on the data used. An analysis of Census data on family income for 2001 and 2011 showed that New South Wales (NSW) was the most unequal state and the coefficient increased from 0.39 to 0.42 in that period. The review went on to calculate the coefficient by local government area. The most unequal areas in Australia were Burwood where the coefficient increased from 0.40 to 0.44; Kogarah (0.42 to 0.44); Strathfield (0.39 to 0.43); and Sydney (0.40 to 0.43) (Fleming and Measham, 2015). This has had a distinctive spatial outcome: a wealthier north and east plus some western fringe suburbs contrasting with less advantaged middle suburbs and those to the west and south-west (figure 4.1). This reflects several decades of employment restructuring relating to continued loss of manufacturing jobs and the growth of new 'knowledge-based' employment, with the latter increasingly associated with the central business district (CBD) and

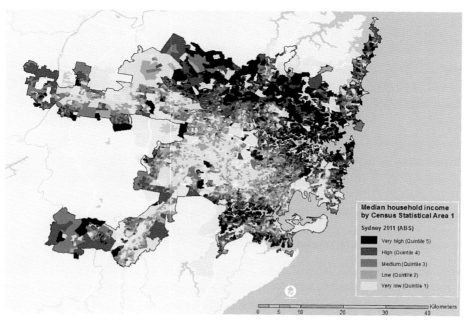

Figure 4.1. Median household income in metropolitan Sydney, 2011. (*Source*: Based on ABS Census, 2011)

inner-city areas (Kelly, *et al.,* 2013). With the 'urban inversion' (Ehrenhalt, 2013) acting to clear the inner suburbs of lower income households, disadvantage has become increasingly synonymous with the middle and outer suburbs (Pawson and Herath, 2015; Randolph and Tice, 2016). In Sydney this has not been helped by the sale of public housing stock in 'The Rocks', an iconic heritage precinct in the shadow of the Harbour Bridge contiguous to the CBD, and relocating displaced residents to new housing, built with the proceeds, on the fringe of the city. In a market-driven context, household income and the related capacity to pay for housing, become the major determinant of development opportunities. The geography of income correlates strongly with property values that underpin development activity – and household income depends, primarily, on the distribution and quality of job opportunities and the ability of people to get to those jobs. Better understanding of this polarization process and implications for the concentration of new jobs have only emerged incrementally since 2000.

The third major change has been the growing significance of higher density multi-unit development. The mix of dwellings across metropolitan Sydney has changed significantly since the turn of the century with a decline in freestanding family homes and increasing proportions of medium- and high-density housing, both notably above national averages (table 4.2).

Table 4.2. Changing dwelling structure in metropolitan Sydney 2001–2011.

Metro Sydney Dwelling type	2001			2011			Change
	Number	%	Australia %	Number	%	Australia %	2001 to 2011
Separate house	960,326	62.1	74.8	1,013,440	58.9	73.8	+53,114
Medium density	282,816	18.3	16.1	338,186	19.7	17.0	+55,370
High density	273,707	17.7	6.3	356,208	20.7	7.6	+82,501

Source: Id, 2016.

Fourth, and interrelatedly, is the almost intractable problem of housing affordability. Both home ownership and private rental costs have become steadily unaffordable on almost every indicator. This is a larger issue for metropolitan Australia but is particularly pressing in Sydney where median house prices and weekly rents have been consistently above national averages (O'Flynn, 2011). By late 2016, although housing supply reached record levels across Sydney, there is little evidence that this has impacted on dwelling prices and hence affordability, except for some apartment sub-markets in central Sydney where oversupply might be occurring. Other than a major financial shock to the macro-economy, there seems little prospect of significant amelioration of dwelling prices and rents.

While these are not the only processes that have impacted on Sydney in recent years, sustained growth, social polarization, densification, and rising housing costs are among the most significant relative to development of the strategic planning frameworks to which we now turn.

The Metropolitan Strategies of 2005, 2010 and 2014

Sydney's recent planning has reflected the current orthodoxy for economic development and growth to be managed through a transition to a more compact city in the context of a market-based neoliberal policy environment. In parallel with this shift in means and ends there have been changes in the methodology for constructing metropolitan strategies. The important trend is the mix of prescription and symbolism. Prescription comes from an earlier time when metropolitan plans could specify desired outcomes with real confidence because the state controlled the infrastructure and most growth was on greenfield land. Outcomes have now become less certain but, as planning and development control powers remain with the state, the convention of detailed sub-regional and local planning has continued as a means of implementation (Searle and Bunker, 2010). Symbolism is evident through graphic representation of the visions driving the plan. The drive to enhance Sydney's role as a global city is most obviously captured through an indicative 'global economic corridor' linking key localities contributing significantly to Australia's Gross Domestic Product (Wade, 2017). This technique has been called 'relational' planning (Healey, 2007). Rogers (2014) argues that this graphic vocabulary (figures 4.2 to 4.4) belies the socio-economic heterogeneity of the city in simplifying the quest for global connectedness. Regardless, this mixture of prescription and ambition helps in part to explain the frequent need to develop new strategies while still keeping or modifying important conceptual constructs.

Three metropolitan strategies for Sydney have been constructed in 9 years, those of 2005 (*City of Cities*) and 2010 (*Metropolitan Plan for Sydney 2036*) by a Labor Government and the most recent in 2014 by a Coalition (Liberal and Country Party) elected in 2011 (*A Plan for Growing Sydney*). Table 4.3 summarizes the key elements of these three major statements. The manner in which the 2010 plan built on the 2005 scheme is evident, but the 2014 plan pulled back on growth aspirations within a foreshortened planning period, in the process simplifying the objectives and hence outcomes in the interests of attainability. A fourth comprehensive strategy is in the offing for 2017, previewed in draft form in late 2016 and discussed below.

City of Cities: A Plan for Sydney's Future

City of Cities (NSW Government, 2005) was the first comprehensive strategy addressing Sydney's growth and development needs since *Cities for the 21st Century* in 1995 (Hamnett, 2000) and arguably the most significant spatial strategy since the 1968 Sydney Region Outline Plan (figure 4.2). Earlier, *Shaping Sydney's Future* (1998) was less a definitive spatial strategy than a marketing update. Indeed,

Table 4.3. Summary of key features of major metropolitan plans 2005–2014.

	City of Cities (2005)	Metropolitan Plan for Sydney 2036 (2010)	A Plan for Growing Sydney (2014)
Premier	Morris Iemma (Labor)	Kristina Keneally (Labor)	Mike Baird (LNP)
Planning Minister	Frank Sartor	Tony Kelly	Pru Goward
Project Coordinator	Gail Connolly	Norma Shankie-Williams	Halvard Dalheim
Time frame	25 years	25 years	15 years
Date	2031	2036	2031
Population	5.3 million	6.0 million	5.9 million
New houses	640,000	770,000	664,000
New jobs	500,000	760,000	689,000
% new housing in existing urban areas	65%	70%	'Significant proportion'
Key features	• City of 5 Cities (Sydney, North Sydney, Parramatta, Liverpool, Penrith) • Centres & Corridors • Global Economic Corridor • Contain urban footprint • Jobs in Western Sydney • Growth Centres • Parks and Public spaces	• Strengthen City of 5 Cities • Multi-centred city • Compact and networked • Western Sydney Employment Area • Urban renewal • Climate change • Urban fringe land use • Social inclusion	• International competitiveness • Expand Global Economic Corridor • Priority growth areas • Strategic centres • Transport gateways & enterprise corridors • Badgerys Creek Airport
Strategic Directions	7	9	4
Objectives	34	54	22
Implementation	• Metropolitan CEOs Group • Sub-regional plans	• Sydney Metropolitan Development Authority • Sub-regional plans	• Greater Sydney Commission • Monitoring & Reporting • Sub-regional plans

metropolitan planning took a back seat in Sydney's planning agenda from the late 1990s as other issues grabbed centre stage including the maturing of sustainability objectives, staging of the Olympic Games in 2000, and broader reforms for state-wide hierarchical governance under the banner of 'Plan First' (NSW Government, 2001). The Carr Labor Government, at least initially, was inclined to control growth simply by 'turning off' housing supply, but attention soon turned to the appropriate policy balance between urban renewal and planned greenfield growth. The latter was to be overseen by a new Growth Centres Commission established in mid-2005. The Commission was a development corporation established to ensure that development in the North West and South West Growth Centres shown in figure 4.2 'proceeded with infrastructure and services planned, funded and linked to the sequence of land release' (NSW Government, 2005, p. 261). This period saw lobbying by developer and other interest groups for a stronger spatial

82 • PLANNING METROPOLITAN AUSTRALIA

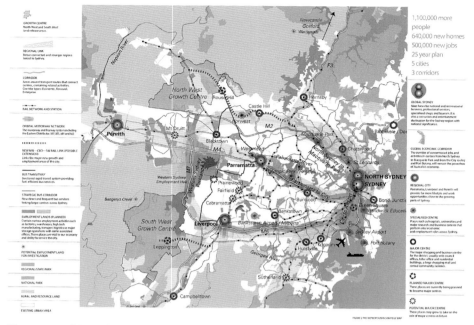

Figure 4.2. City of Cities plan (2005). (*Source*: NSW Government, 2005)

framework for the city's planning and land releases (McGuirk, 2007). The new strategy eventually emerged in late 2005.

City of Cities was a substantive document of over 300 pages, admirably presented and driven by purpose and confidence. Conceived originally as a series of separate documents, the plan drew inspiration from comparable cities, including Melbourne, London and New York, with an emphasis on urban design principles in supporting a compact urban form. Figure 4.2 shows the essential spatial arrangements: a polycentric metropolis whose global status is reinforced by a 'global economic corridor', an archetypal relational metaphor picking up ideas that were then in the air (Searle, 2013). It extended in an arc from the Norwest Business Park through the CBD and south to the airport. Presuming an anticipated population growth of 1.1 million by 2031, the plan envisaged 65 per cent of this expansion coming from infill and renewal in established areas. The same principles were used to distribute future dwellings as targets by sub-region, to be further broken down by local government area in subsequent detailed sub-regional plans. The centres were organized mainly by hierarchy and secondly by type. They comprised two centres in global Sydney (Sydney and North Sydney), three regional cities, nine specialized centres and twelve major centres joined by corridors of more dense development, all with capacity targets to 2031. The regional cities of Parramatta, Liverpool and Penrith were meant to provide higher density and strategic concentrations of services, businesses and housing for surrounding suburban populations. To this end they were to have improved public transport services and appropriate infrastructure. McGuirk (2007, p. 184) argues that the 'centre and corridor' strategy was in part 'an institutional compromise' which provided a contained solution to the conflict over how compact city policies might be implemented in practice while also justifying the focus on the global corridor as the epicentre for economic growth. The result is a highly articulated, spatially interlocking series of detailed proposals driven by the pragmatic imperative to produce a 'workable document' (Mitchell, 2015).

The 2005 plan claimed that its guiding principles were economic, social and environmental sustainability and these were expressed in its five aims of enhancing liveability, strengthening economic competitiveness, ensuring fairness, protecting the environment and improving governance (NSW Government, 2005, p. 6). Peter Newman, co-author of the influential book *Cities and Automobile Independence* (Newman and Kenworthy, 1989) and appointed a Sustainability Commissioner by the NSW Government from 2004 to 2005, signed off on the plan, although there were still only limited measures to address climate change through reduction of emissions.

The 2005 plan was also weakened by an approach to implementation that lacked follow-through by a government which assumed the market would deliver required outcomes. This was not helped by changes in senior Ministers (including both the Premier and Planning Minister) as well as more general governmental resistance. The expectations placed on a steering group of metropolitan CEOs were never realized. Moreover, Mahjabeen (2013) has argued that the plan-making process centralized decision-making, exploited opportunities for the purpose of serving developer interests, and marginalized community groups. By the time more detailed draft sub-regional plans actually emerged, the global financial crisis (GFC) of 2008 resulted in an emergency budget that rethought the public transport proposals intended to complement the land-use strategy.

Metropolitan Plan for Sydney 2036

The 2005 Strategy underwent a review that was released as a discussion paper early in 2010 complementing new transport proposals with a view to delivering a fully integrated land use and transportation plan by year's end (figure 4.3). The review acknowledged emerging new challenges – the impact of the GFC, climate change, housing affordability, higher population forecasts, planning and delivery of transport infrastructure and failing employment opportunities in western Sydney. It also noted the need to protect land for primary production, open space and conservation on the urban fringe (NSW Government, 2010*a*).

The final 2010 metropolitan plan released to announce the 'robust and visionary framework' of the new State Premier Kristina Keneally – the fourth Labor premier since 2005 – was essentially a revision of the 2005 plan (NSW Government, 2010*b*). It used updated population and employment targets for 2036 by sub-region and increased slightly the target for new housing in established urban areas (table 4.3). In contrast to *City of Cities*, the 2010 plan was linked to a formal

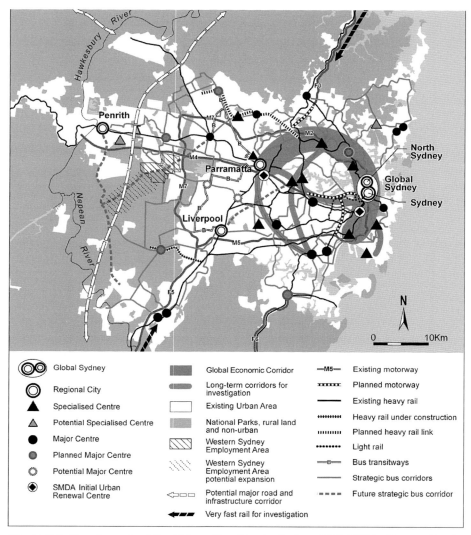

Figure 4.3. Key elements of the Metropolitan Plan for Sydney 2036 (2010). (*Source*: Searle, 2013)

metropolitan transport strategy claimed to be a 10 year fully funded transport plan (NSW Government, 2010c). Accordingly it envisaged improved connectivity as crucial to strengthening Sydney as a global city. The new plan identified forty-six key transport corridors and proposed urban renewal opportunities supported by the existing and expanded rail network, but a second Sydney airport was excluded because of the federal government's reluctance to commit to the project. However, it took the relational elements further with the global economic arc extended to Parramatta, a gesture symbolizing the rising planning significance and political importance of western Sydney (Searle, 2013). But overall, this was a stocktaking document lacking the game-changing gravitas of the 2005 Strategy and its weak implementation plan proved more hopeful than realistic.

A Plan for Growing Sydney

In March 2011 the Labor Government in power since the mid-1990s lost office, with inaction and indecision about metropolitan transport and a succession of planning scandals playing a decisive role (Freestone and Williams, 2012; Freestone *et al.*, 2012). For nearly twelve months the new Liberal-National Party Government nonetheless appeared content with the forward planning of the 2010 document, but in May 2012 released a discussion paper announcing 'a fresh start' with a major focus on 'housing affordability and transport problems across the metropolitan area' (NSW Government, 2012). In March 2013 a draft plan was released with a strong pro-investment orientation (NSW Government, 2013). It identified nine 'city shapers' critical to Sydney's growth – Global Sydney, Global Economic Corridor, Sydney Harbour, Parramatta, Parramatta Road Corridor, Anzac Parade Corridor, North West Rail Corridor, Western Sydney Employment Area and the Metropolitan Rural Area – and the intensification of housing and employment in a series of 'activation precincts'.

A *Plan for Growing Sydney*, the strategy released in December 2014, built on the draft document and its predecessors but departed in some significant ways (figure 4.4). Fensham (2015, p. 47) maintained that it was 'not as clear in describing its

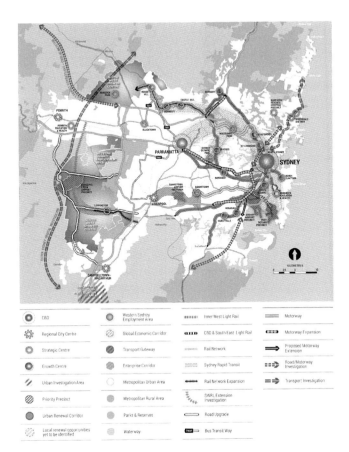

Figure 4.4. A Plan for Growing Sydney (2014). (*Source:* NSW Government, 2014)

key elements' as the two earlier strategies. It was also for a shorter time period and centres were treated in more generic fashion than as an ordered hierarchy. The aims and initiatives were pared back, and the schematic plan had noticeably fewer aspirations than earlier visions, arguably a statement on the circumscribed role of the state government in decisively delivering outcomes (Fensham, 2015, p. 48). While long-term household, dwelling and employment targets for 2031 were still in the plan, there was much more flexibility in how these might be achieved. Sub-regional planning was the vehicle for driving housing supply and choice with further work needed to define areas capable of additional housing capacity. An urban feasibility model was to be used to test the practicability of development options for each sub-region and to set housing targets for councils. Housing production was seen as a purely private sector responsibility and 'on rezoned sites [with] sufficient consumer demand for it, at a price that provides a return to the developer' (NSW Government, 2014, p. 66). A precise split between greenfield and brownfield was foregone. Despite an emphasis on home–job connectivity, the discussion of transport infrastructure and options was limited, effectively deferring to decisions already made in the *State Infrastructure Strategy* (Infrastructure NSW, 2012, 2014) with considerable developmental work, funding commitments, and partnership agreements required. Much future work was deferred to a projected new body, the Greater Sydney Commission, discussed below.

Some Key Features of Sydney's Planning since 2000

While the metropolitan planning strategies set a broad vision, spatial arrangements and targets for population and employment growth, there are other actors and issues in the metropolitan scene that have affected or amended these proposals. Typically, these are recognized in the strategies, but have something of a life of their own. It is a complex and evolving picture as the brief and selective account in this section is intended to convey.

Western Sydney

The problem and potentialities of Western Sydney as a major distinctive sub-region of metropolitan Sydney have been intertwined since at least the release of an initial planning strategy in the late 1990s (NSW Government, 1998). Western Sydney has accommodated much of Sydney's population expansion since the post-war years and the two peripheral 'growth centres' to the north-west and south-west of the city shown in all three strategy plans have been the foci of greenfield development since 2004, with planned major centres at Leppington and Rouse Hill as shown in figure 4.2. They were to be supported by railway extensions since largely completed or under construction. All strategies have addressed issues of employment, housing and connectivity and *A Plan for Growing Sydney* pays particular attention to transforming the productivity of Western Sydney through growth and investment.

Parramatta is promoted as Sydney's second CBD and some government functions have been transferred there. One important development that is increasingly recognized as a 'game changer' is the second Sydney airport at Badgery's Creek. The federal government initially announced that such an airport would be located there in 1986 but resisted any formal commitment until April 2014. *A Plan for Growing Sydney* is the first plan to explicitly recognize the new airport projected to open in 2025.

In environmental terms, Western Sydney is at some disadvantage. The climate is more extreme than the coastal strip and conditions in summer can be difficult as onshore cooling breezes struggle to penetrate inland. Air quality is not as good and the area is distant from the coast and its attractions. Planning policies do address these issues, with extensive attention to parklands, as in *City of Cities*, the enhancement of river and water features, and greening strategies to mitigate the urban heat island effect.

Transport and Infrastructure Planning

Despite the obvious importance of providing more infrastructure to support a denser city, this has been a critical shortcoming of compact city planning for Sydney, particularly for travel and transport needs. *City of Cities* in 2005 was not linked with a transport plan but plans for infrastructure projects and transport were issued the following year. However these were disrupted by the GFC and competing ideas about the provision of public transport. Confusion about transport planning attended the remaining years of the Labor Government and the early years of the succeeding Coalition Government saw much the same. However, in the last 3 years a suite of important transport projects has been announced with committed funding, including light rail, heavy rail and major roads. The most significant of these is the Western Sydney airport project. A second is WestConnex, an ambitious and controversial high-capacity road connection between Parramatta and the central city. The third is a 'metro' high-speed rail spine supporting an expanded global arc. This will be achieved partly by upgrading existing tracks and partly by a new harbour tunnel and underground route through the CBD. This would begin to provide the high-speed, frequent and reliable underground connections characteristic of alpha global cities such as London, New York, and Tokyo.

Rearrangement of Port Functions

Sydney Harbour has been a working port since the arrival of the First Fleet in 1788. An important rearrangement of port functions in the last two decades has had significant effects on Sydney's development. Freight handling operations have been increasingly relocated from the Harbour with Botany Bay expanding as the major container port. The changed and increased land freight movement patterns consequent on these rearrangements were an important part of *City of Cities*, and improvement of the Port Botany freight line and expansion of important rail yards continued in the following plans. At the same time the regional ports of Newcastle to the north and Port Kembla to the south were also reconstructed in their functions and capacities. This enabled space to be made for the knowledge and lifestyle industries seen as so essential for Sydney's future. The Bays Precinct in the inner harbour is a current planning hotspot and for the time being has been used to accommodate the growing number of cruise ships.

Development Corporations

Development corporations have played a significant role in Sydney's development in strategic locations since 2000 (Searle, 2005). They have generally been given power to plan, acquire and dispose of land commercially for redevelopment. They operate outside the normal planning system and have been frequently criticized for lack of accountability and the domination of business interests in their operation. One of the oldest is Landcom, formed in 1975 to provide fully serviced affordable land on the fringe of Sydney. It was corporatized in 2001 and now operates much like a for-profit business. UrbanGrowth NSW is a development corporation formed in 2013 by combining Landcom and the Sydney Metropolitan Development Agency. The new arrangements are designed to facilitate urban renewal in strategic locations by partnerships with the private sector and councils. The Barangaroo Delivery Authority was established in 2009 to redevelop redundant wharf areas immediately to the west of the CBD. Numerous changes have taken place in the original proposals emerging from a 2005 international ideas competition subsequent to Lend Lease being appointed the preferred developer for the southernmost section of the site. The upscaling of commercial towers and the siting and bulk of a mixed-use casino, apartment and hotel tower for James Packer's Crown Group, planned to reach 275 metres and positioned on what was public land on the harbour waterfront, have been prominent concerns, with strong opposition from the City of Sydney and other critics concerned at the diminution of the public realm (Stickells, 2010).

Reforming the Planning System

The provisions of the metropolitan strategies are implemented in regions and localities by various statutory mechanisms including State Environmental Planning Policies (SEPPs) and the provisions of Local Environmental Plans (LEPs) also ultimately requiring the imprimatur of the state government. SEPPs are powerful and flexible instruments and override all other planning controls. They include such matters as urban renewal, affordable housing, transport infrastructure and land fill. Under the Labor Government until 2011 they were often used in an arbitrary manner which at its most blatant amounted to little more than ministerially driven rezoning mechanisms (Freestone *et al.*, 2012).

From 2004 the NSW planning system has been the target of waves of planning reform intended to 'focus on strategic planning for growth areas, simplify planning controls [and] improve development assessment processes' (NSW Government, 2005, p. 12). The planning system has been seen as stifling competition and an impediment to economic activity. This is a continuing criticism largely supported by the Productivity Commission (2011).

Planning reform is a continuing and complex issue, involving a diminished role for local government and an increased involvement by state officials and professional appointees (Freestone *et al.*, 2012; MacDonald, 2015; McFarland, 2011; Ruming and Davies, 2014). Part 3A of the amended *Environmental Planning and Assessment Act* 1979 commenced in August 2005 with the intention of fast-tracking major job-generating projects under the banner of state significance to bypass the normal assessment and approval process. The use of this power by the Labor Government aroused so much criticism that the then Opposition promised to repeal it and did so when elected to office in 2011. However, considerable decision-making of this kind still remains in the province of the minister. A new Planning Assessment Commission was constituted to review and determine, under delegation, major developments in NSW. Joint Regional Planning Panels were also established and given planning and approval powers for projects of regional significance. At the local level, some councils have also instituted independent development assessment panels to determine significant applications.

Funding Infrastructure

The enormous sums needed for major metropolitan infrastructure projects have been a determining influence on funding models. WestConnex is currently estimated to cost $16 billion and is financed by a mixture of federal, state and private sector funding. The ambitious new metro rail proposals are underwritten by the sale of part of the state's electricity distribution system. Public-private partnerships have also been used to build toll roads and the airport line to serve the 2000 Olympics. Some projects such as the cross-city tunnel opened in 2005 have failed financially because of overambitious traffic projections (Phibbs, 2008; Haughton and McManus, 2012), a not atypical scenario for large-scale infrastructure projects of the neo-liberal era (Flyvbjerg *et al.*, 2003).

Federal–State Financial Relations

Because of its superior revenue-raising capacity, the federal government makes loans and grants to the states for many purposes including infrastructure. This provision is somewhat hit and miss and depends not only on federal budget circumstances but also on the views and working relationships of senior politicians at both state and federal level. Liberal Prime Minister Tony Abbott restricted transport subventions to the states to road proposals and kick-started WestConnex.

He also made funds available to start the infrastructure to support a second Sydney airport through a A$3.6 billion Western Sydney Infrastructure Plan. Abbott's successor Malcolm Turnbull signed a memorandum of understanding with then NSW Premier Mike Baird in October 2016 to use the new Western Sydney airport as a catalyst to stimulate new jobs and businesses as part of a new British-inspired 'city deal' partnership.

State–Local Relations

These assume a number of dimensions. There has been some tension in the relations between the state and local governments in the planning reforms outlined above. In December 2015 the state government announced it intended to amalgamate the forty-five local councils in Sydney into twenty-three and this began in May 2016 and has continued with considerable acrimony and opposition. State government relations with local publics and communities of interest have also been lively. The organization of community opposition to the proposed reforms of 2012–2013 was extremely effective. Local groups continue to protest about the construction of WestConnex and other major projects. Despite what appears to be widespread professional support for the state government's planning directions, led through 2015–2016 by Premier Baird and Minister Rob Stokes, a growing wave of criticism about anti-democratic intervention is evident (figure 4.5). The media commentator Elizabeth Farrelly has been a prominent critic of a 'war on

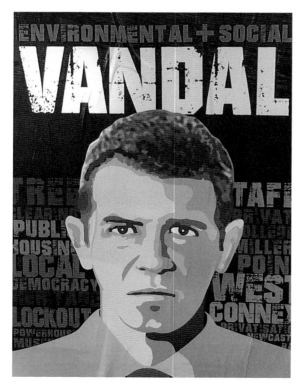

Figure 4.5. Poster critical of the planning and environmental policies of the NSW State Government led by Liberal Premier Mike Baird (April 2014–January 2017). (*Source*: Authors)

the public realm' (e.g. Farrelly, 2016). Baird resigned suddenly in January 2017 citing personal reasons and any reverberations into planning and local government matters are yet to play out.

Appraisal

Taking the above discussion further, how far and in what way have the main goals of Sydney's planning since 2000 been realized? The COAG Reform Council's 2011 national survey of capital city planning systems revealed critical structural weaknesses in Sydney metropolitan planning. While 'high-quality planning content' was acknowledged, this was not complemented by 'hard-edged measures to deliver this in an integrated way' (COAG Reform Council, 2011, p. 97). The scorecard by planning consultant Pat Fensham (2015) is also less than fulsome. He gave a 'pass' mark for some aspects, notably land-use regulation but recorded 'fails' on several key issues including development of road and transportation pricing policies, proactive public transport initiatives, education and engagement initiatives, unconvincing commitment to the polycentric city agenda, and weak metropolitan governance. Our assessment focused on broader cross-cutting issues is similarly mixed. Sydney's planning experience since 2000 reflects many of the features of neoliberal planning mentioned briefly at the start of this chapter, as applied to the compact city

A Global City

Strengthening Sydney's role as a global city has been a centrepiece of high-level planning since the late 1990s (Searle, 1996). What evidence is there to mark progress on this? Different indicators produce varied outcomes. *City of Cities* cited the Globalisation and World Cities Research Group (GaWC, 2016) ranking for Sydney. This uses measures of the connectivity of advanced producer services in cities around the world. The current website has data for 2000, 2004, 2008, 2010 and 2012. Between 2004 and 2008 Sydney advanced its ranking from Alpha to Alpha plus and in 2012 was one of eleven such world cities in that second rank behind London and New York in top place. Another periodic world ranking is that of PriceWaterhouseCoopers (2016) called *Cities of Opportunity*. It ranked Sydney tenth in the thirty cities surveyed in 2016. Questions over transport infrastructure, housing affordability and terrorism have deleteriously affected other rankings.

The City of Sydney Local Government Area remains the core of the city's international standing, its reputation intensified through 'concerted planning action among major stakeholders' (Hu, 2012, p. 347). In more concrete terms, there is evidence from longitudinal floor space and employment surveys recording Sydney's confirmation as a global city (Hu, 2014). In the period 1991–2006 employment in central Sydney (CBD and, significantly, the renewing city fringe neighbourhoods of Pyrmont and Ultimo) grew from 204,000 to 300,000. There were marked increases in advanced producer services such as finance, banking, accountancy, advertising, marketing and management consultancy, the 'knowledge services' typical of a global city. Another noticeable feature was a growing capacity in 'experience services' such as amenity facilities and cultural and recreational activities, as well as accommodation. More recent analyses are for an extended survey area and so are not directly comparable with Hu's (2014) review, but report employment of 438,000 workers in 2012 (City of Sydney 2012).

Progressive expansion of the spatial conception of global Sydney deeper into the metropolitan area has also been a feature of successive strategies, most obviously through increasing the tentacles of the global economic corridor. There remains a tension between continued strong growth in the global economic corridor forecast and competing aspirations for employment growth in western Sydney. Overall since 2001 employment growth has occurred primarily in accordance with the metropolitan planning framework: 96 per cent of metropolitan employment growth was in designated centres with 44 per cent in four key centres: CBD, North Sydney, Parramatta, and Macquarie Park (Miller, 2014).

A Compact City

While Sydney's footprint has continued to expand through new greenfield estates concentrated in the north-west and south-west growth centres, the dominance of this growth process has been checked by a continuation of the turn to urban consolidation first evident nationally in the 1980s (Forster, 2006). As noted earlier, shares of medium and higher density housing have grown. As another expression, figure 4.6 illustrates the substantial increase in the approvals of 'other-residential'

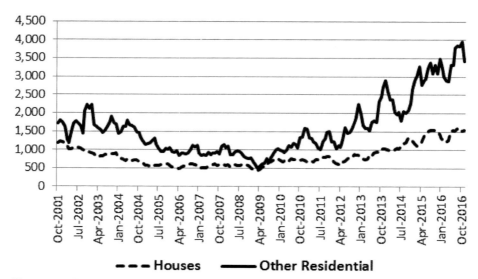

Figure 4.6. Total monthly approvals for 'houses' and 'other residential' dwellings, Sydney, 2001–2016 (4 month rolling averages). (*Source:* ABS (2017) 8731.0. Building Approvals)

(i.e. attached and multi-unit) dwellings in recent years compared with those for houses. The metamorphosis of Landcom into UrbanGrowth NSW is a reflection of this substantial shift in market preferences and government priorities. Steadily and inexorably the processes of densification have made urban renewal linked to transit-oriented development a key focus for strategic metropolitan planning. A ready – but ultimately finite – supply of large-scale former industrial sites, many along the Parramatta River corridor, has facilitated the urban renewal agenda to date, but the financial viability of renewing older apartment blocks near transport nodes is a pressing policy challenge (Troy *et al.,* 2015).

Among Australian cities, travel in Sydney in 2011 had 'by far the lowest mode share for car driving, the highest share for public transport and above-average rates of walking' (Mees and Groenhart, 2012, p. i). While density is but one of the variables affecting choice of travel mode (Rickwood and Glazebrook, 2009), data from household travel surveys show that over the decade commencing 2002, Sydney's population increased by 13 per cent, train trips by 24 per cent, bus trips by 19 per cent and vehicle trips by 5 per cent (Transport for NSW, 2014).

Transport Infrastructure

Much of Sydney's growth through redevelopment and renewal to higher densities was not supported by any substantial attention to travel demands. Increased congestion is another common feature of the more compact city (OECD, 2012). It is only in the last 2 or 3 years that decisions have been locked-in about major strategic road and rail infrastructure projects, most feeding into central Sydney. This raises the issue of the important transport connections needing to be put in place to support the further growth of western Sydney and its internal and external connections. Travel patterns are less channelled and focused than in inner and middle Sydney. *City of Cities* planned for a number of strategic bus corridors to connect centres, and bus services (largely privatized) have been expanded and extended in western Sydney.

This area of travel management and transport infrastructure may well be the most important issue in future metropolitan strategies. There are significant challenges ahead about the provision of major transport infrastructure with competing demands needing to be reconciled. Of considerable importance is the sequencing and financial implications of these decisions. The colossal sums needed to fund these have already led to some important initiatives. WestConnex is funded by federal and state governments and intends to attract some private investment. The first stage of the metro project is publicly funded but there are increasing calls for 'value capture' to be levied from developers benefiting from the provision of this high-grade transport infrastructure, although the development industry is already questioning this approach (Stapledon and Fox, 2016).

Sustainability

City of Cities in 2005 was driven by principles of economic, social and environmental sustainability. How far these have been achieved is difficult to briefly appraise. As far as economic and social sustainability go, earlier discussion enables some summary conclusions to be drawn. Economic sustainability is on track given the continued role of Sydney as a global city and the resilience shown in recovering from the economic impact of the GFC, with Sydney resuming its leading role with Melbourne in driving increases in Australia's Gross Domestic Product. In contrast social sustainability is at risk, given the increasing disparities that characterize Australia's most unequal city.

Although increasingly a centrepiece of official and insurgent thinking (Rauscher and Momtaz, 2016; Total Environment Centre, 1999), the record in environmental sustainability is more complex. There is little explicit comment on climate change and indirect measures to address it prevail, notably in the assumptions regarding the compact city. As Davidson and Arman (2014) observe, the compact city is assumed to be associated with more sustainable transport leading with less use of fossil fuel and lower greenhouse gas emissions. As they observe, the principle of sustainable transport was mainstreamed into all planning documents and closely tied to metropolitan transport planning from 2010. Unfortunately, while Mees and Groenhart (2012) saw Sydney as having the most sustainable transport system, they also noted a regression at that time to Infrastructure NSW's 2012 endorsement of a predominantly road-based system for public transport planning (later reversed by direction of the Premier in their 2014 report). It was another 5 years before some cohesion was restored into sustainable transport planning to support a more compact city.

The compact city is assumed to lead to savings in energy consumption (both within the household and in travel), and in water use. Some of these assumptions are debatable (Randolph and Troy, 2011) but there have been some important initiatives in this field. Seeded more successfully was the introduction of BASIX online standards in 2004, which set explicit and demanding targets for water and energy efficiency in all new and substantially modified dwellings. It originally aimed to reduce greenhouse gas emissions from houses by 40 per cent (although only 20 per cent for apartments) and has since been refined and extended (NSW Government, 2011). Stormwater sensitive urban design at dwelling, locality and neighbourhood scale is also facilitated through planning and development assessment of development proposals. Planning documents are strong on protecting diversity and managing natural resources and there is also consistent attention to providing linked green and open spaces.

Governance

Governance is seen as 'the Achilles heel' of metropolitan planning (Fensham, 2015, p. 60). Metropolitan level of governance has been needed to fully assert and implement the imperatives of metropolitan strategies, and Sydney has lacked this dimension since abolition of the Cumberland County Council in the early 1960s. One of the key announcements in the *Plan for Growing Sydney* was the Government's intention to establish a new independent body to further develop, articulate, refine and drive implementation of the strategy. The Greater Sydney Commission (GSC) was established by legislation in November 2015. In its enabling Act the first of its principal objectives is 'to lead metropolitan planning for the Greater Sydney Region' (Section 9 (a)).

The GSC consists of three Commissioners appointed for their experience and expertise in economic, environmental and social concerns. A fourth Commissioner is the Chief Commissioner and the initial appointment was Lucy Turnbull, wife of the Prime Minister and a former Lord Mayor of Sydney. Six District Commissioners each represent a particular part of Greater Sydney for which district plans are being prepared. The other members of the Commission are the secretaries of the NSW Treasury, Transport for NSW, and the Department of Planning and Environment.

In November 2016 the GSC released a draft amendment to *A Plan for Growing Sydney* that reconceptualizes metropolitan Sydney as a metropolis of three cities to 'collectively create Global Sydney': the Eastern Harbour City, the Central Parramatta River City, and the Western City in and around the new airport (figure 4.7). The metropolis of three cities is a new relational schematic capturing the

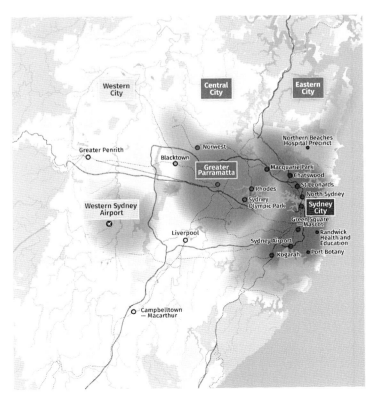

Figure 4.7. 'A metropolis of three cities'. (*Source:* NSW Government, 2016)

challenge of organizing the planning of Sydney as a productive, liveable and sustainable polycentric '30 minute' metropolis of 8 million people by 2056 (NSW Government, 2016). A hierarchy of centres is also reinstated. Productivity comes first with the objective of increasing the metropolitan area's economic activity by 75 per cent to approximately A$655 billion per annum by 2036. Supporting the initial implementation of this vision is the new intergovernmental 'city deal' referred to above, with its emphasis on major transport infrastructure provision associated with the planned Western Sydney Airport.

A weakness of previous metropolitan strategies concerned the sub-regional plans to guide local plan-making. Earlier initiatives were delayed and failed to make the links into the strategic and statutory planning of local councils. Hence, alongside the draft amendment come six draft district plans translating the broader metropolitan vision into more detailed strategies to be given effect through Local Environmental Plans, housing and job targets, urban renewal plans, and policy directives around affordable housing, zero net carbon outcomes, and networked open space provision.

Conclusion

This chapter has been built around the succession of planning strategies guiding the development of metropolitan Sydney since the early 2000s and their intersection with a raft of other issues with implications for planning. The overarching economic agenda is the strongest narrative, articulated through policies driving a transition to a more compact, multi-centred global metropolis. The dominant complexion is neoliberal but within a messy, often opportunistic and inevitably hybridized, set of processes (Brenner, 2004; McGuirk, 2005).

Strategies have sought appropriate balances of 'blueprint' and 'relational' elements to mediate respectively the demands of 'traditional determinism' and 'fluidity' (Searle, 2013). While using much the same methodology, there has been a progression from the detailed prescriptions of *City of Cities* to a more pragmatic and adaptable approach as planners work more with the private sector and learn to cope better with uncertainty. The visionary content of the 2005 plan with its 'five cities, three corridors, one global city' is matched if not exceeded by the draft 2016 amendment to the 2014 plan with a 'positive transformation' towards a re-imagined tripartite metropolitan form.

The achievements over a decade and a half have been mixed, with implementation let down by weak metropolitan governance. Successive strategies have not been seen definitively as key reference documents across government (Fensham, 2015). Economic sustainability has emerged as the major driver and preferred means to a more socially and environmentally sustainable metropolis. However, a by-product of the transition to a more compact city has been a more unequal city, in that lower income and disadvantaged communities are becoming increasingly marginalized. But the lack of attention to transport and accessibility is being redressed with ambitious new or augmented transport infrastructure seen as the catalyst for higher density redevelopment. The new airport in Western Sydney is expected to generate thousands of jobs directly and indirectly and will be 'city-shaping'.

There is now a renewed vigour and purpose in strategic planning. Missing pieces of the governance puzzle have finally fallen into shape. The federal government is taking a close interest in Western Sydney and helping to fund major infrastructure projects. The new Greater Sydney Commission assumes the role of a 'champion' for metropolitan planning that has long been missing (Fensham, 2015). But it is early days still and fresh challenges are destined to surface for this new institution, particularly in relation to how it will deliver better coordination between state and local planning, its equitable balancing of competing demands for development across the metropolitan area, and perceptions of its democratic mandate as a fully appointed body. The litmus test for the new Commission and the comprehensive review of the metropolitan strategy to be undertaken in 2017 will be the ability of the new plan to address the heterogeneity of Sydney such that the benefits of economic growth and environmental amenity can be more evenly distributed across the city.

References

ACOSS (Australian Council of Social Service) (2015) *Inequality in Australia: A Nation Divided.* Sydney: Australian Council of Social Service.

Australian Bureau of Statistics (2017) *8731.0 Building Approvals, November 2016.* Canberra: ABS.

Brenner, N. (2004) Urban governance and the production of new state spaces in Western Europe 1960–2000. *Review of International Political Economy*, **11**(3), pp. 447–488.

Brenner, N. and Theodore, N. (2002) The urbanization of neoliberalism: theoretical debates. *Antipode*, **34**(3), pp. 349–379.

Bunker, R. and Searle, G. (2009) Theory and practice in metropolitan strategy: situating recent Australian metropolitan planning. *Urban Policy & Research*, **27**(2), pp. 101–116.

City of Sydney (2012) *Floorspace and Employment Survey Report.* City of Sydney. Available at: http://www.cityofsydney.nsw.gov.au/learn/research-and-statistics/surveying-our-community/floor-space-and-employment-survey.

COAG Reform Council (2011) *Review of Capital City Strategic Planning Systems. Report to the Council of Australian Governments.* Sydney: COAG Reform Council.

Cui, T. and Gurran, N. (2015) Planning Reform, Interest Group Participation and Influence: the Case of New South Wales. Paper presented to the State of Australian Cities Conference, Gold Coast. Available at: http://apo.org.au/search/site/cui%20and%20gurran.

Davidson, K. and Arman, M. (2014) Planning for sustainability: an assessment of recent metropolitan planning strategies and urban policy in Australia. *Australian Planner*, **51**(4), pp. 296–306.

Davidson, K. and Gleeson, B. (2014) The sustainability of the entrepreneurial city? *International Planning Studies*, **19**(2), pp. 173–191.

Ehrenhalt, A. (2013) *The Great Inversion and the Future of the American City.* New York: Knopf Doubleday.

Farrelly, E. (2016) Sydney's planning storm is building to a tempest. *Sydney Morning Herald*, Available at: http://www.smh.com.au/comment/sydneys-planning-storm-is-building-to-a-tempest-20160623-gpq1w6.html.

Fensham, P. (2015) The Sydney Metropolitan Strategy: implementation challenges, in Buček, J. and Ryder, A. (eds.) *Governance in Transition.* Dordrecht: Springer, pp. 41–64.

Fleming, D. and Measham, T. (2015) Income inequality across Australia during the mining boom 2001–11. *Australian Geographer*, **45**(2), pp. 203–216.

Flyvbjerg, B., Bruzelius, N. and Rothengatter, W. (2003) *Megaprojects and Risk: An Anatomy of Ambition*, Cambridge: Cambridge University Press.

Forster, C. (2006) The challenge of change: Australian cities and urban planning in the new millennium. *Geographical Research*, **44**(2), pp. 173–182.

Freestone, R. and Williams P. (2012) Urban planning, in Clune, D. and Smith, R. (eds.) *From Carr to Kenneally: Labor in Office in NSW 1995–2011*. Sydney: Allen and Unwin, pp. 193–206, 363–367.

Freestone, R., Williams, P. and Moore, N. (2012) From Carr to Kenneally: the business of planning in New South Wales 1995–2011, in Gaynor, A., Gralton, E., Gregory, J. and McQuade S. (eds.) *Urban Transformations: Booms, Busts and Other Catastrophes*. Proceedings of the 11th Australasian Urban History/Planning History Conference, University of Western Australia, pp. 115–130.

GaWC (2016) *Globalization and World Cities Research Network*. Loughborough University. Available at: http://www.lboro.ac.uk/gawc/.

Gleeson, B. and Low, N. (2000) *Australian Urban Planning: New Challenges, New Agendas*. Sydney: Allen and Unwin.

Hamnett, S. (2000) The late 1990s: competitive versus sustainable cities, in Hamnett, S. and Freestone, R. (eds.) *The Australian Metropolis: A Planning History*. Sydney: Allen and Unwin, pp. 168–188.

Haughton, G. and McManus, P. (2012) Neoliberal experiments with urban infrastructure: the Cross City Tunnel, Sydney. *International Journal of Urban and Regional Research*, **36**(1), pp. 90–105.

Healey, P. (2007) *Urban Complexity and Spatial Strategies: Towards a Relational Planning for Our Times*. London: Routledge.

Hu, R. (2012) Shaping a global Sydney: the city of Sydney's planning transformation in the 1980s and 1990s. *Planning Perspectives*, **27**(3), pp. 347–368.

Hu, R. (2014) Remaking central Sydney: evidence from floor space and employment surveys in 1996–2006. *International Planning Studies*, **19**(1), pp. 1–24.

Id (2016) *Id: The Population Experts*. Melbourne. Available at: http://home.id.com.au/.

Infrastructure NSW (2012) *State Infrastructure Strategy*. Sydney: Infrastructure NSW.

Infrastructure NSW (2014) *2014 State Infrastructure Strategy Update*. Sydney: Infrastructure NSW.

Kelly, J-F., Mares, P., Harrison, C., O'Toole, M., Oberklaid, M. and Hunter, J. (2013) *Productive Cities*. Melbourne: Grattan Institute.

Kübler, D. and Randolph, B. (2007) Metropolitan governance in Australia: the Sydney experience, in Hambleton, R. and Gross, J. (eds.) *Governing Cities in a Global Era: Urban Innovation, Competition and Democratic Reform*. New York: Palgrave Macmillan, pp. 139–150.

Leigh, A. (2013) *Battlers and Billionaires: The Story of Inequality in Australia*. Melbourne: Redback.

MacDonald, H. (2015) Fantasies of consensus: planning reform in Sydney, 2005–2013. *Planning Practice and Research*, **30**(2), pp. 115–138.

McFarland, P. (2011) The best planning system in Australia or a system in need of review? An analysis of the New South Wales planning system. *Planning Perspectives*, **26**(3), pp. 403–422.

McGuirk, P. (2005) Neoliberalist planning? Rethinking and re-casting Sydney's metropolitan planning. *Geographical Research*, **43**(1), pp. 59–70.

McGuirk, P. (2007) The political construction of the city-region: notes from Sydney. *International Journal of Urban and Regional Research*, **31**(1), pp. 179–187.

Mahjabeen, Z. (2013) Community Participation in Planning Practice: Analysis of Sydney Metropolitan Strategy 2005. PhD thesis, University of New South Wales.

Mees, P. and Groenhart, L. (2012) *Transport Policy at the Crossroads: Travel to Work in Australian Capital Cities 1976–2011*. Melbourne: RMIT University.

Miller, S. (2014) Employment Distribution and Centres-based Strategic Planning: Sydney 2001–2011. BPlan thesis, University of New South Wales.

Mitchell, D. (2015) Defining the Inevitable: Micro-Practices of Strategic Spatial Planning. Paper presented to the State of Australian Cities Conference, Gold Coast. Available at: http:soacconference.com.au/wp-content/uploads/2016/02/Mitchell.pdf.

NSW Government (1998) *Shaping Western Sydney: The Planning Strategy for Western Sydney*. Sydney: NSW Department of Urban Affairs and Planning.

NSW Government (2001) *Plan First: Review of Plan Making in NSW White Paper*. Sydney: DUA (Department of Urban Affairs and Planning).

NSW Government (2005) *City of Cities: A Plan for Sydney's Future*. Sydney: NSW Department of Planning.

NSW Government (2010a) *Metropolitan Strategy Review: Sydney Towards 2036*. Sydney: NSW Government.

NSW Government (2010b) *Metropolitan Plan for Sydney 2036*. Sydney: NSW Government.

NSW Government (2010c) *Metropolitan Transport Plan: Connecting the City of Cities*. Sydney: NSW Government.

NSW Government (2011) *2006–09 Multi-Dwelling Outcomes: BASIX Ongoing Monitoring Program*. Sydney: NSW Department of Planning.

NSW Government (2012) *Sydney over the next 20 years: A Discussion Paper*. Sydney: NSW Department of Planning and Infrastructure.

NSW Government (2013) *Draft Metropolitan Strategy for Sydney to 2031*. Sydney: NSW Department of Planning and Infrastructure.

NSW Government (2014) *A Plan for Growing Sydney*. Sydney: NSW Department of Planning and Environment.

NSW Government (2016) *Towards our Greater Sydney 2056: A Draft Amendment to Update a Plan for Growing Sydney*. Sydney: Greater Sydney Commission.

Newman, P. and Kenworthy, J. (1989) *Cities and Automobile Dependence: An International Sourcebook*, Aldershot: Gower.

O'Flynn, L. (2011) *Housing Affordability*, Briefing Paper No 04/2011. Sydney: NSW Parliamentary Library.

OECD (Organisation for Economic and Cultural Development) (2012) *Compact City Policies: A Comparative Assessment*. OECD Green Growth Studies. Paris: OECD.

Pawson, H. and Herath, S. (2015) Dissecting and tracking socio-spatial disadvantage in urban Australia. *Cities*, **44**, pp. 73–85.

Peck, J. and Tickell, A. (2002) Neoliberalizing space. *Antipode*, **34**(3), pp. 380–404.

Phibbs, P. (2008) Driving alone – Sydney's Cross City Tunnel. *Built Environment*, **34**(3), pp. 364–374.

PriceWaterhouseCoopers (2016) *Cities of Opportunity* 7. Available at: www.pwc.com/cities.

Productivity Commission (2011) *Performance Benchmarking of Australian Business Regulation: Planning, Zoning and Development Assessment*. Research Report. Canberra: Productivity Commission.

Randolph, B. and Tice, A. (2016) Relocating disadvantage in Australian cities: socio-spatial polarisation under neo-liberalism. *Urban Policy and Research*. Published online at: http://www.tandfonline.com/doi/full/10.1080/08111146.2016.1221337.

Randolph, B. and Troy, P. (2011) Factors in energy and water consumption, in Newton, P. (ed.) *Landscapes of Urban Consumption*. Melbourne: CSIRO Publishing, pp. 215–236.

Rauscher, R.C. and Momtaz, S. (2016) *Cities in Global Transition: Creating Sustainable Communities in Australia*. Cham, Switzerland: Springer.

Rickwood, P. and Glazebrook, G. (2009) Urban structure and commuting in Australian cities. *Urban Policy and Research*, **27**(2), pp. 171–188.

Rogers, D. (2014) The Sydney Metropolitan Strategy as a zoning technology: analyzing the spatial and temporal dimensions of obsolescence. *Environment and Planning D*, **32**(1), pp. 108–127.

Ruming, K.J. and Davies, P.J. (2014) To what extent 'an entirely new approach to how planning is done'? Tracing planning system reform in New South Wales. *Australian Planner*, **51**(2), pp. 122–131.

Searle, G. (1996) *Sydney as a Global City*. Sydney: NSW Department of Urban Affairs and Department of State and Regional Development.

Searle, G. (2005) The Sydney-Waterloo Authority: Sydney's Continuing Use of Development Corporations as a Primary Method of Urban Governance. Paper presented to the State of Australian Cities Conference, Brisbane. Available at: http://apo.org.au/resource/refern-waterloo-authority-continuing-se=development-corporations-primary-mode.

Searle, G. (2013) 'Relational' planning and recent Sydney metropolitan and city strategies. *Urban Policy and Research*, **31**(3), pp. 367–378.

Searle, G. and Bunker R. (2010) New century Australian spatial planning: recentralization under Labor. *Planning Practice and Research*, **25**(4), pp. 517–529.

Stapledon, N. and Fox, K. (2016) *Value Capture is not a Magic Pudding: Options for Funding Infrastructure*. Sydney: Urban Taskforce Australia.

Stickells, L. (2010) Barangaroo. Instant urbanism: just add water. *Architecture Australia*, **99**(3), pp. 47–51.

Total Environment Centre (1999) *Greenprint: An Environmental Strategy for the 21st Century*. Sydney: TEC.

Transport for NSW (2014) *2012/13 Household Travel Survey (HTS): Key Transport Indicators for Sydney*. Sydney: Transport for NSW.

Troy, L. (2013) Clothed in Green: Growth Politics and Sustainability. PhD dissertation, University of Sydney.

Troy, L., Randolph, B., Pinnegar, S. and H. Easthope (2015) Planning the End of the Compact City? Paper presented to the State of Australian Cities Conference, Gold Coast. Available at: http://apo.org.au/files/Resource/troy-l.compressed2.pdf.

Wade, M. (2017) Three inner-Sydney districts contributed a quarter of Australia's GDP growth in 2015–16. *Sydney Morning Herald. 28 February.* Available at: http://www.smh.com.au/business/the-economy/three-innersydney-districts-contributed-a-quarter-of-australias-gdp-growth-in-201516-20170228-gumztb.html.

Acknowledgements

Our thanks to John Brockhoff, Gail Connolly, Halvard Dalheim, Pat Fensham and Norma Shankie-Williams for sharing their thoughts and recollections in a series of interviews conducted between August and November 2016, and Bob Meyer for his critique of a draft, but we absolve them from responsibility for the assertions and conclusions made here which remain ours alone. Figures 4.2, 4.4, and 4.7 are reproduced with the kind permission of the Greater Sydney Commission. Figure 4.3 is reproduced by kind permission of Glen Searle and Taylor & Francis.

Chapter 5

Adelaide:
Tough Times in the City of Light

Stephen Hamnett and *Jon Kellett*

South Australia has a long tradition of purposeful government planning and social reform which is commonly traced back to its establishment as a planned free settlement in 1836 (Hutchings and Bunker, 1986; Hutchings, 2007). Elements of this tradition were still apparent in the early 1990s following a major review of the planning system which emphasized the importance of strategic planning for metropolitan Adelaide (Hamnett, 2000, p. 179). Some components of the planning system introduced at that time survive but it has been weakened by the imperatives of neoliberalism and by the particular pressures arising from South Australia's increasingly challenging economic circumstances which have led to an aggressively pro-development climate in the state in recent years.

Adelaide has the smallest population and the lowest rate of population growth of the mainland state capitals discussed in this book (ABS, 2016a). While there has been some increase in population density in the inner suburbs in the early twenty-first century (Coffee *et al*., 2016), Adelaide still has one of the lowest overall population densities of the capitals (Government of South Australia, 2016a) and the highest level of car use (ABS, 2013a).

After a short historical prelude, this chapter summarizes the principal economic and demographic trends in Adelaide in the early twenty-first century. Since 2002 South Australia has been governed almost entirely by Labor Governments, led first by Mike Rann and then, from 2011, by Jay Weatherill. The main focus of the chapter is on a chronological analysis of the principal metropolitan plans released in 2003, 2006, 2010 and 2016, interwoven with a discussion of accompanying reforms to planning processes and legislation. Some particular elements are identified which serve to differentiate Adelaide's recent metropolitan policy reforms and regulatory experiments from those of Australia's other major cities. Overall, however, the chapter observes a tendency for South Australian planning to converge with practice elsewhere, with a consequential weakening of the state's once distinctive planning tradition.

Recent Economic and Population Trends

The South Australian economy is more reliant on agriculture and manufacturing than is Australia generally. Because of its small size the state is highly dependent on the health of the national economy, with many factors affecting its growth lying beyond its control (Hampton *et al.*, 2013, p. 11). The mining boom of the early twenty-first century, which carried Australia largely unscathed through the Global Financial Crisis, offered South Australia a brief prospect of prosperity when a massive expansion of the Olympic Dam copper and uranium mine, near Roxby Downs in the north of the state, was proposed in 2008. This was predicted to contribute more than A$45 billion to Gross State Product over its 40-year life (Minister for Mineral Resources Development/ Minister for Urban Development and Planning, 2011, p. 3), but these expansion plans were shelved in 2012.

A second blow to the South Australian economy has been the demise of the motor industry, a major bulwark of the state's manufacturing sector throughout the second half of the twentieth century. The last remaining manufacturer, General Motors Holden, will cease vehicle production at its Elizabeth plant in the northern suburbs of Adelaide in 2017.

In November 2016 South Australia reported an unemployment level of 7.0 per cent, the highest amongst Australian states (ABS, 2016*b*). A much-needed boost came in 2016 with a major Commonwealth contract to build submarines, but the state government has recognized the urgent need to diversify the economy by supporting the export of high-value agricultural and horticultural products; developing 'knowledge industries'; attracting more international students; and drawing additional tourists to Adelaide's arts and music festivals and to South Australia's internationally renowned wine-producing areas, most of which are fairly accessible from the capital city. As a particular indication that desperate times require desperate measures, serious consideration was given recently to the establishment of dumps to store imported nuclear waste (Nuclear Fuel Cycle Royal Commission, 2016, p. xiii).

Between 2000 and 2016 South Australia's total population grew from 1.5 to 1.7 million people (Government of South Australia, 2016*b*). Part of this period saw a higher than average rate of population growth, with implications for planning policy. Metropolitan Adelaide retains a high degree of primacy within the state's settlement system, with nearly 80 per cent of the total resident population. The metropolitan area grew from 1.06 million to 1.225 million people over the period 2001–2016 (ABS, 2006; 2013*b*), with changes to statistical boundaries introduced at the time of the 2011 census accounting for around 123,700 of this. The post-millennium period has seen an increase in the number of migrants of Asian origin settling in the city, although a higher proportion than in other states was still of European descent in 2011 (ABS, 2013*b*).

The City of Adelaide, the central part of the metropolitan area, has grown more quickly in recent years, almost doubling its resident population from fewer than

13,000 in 2001 to 23,000 by 2015. With three major universities having campuses in the central city, international students comprise a significant proportion of this growth, and the population is now dominated by the 15–44 age group. There has been an accompanying change to the skyline. The City of Adelaide has long been distinguished from other mainland capitals by its low-rise city of stone heritage buildings, but tall, bland apartment blocks, predominantly designed to meet minimal space standards, are now changing this character, with higher-quality design limited mainly to new government and, in particular, university buildings.

Figures 5.1a and **5.1b**. Old and new in the City of Adelaide. (*Photos*: Stephen Hamnett)

Precursor: Adelaide's Planning Tradition

Adelaide was founded in 1836 as part of a deliberate process to establish a new South Australian colony 'as like as possible to a country which is perfectly civilized but not over-peopled' (Mill, 1834). It was laid out according to Colonel William Light's celebrated city plan which later helped to shape the ideas of the international garden city movement. Since its establishment Adelaide has generally grown at a slower rate than other Australian state capitals for reasons to do with its relative isolation and limited economic opportunities. These circumstances have led to a long history of activist and interventionist state governments. The particular conditions of the Great Depression in the 1930s led to the establishment of the South Australian Housing Trust (SAHT), a public housing agency which built cheap housing for workers to support the state's industrialization. South Australia's public rental housing stock reached a peak of about 63,000 dwellings in 1992 (Marsden, 2011, p. 262), although it has declined substantially since then in accord with the move nationally away from government ownership of dwellings to a range of other policy instruments to meet housing objectives (Beer and Paris, 2005). In the post-war years the SAHT undertook larger-scale projects which reshaped Adelaide in a way that demonstrated a 'practical and powerful' approach to metropolitan planning (Stretton, 1970, p. 142; see also Howe, 2000). South Australia was also a major beneficiary in the 1970s of the Whitlam Government's land commission funds for public land acquisition in support of 'comprehensive and orderly urban development' (Forster and McCaskill, 2007, p. 99). By the late twentieth century South Australia had a well-entrenched reputation amongst Australian states as a developmental social democracy with a distinctive planning tradition (Badcock, 1986; Hutchings and Bunker, 1986).

Adelaide's Planning in the 1990s

The main elements of the South Australia planning system in 2000 had been established in the early 1990s, following a major review conducted by the Bannon Labor Government (Planning Review, 1992*a*). One output of this review was the proposal for a series of new planning strategies for the various regions of the state, commencing with a new metropolitan strategy. This would replace the traditional 'end-state' plan, which had shaped Adelaide's growth since the 1960s, with a more flexible and indicative spatial framework for development. It anticipated a metropolitan population of between 1.23 million and 1.38 million by 2021. It argued that most of the housing to meet this growth could be built on vacant land within the existing metropolitan boundary (Planning Review, 1992*b*, p. 25), with the government's land agency, the South Australian Urban Land Trust, expected to play a strong role in joint venture developments between the public and private sectors in both inner and outer areas. Other key elements of the 1992 strategy included a reaffirmation of the importance of a strict hierarchy of centres within a polycentric metropolis; the renewal of Adelaide's extensive old public housing estates to address issues of social disadvantage; and an acknowledgment of the new imperatives of sustainability. Overall, the review proposed a shift from reactive, short-term thinking to a long-range, citizen-oriented style of planning which would aspire '… to place equity considerations back on the metropolitan planning agenda and to resolve tensions between economic investment and environmental planning' (Lennon, 2000, p. 164).

However, the lofty ambitions of the Bannon Government's planning review soon proved to be out of step with a strengthening trend towards greater reliance on market outcomes (Lennon 2000, p.165). Labor lost office in 1993 and metropolitan strategy became the responsibility of a Liberal Government which showed little enthusiasm for the strategy that it had inherited. The period from 1993 to 2002 was one of 'broad ideology and ad hoc projects' (Bunker and Hutchings, 1996, p. 48).

The Liberals revised the metropolitan planning strategy in 1998 and this was the plan in force in 2000 (Premier of South Australia, 1998). Its emphasis was squarely on supporting the government's economic imperatives, primarily by ensuring the availability of serviced land and by building roads. There had been no substantial new investments in public transport infrastructure in South Australia since the mid-1980s and, over the period 1986–1999, the mode share of public transport plunged by 32 per cent (Transport SA, 2002, p. 2). The 1998 strategy did express support, however, for development 'at higher densities around centres of activity and along major transport routes' (Premier of South Australia, 1998, p. 66) and, over time, it foresaw a shift towards 'a multi-centred city' (Premier of South Australia, 1998, p. 67). Given their pro-market tendencies, a surprising proposal by the Liberals the following year was for an urban growth boundary for Adelaide, eventually introduced in 2002 (DTUPA, 2002).

Strategic Planning under the Rann Labor Government 2002–2011: 'Prosperity Through People'

Metropolitan Planning 2003–2007

A Labor government led by Mike Rann took office in 2002 and Labor have remained in power in South Australia ever since (see table 5.1 overleaf).

The Rann Government oversaw substantial changes to metropolitan planning strategy and to the state planning system more generally. An updated metropolitan planning strategy was adopted in January 2003 (Premier of South Australia, 2003) which restated earlier commitments to urban consolidation, retaining the growth boundary, the use of surplus government land for development and a strong centres policy (see figure 5.2). But, even while adopting the 2003 strategy, the government indicated that this was just a set of 'discrete amendments' (Government of South Australia, 2005, p. 2) pending a more comprehensive review.

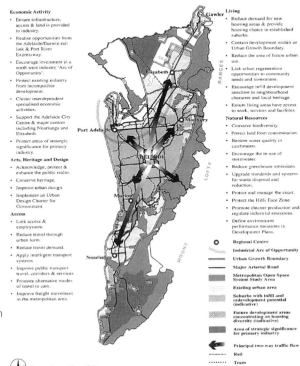

Figure 5.2. Summary of Planning Strategy Priorities 2003. (*Source*: Premier of South Australia, 2003, p. 4. Image courtesy of the Department of Planning, Transport and Infrastructure, South Australia)

Table 5.1. Governments, plans and planning reforms 2000–2016. (*Source*: The authors)

Year	Government	Legislation and Principal Planning Agencies	Plans and Strategies	Planning Reform
2001	Liberal (in power since 1993) Premier Olsen, then Kerin	Department of Transport, Urban Planning and the Arts		Development Assessment Panels (DAPs) introduced
2002	Labor elected Premier Rann	Department of Transport and Urban Planning		Economic Development Board established
2003			Planning Strategy for Metropolitan Adelaide	
2004			State Strategic Plan	
2005		Planning SA (Department of Primary Industry and Resources)	Strategic Infrastructure Plan	
2006	Labor re-elected Premier Rann	Development (Panels) Amendment Act, 2006	Planning Strategy for Metropolitan Adelaide	DAP powers amended to ensure a minority of elected members
2007		Climate Change & Greenhouse Emissions Reduction Act, 2007	Planning Strategy for Metropolitan Adelaide Tackling Climate Change: South Australia's Greenhouse Strategy, 2007–2020	
2008		Department of Planning and Local Government		Planning and Development Review
2009				
2010	Labor re-elected Premier Rann		30 Year Plan for Greater Adelaide	
2011	Rann replaced as Premier by Weatherill	Department of Planning, Transport and Infrastructure		
2012				
2013				
2014	Labor re-elected Premier Weatherill			Expert Panel on Planning Reform 2013–2014
2015			Integrated Transport and Land Use Plan South Australia's Climate Change Strategy 2015–2050	
2016		Planning, Development & Infrastructure Act 2016	30 Year Plan Update	

Soon after coming to office, Rann established a new Economic Development Board (EDB) and this recommended establishing a high-level, visionary State Strategic Plan (EDB, 2003, p. 26). Early in 2004 the state government published a population policy entitled 'Prosperity through People' (Government of South Australia, 2004*a*). Its ambitious target of 2 million people for South Australia by the middle of the twenty-first century was central to the first State Strategic Plan, released in May 2004 (Government of South Australia, 2004*b*) and also informed the continuing task of revising the metropolitan planning strategy. But the latter also placed a much greater emphasis than previously on ecologically sustainable development as a foundation of planning and 'not just another issue which needs ticking off on a checklist' (Bellette, 2003, p.12). Unusually, the planning team was led by an environmental scientist and the resulting draft strategy was particularly rich in its analysis of water, waste, energy and biodiversity, and in its understanding of the links between these elements and urban development.

The draft metropolitan planning strategy was released for public comment in April 2005. 'Integration' was a key aspiration, with three strategic planning priorities expressed as 'integrated energy provision, transport planning and land use planning'; 'integrated land and water use planning and development'; and 'urban containment' (Government of South Australia, 2005, pp. 10–12). Growth was to be contained within an urban boundary although it was acknowledged that 'broad hectare' land would be exhausted within 12 to 15 years at current rates of development. If urban sprawl was to be contained, therefore, it would be necessary to achieve higher urban densities through 'transit-focused development'. When finalized in August 2006 (Government of South Australia, 2006), however, the strategy included a modest target of only 10 per cent of weekday travel by public transport by 2018 and no substantial public transport investments were proposed.

The 2006 Planning Strategy was a well-crafted document, in the general style of earlier post-1990 South Australian strategies. It included an indicative 'Metropolitan Spatial Framework' for the next 30 years (figure 5.3) which was to provide a flexible long-term context for the more detailed planning of land release in the shorter-term. The latter was outlined in the government's Residential Metropolitan Development Program, a well-established programme for monitoring trends in land supply and allocating land for suburban expansion over the coming 8–10 years. This seemed to strike an appropriate balance between longer-term flexibility and shorter-term specificity, although the Planning Institute of Australia found the 'spatial framework' to be too abstract, lacking as it did specific indications of priority areas for urban redevelopment or targets for population and jobs (PIA, 2005).

Over the period 2005–2007, much effort went into the preparation of South Australia's Greenhouse Strategy, published in 2007 as 'Tackling Climate Change'. A key underlying assumption was that more compact settlements could encourage shorter journeys and thus reduce harmful emissions (Government of South Australia, 2007*b*, p. 36). This was one of several important state government

Figure 5.3. Adelaide Metropolitan Spatial Framework 2006. (*Source*: Government of South Australia, 2006, p. 26. Image courtesy of the Department of Planning, Transport and Infrastructure, South Australia)

policy documents published between 2004 and 2007. Another was the 'Strategic Infrastructure Plan for South Australia', released in 2005 (Office for Infrastructure Development, 2005, p. 6). This incorporated matters traditionally associated with land-use and spatial planning, including increased housing densities in strategic locations well served by public transport. Proposed improvements to transport infrastructure within the metropolitan area continued to give priority to road construction, however.

The metropolitan planning strategy came to sit rather uneasily alongside these other strategic statements. Rather than guiding the provision and staging of infrastructure, it now had the somewhat lesser role of expressing the spatial consequences of infrastructure decisions already taken elsewhere. The marginalization of spatial planning was further symbolized at this time by the relocation of the state government planning function from a Department of

Transport and Urban Planning to become a relatively minor part of the large Primary Industries and Resources portfolio (Bunker, 2015, p. 383).

Consultation on the draft metropolitan planning strategy in 2005 was more limited than previously (O'Leary, 2005) and legislative changes around this time also contributed to a loss of local democratic input into planning decisions. In 2001 the state Liberal Government had established 'Development Assessment Panels' to replace elected councils as the planning authorities for local government areas. Amendments in 2006 specified that, henceforth, these were to have a majority of independent expert members. Development assessment panels of various types have subsequently been established in other states, sometimes as a response to concerns about corrupt practices on the part of local councils. Corruption does not seem to have been a significant factor in South Australia, however. The impetus came, rather, from a desire to reduce the capacity for local councils to delay developments by taking frivolous or parochial decisions. There are nineteen local councils responsible for parts of the Adelaide metropolitan area, ranging in population size from nearly 170,000 to less than 10,000. Local government reform to reduce the number of councils is regularly canvassed 'to allow metro Adelaide to operate as a city rather than as a series of parishes' (Landry, 2004, p. 30; see also Property Council, 2016) but successive state governments have shown little enthusiasm for this, primarily because of its likely electoral unpopularity.

The Rann Government maintained a strong commitment to ecologically sustainable development while simultaneously pursuing the economic growth priorities of the State Strategic Plan. The integration of these conflicting strategic purposes was and remains an elusive goal. Nevertheless, Rann can claim some impressive achievements in the pursuit of sustainability. These included laying the basis for obtaining around 40 per cent of South Australia's electricity from renewable sources – especially wind farms – by 2014; construction of a desalination plant powered by renewable energy; encouraging the highest national adoption rates for both domestic rain water tanks and solar photovoltaic panels; providing recycled water to several suburbs; ensuring that office developments meet high energy efficiency standards; and pioneering energy efficient housing.

However, the compact city, a central plank of 'Tackling Climate Change' and also of the 2006 Planning Strategy, soon came under strong pressure from the land development industry, which was increasingly critical of the limited amount of land identified for residential development at and beyond the metropolitan fringe, especially in the face of stronger than anticipated population growth. Pressure to release more land also became increasingly linked to the growing political salience of housing affordability and land supply concerns in the lead up to the 2007 Federal election.

In response, less than a year after adopting the 2006 planning strategy, the state government announced that it was extending Adelaide's urban boundary to include an additional 2,000 hectares of land (Hansard, 2007) and the metropolitan planning strategy was updated to incorporate this in December 2007.

The Planning and Development Review 2008: Planning as 'Sustainable Economic Enabler'

The dominant characteristic of the period between the adoption of the 2006 metropolitan strategy and the next significant plan, the 30-Year Plan of 2010, was the growing ascendancy of the property development industry as a major influence on government planning policy. A 'Planning and Development Review' was announced in June 2007 and this was overseen by a steering group with strong industry links.

Despite the Global Financial Crisis, the economic prospects for South Australia still appeared promising in 2008. In addition to the projected expansion of the Olympic Dam mine, the state had some significant defence contracts, and population growth was being driven by increased levels of net overseas migration (Hugo, 2008). To accommodate anticipated growth, therefore, the Review advocated yet another expansion of the urban boundary, noting that the boundary 'must be seen as a dynamic management tool, not a fixed line on a map' (Planning and Development Review Steering Committee, 2008, p. 80). It also recommended a reinvigorated metropolitan planning strategy to assist in restoring the planning system 'to its intended role of a sustainable economic enabler' (2008, p. 54) and it proposed a new 30-Year Plan for 'Greater Adelaide', an expanded metropolitan region encompassing about 85 per cent of South Australia's population. The Review also acknowledged the government's climate change agenda and proposed substantial increases in residential densities at locations served by transit. These policies were to be driven by 'a reinvigorated and separate state planning department' (*Ibid.*, p. 52) although, given the composition of the review team, it was unsurprising that it sought a reduced role for the government's land development agency, by now known as the Land Management Corporation (*Ibid.*, p. 148). A further proposal was for a new residential code to speed up the approval of housing developments.

On 10 June 2008, the government announced its acceptance of most of the Review's proposals. The 2008–2009 State Budget also proposed significant investment in the metropolitan rail system, the electrification of suburban lines to support transit-oriented development and the staged extension of Adelaide's only tram line to Port Adelaide.

As part of the preparation of the new 30-Year Plan, additional priority areas for housing beyond the urban fringe were to be identified. Private consultants were quickly commissioned to prepare a Growth Investigation Areas (GIA) report on the grounds that 'Planning SA was short staffed and would not be able to deliver the GIA report within the tight time frame required' (Ombudsman SA, 2013, p. 19; see also Bunker, 2015, p. 386).

The 30-Year Plan for Greater Adelaide 2010

A draft of the 30-Year Plan for Greater Adelaide was released for public comment in July 2009 (DPLG, 2009*a*) and finalized, with relatively few changes, in February

2010 (DPLG, 2010). It combined a very generous amount of residential land for urban expansion with heroic aspirations for urban infill in a more compact city. There was an obvious conflict between these two principal strategic thrusts of the plan.

The 30-Year Plan noted that population was growing more rapidly than had been forecast in 2004 and that the date for achieving a state population target of 2 million had now been brought forward from 2050 to 2027 (DPLG, 2009b, p. 16). This was translated into an additional 560,000 people for Greater Adelaide by 2036, requiring an additional 258,000 dwellings and 282,000 jobs.

The overall planned growth of Greater Adelaide was disaggregated into a series of detailed housing and employment targets across eight regions. The greater part of new fringe growth was directed to the northern region and to an expanded Barossa region. Large new development areas were identified at Mount Barker, Roseworthy and, controversially, at Buckland Park, a fairly remote tract of flood-prone land north-west of the metropolitan area, where a 'country township' had been proposed by a large private development company (Hamnett and Hutchings, 2009; Hutchings and Kellett, 2013).

Within the existing metropolitan area, locations for fourteen new transit-oriented development sites (TODs) were identified. Over the life of the Plan it was intended that 70 per cent of all new housing would be built within the existing urban area, with 50 per cent of the region's growth concentrated in transit corridors (see figure 5.4) where densities were projected to increase 'on average from 15 to 25–35 dwellings per hectare' (DPLG, 2009a, p. 74).

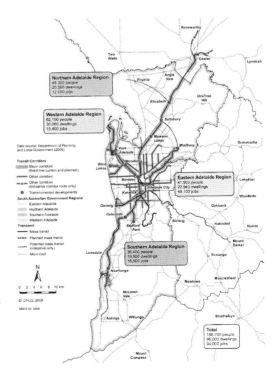

Figure 5.4. The 30-Year Plan for Greater Adelaide 2010. Map D2 Targets for Transit Corridors. (*Source*: DPLG, 2010, p.75. Image courtesy of the Department of Planning, Transport and Infrastructure, South Australia)

The population projections adopted for the 30-Year Plan were higher than the highest contemporary forecasts of the Australian Bureau of Statistics (see Hutchings and Kellett, 2013). The Planning Minister suggested that 'if you over-achieve or underachieve on these targets … all it will do is simply adjust the timing of the plan' (Hansard, 2010, p. 1554). The Planning Institute pointed out, however, that it might be difficult to achieve the increased level of infill housing sought in the short to medium term and that this would lead to greenfield development being prioritized, with associated increases in car use (PIA, 2009). Since 2004–2005, public transport's share of weekday vehicle kilometres travelled in metropolitan Adelaide had remained consistently low at only 7.5 per cent (South Australia's Strategic Plan Audit Committee, 2012, p.111). A comparative analysis of census data on travel to work patterns in Australia's capital cities was published in 2012 (Mees and Groenhart, 2012) and noted that Adelaide had the highest mode share for car driving of any of the capital cities, the third-lowest rate of public transport use (after Canberra and Hobart) and the second-lowest rate of active transport use (after Perth). The early provision of a high quality public transport system seemed essential if Adelaide was to achieve a substantial shift from greenfield development to higher density infill over time and to lose its label as 'Australia's car capital' (Mees and Groenhart, 2012, p. ii).

The Weatherill Government: Towards a More 'Vibrant' Adelaide

In October 2011 Rann was replaced as Labor Premier by Jay Weatherill and this led to some further changes in emphasis in metropolitan planning policy. The focus shifted from transit-oriented development across a multi-centred city towards accelerated redevelopment at substantially greater densities and heights in central Adelaide and along inner arterial roads. As an indication of the state government's shift in focus, the Land Management Corporation became the 'Urban Renewal Authority' in 2012. 'Vibrancy' in the inner city became a rhetorical centrepiece of planning policy under Weatherill and, in pursuit of this, substantial investment went into the redevelopment of key sites in the city centre, including the Riverbank area, adjacent to an upgraded Adelaide Oval. Regulatory reforms were also made to encourage the growth of small bars in the city, linked to the revitalization of 'laneways' (explicitly drawing on the experience of central Melbourne). As noted earlier, the resident population of the City of Adelaide more than doubled between 2001 and 2015 and changes to planning policy in 2012 sought to encourage further growth by allowing dramatic increases in permitted height limits in the central area.

Also in 2012, however, it was conceded that a population of 2 million for the state was now unlikely to be achieved by 2027 (South Australia's Strategic Plan Audit Committee, 2012, p. 95). The target of 258,000 dwellings set in the 30-Year Plan required an average annual net growth of 8,600 dwellings, whereas the average from 2006 to 2011 was 8,000 a year and this dipped in 2012–2013 to just under

Figure 5.5. Vibrant Adelaide – street art in Stafford Street. (*Photo*: Stephen Hamnett)

6,000 (DPTI, 2013*b*, p. 24). The upgrading of the rail network was also proceeding more slowly than planned. The electrification and extension of Adelaide's southern suburban rail line was completed in 2014, but plans to electrify the main northern and north-western lines were postponed in the 2012–2013 budget, as was the extension of the tram network in the face of what the State Treasurer described as 'a record revenue write-down' (Government of South Australia, 2012).

The electrification of suburban rail lines is likely to be completed eventually. In 2013, however, the state government released a draft 'Integrated Transport and Land Use Plan' (ITLUP) which refocused priority for new tramlines on routes within the CBD and extending into nearby inner suburbs (Minister for Planning and Minister for Transport, 2013, p. 4).

Figures 5.6a and **5.6b**. (*a*) Adelaide's 'coast to coast' tram (currently stalled at Hindmarsh); (*b*) New electric train on the Adelaide-Seaford line. (Photos: Stephen Hamnett)

Meanwhile, the development industry continued to lobby for the further streamlining of the planning system. In response, and also in the broader context of growing support for planning reform at national level (Productivity Commission, 2011; COAG, 2012), another review of the South Australian planning system was conducted (Expert Panel on Planning Reform, 2014; Hamnett and Kellett, 2016). This drew heavily on recent reforms in other Australian states. It led to a new Act of Parliament in April 2016 (Planning, Development and Infrastructure Act, 2016) which made provision for the establishment of a new State Planning Commission, drawing in part on the experience of the Western Australian Planning Commission and bringing together existing state policy and assessment bodies. The centrepiece of the new Act was a proposed Planning and Design Code, intended to increase the number of development types for which no approval was required and to allow for faster assessment of development proposals against a checklist of standardized built-form criteria. A statutory requirement was introduced that there should be a strengthened urban growth boundary to protect what were called 'Environment and Food Production Areas' from urban encroachment. The Act also foreshadowed a 'Community Engagement Charter', although this sat uncomfortably alongside further radical proposals for substantial reductions to the rights of third parties to appeal against planning decisions and for the almost complete removal of elected local councillors from development assessment panels. In effect, the latter meant that local government would lose its already diminished role in the assessment of all but the most minor development applications, a very significant shift in the planning responsibilities of state and local governments.

The 30-Year Plan for Greater Adelaide 2016 Update

A final version of the ITLUP was released in 2015. This indicated that spatial planning strategy was now expressed in three separate plans which needed to be read together: the planning strategy; the strategic infrastructure plan; and the ITLUP (Minister for Planning and Minister for Transport, 2015, p. 19).

In the same year significant changes were made which weakened the long-established policy of reinforcing a hierarchy of centres within the metropolitan area, on the basis that 'excessive oversight' of the location of retail activities might discourage investment (DPTI, 2015). These were subsumed into a more comprehensive update to the 30-Year Plan (figure 5.7) released for public comment in August 2016 (Government of South Australia, 2016a).

The 30-Year Plan Update is an accessible document, with some similarities in style to the indicative planning strategies produced for Adelaide between 1993 and 2006. It is replete with cartoon-like visual cues to emphasize its main principles and its mantra of vibrancy. The 2010 Plan was a much more detailed plan with eighty-nine targets which have been simplified in the Update to six 'strategic high level targets' (Government of South Australia, 2016a, p. 28), thereby attracting the ire of the land development industry as being 'too generic' (UDIA, 2016, p. 2).

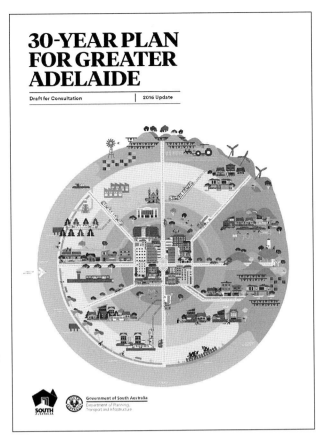

Figure 5.7. The 30-Year Plan Update 2016 – Cover Image. (*Source*: Government of South Australia, 2016b. Image courtesy of the Department of Planning, Transport and Infrastructure, South Australia)

The six new targets for 2045 were all expressed quantitatively:

1. 85 per cent of all new housing to be built in established urban areas;

2. 60 per cent of all new housing to be built within close proximity to quality public transport (rail, tram, O-Bahn – a guided busway built in the 1980s – and bus);

3. 25 per cent increase in the share of work trips made by active transport modes;

4. 25 per cent increase in the percentage of residents living in walkable neighbourhoods (this 'walkability' target applies only in the inner and middle suburbs);

5. 20 per cent increase in tree canopy cover;

6. 25 per cent increase in housing diversity to meet changing household needs.

Adelaide's population growth rate has slowed, with an additional 545,000 people now predicted for Greater Adelaide by 2045. The urban form proposals in the Update anticipate further increases in the overall proportion of new housing to be built within the existing urban area (85 per cent by 2045), more high-rise apartments in the CBD and developments of four to six storeys in the inner and middle suburbs along 'transport boulevards'. Between 2010 and 2014, 75 per cent of dwellings built in metropolitan Adelaide were still detached dwellings, but the Update seeks a more diverse and affordable housing stock. Since 2005 South Australian governments have pursued a target of achieving a minimum of 15 per cent of affordable housing in all significant new developments with some success, although the relative affordability of housing in Adelaide at present is more to do with the overheated housing markets of other, faster-growing cities than with the innovative public housing policies of recent South Australian governments. Affordability and economic competitiveness are linked in the Update (Government of South Australia, 2016a, p. 59), as they were in the 2008 Planning and Development Review (and, indeed, as they have been in South Australia since the 1930s).

The 2010 Plan assumed that an average of 400 hectares of fringe land would be consumed annually, but this has now been shown to have been a substantial over-estimate (Government of South Australia, 2016a, p. 19). With regard to the 2010 Plan's dwelling infill target, the Update asserts that this has already been met – 70 per cent of new housing growth in 2014 was in established urban areas as a result of a combination of factors. About a third of annual growth in housing stock between 2004 and 2014 came from small-scale subdivision, following reductions in minimum allowable allotment sizes (DPTI, 2013b, p. 1; Giannakodakis, 2013). Renewal of older public housing areas was also significant and around a third of all annual growth in new housing development was on brownfield land (DPTI, 2013b, p. 18).

The Update maintains the link with the government's updated climate change strategy (Government of South Australia, 2015) and reasserts the contribution that a more compact city can make to the current target of net zero emissions by 2050. Denser inner and middle suburbs will be 'healthy neighbourhoods that promote cycling, walking and public life' (Government of South Australia, 2016a, p. 67), although the Update is realistic about the challenge of creating 'walkable neighbourhoods', given that metropolitan Adelaide's population density, with fewer than 1,400 people per square kilometre on average, remains amongst the lowest of large Australian cities (Government of South Australia, 2016a, p. 21).

In sharp contrast to the 2010 plan, there are no targets in the Update which relate to employment. Economic policy is now primarily about removing barriers to business growth and accelerating approval processes (Government of South Australia, 2016a, p. 22). Jobs in the 'knowledge economy' are said to agglomerate in the city and to a lesser extent in other employment centres .The priority, therefore, is to 'locate more housing in close proximity to the city and activity centres and better utilize public transport connections to link people with jobs' (Government of South Australia, 2016*a*, p. 71).

There is very little in the Update about planning policy for the outer suburbs. A brief 'case study' of the separate Northern Economic Plan is included (Government of South Australia, 2016*a*, p. 76) and there is a similarly brief reference to how parts of the northern suburbs are being redeveloped (Government of South Australia, 2016*a*, p. 65). The overall presumption appears, however, to be that a shift to a denser urban form will in time provide better access to jobs, reduce the potential for social isolation in low-density outer suburbs and build social capital through interaction (Government of South Australia, 2016*a*, p. 128).

There has been a good deal of scholarly analysis in recent years which has shown that life in the outer suburbs of Australian cities is not simply determined by urban form but by access to jobs, education, health and services (see for example, Forster, 2006; Fagan and O'Neill, 2015; Dodson, 2016). There is also some excellent Australian research on how public transport can be provided more effectively in low-density suburbs (Mees, 2010), recognizing that trends in the distribution of jobs and services have led to more complex travel patterns than can be easily represented in a neat model of centre-based activities. Indeed, the recent weakening of retail policy in metropolitan Adelaide seems to acknowledge the practical difficulties of intensifying economic development in existing centres. The Update does not contain much rigorous analysis to support its assumption that most future jobs will readily concentrate in a few highly accessible centres in a city which, for the most part, will remain low density and car-dominated for years to come. Some optimism is expressed about the potential of 'driverless cars' to contribute to a more compact urban form (Government of South Australia, 2016*a*, p. 14), but, once again, there is no detailed analysis or explanation in the Update of what this might mean. Recent experiences also suggest a need for caution about the capacity of public transport investment, and the other 'active transport' measures in the 30-Year Plan Update, to reduce car dependency in the short to medium term and to keep pace with increases in population and density. Investment in new cycling infrastructure is regularly contested by the influential motoring lobby in Australia's car capital (see Waldhuter, 2017), while public transport investments remain highly sensitive to changing budgetary circumstances and to ideological fashions under Australia's turbulent federal political system.

Overall, the 30-Year Plan Update seems to rest on an unambiguous acceptance of the notion that increases to urban densities are an essential condition for shaping preferred environmental, social and economic outcomes in Greater Adelaide. The greatest capacity for increasing densities is seen in the 'vibrant and attractive' central and inner areas of the city (Government of South Australia, 2016*a*, p. 2) and in transit corridors elsewhere. The main focus of policy in the Update is overwhelmingly on these areas.

Conclusion

The compact city has been a key building block of twenty-first century planning and environmental strategies for metropolitan Adelaide. The metropolitan plans of 2003 and 2006 sought to encourage this through strict limits on the amount of land released at the urban fringe. The 2010 Plan, however, while continuing to advocate a compact city, expanded the urban growth boundary substantially and also rezoned large tracts of land for housing around far-flung townships with no public transport links to Adelaide. Nevertheless, infill development since 2010 has occurred at a much higher rate than forecast, with the consequence that appreciably more greenfield land has been designated than will be required in the foreseeable future. This has made it easier for the most recent set of planning reforms to take a tougher line on urban expansion by designating protected Environment and Food Production areas, the boundaries of which can only be changed with parliamentary approval.

Within these strengthened urban boundaries, the recently released 30-Year Plan Update seeks even higher levels of infill in the future and foreshadows ambitious attempts to increase housing densities in 'walkable' inner and middle suburbs. There is a lack of detail in the Update about how higher levels of infill are to be achieved, however. Recent changes to zoning have been effective in unleashing a substantial boom in apartment buildings in the CBD as well as encouraging the redevelopment of older, larger housing blocks in the inner and middle suburbs. But zoning is a blunt instrument and there is considerable scope for an enhanced and more nuanced role for government in facilitating land assembly in infill areas. The evidence to date suggests that the cost to government of infrastructure for new housing development on infill sites is significantly less than on greenfield sites (Giannakodakis, 2013; Hamilton and Kellett, 2017), although this is not necessarily the case for private developers, nor for every infill location as infrastructure capacity is a key issue. The Urban Development Institute of Australia has criticized the 30-Year Plan Update for assuming too readily the adequacy of existing infrastructure to cope with higher levels of infill (UDIA, 2016, p. 3). Significantly, most large infill sites have now been developed and a major challenge for the Urban Renewal Authority will be to facilitate the assembly of land for medium-density development within existing suburbs where ownership is more fragmented.

What seems to be lacking in the most recent 30-Year Plan Update, as compared to its predecessors, is an overall vision for the future of the entire metropolitan area and its hinterland. The preferred model of dense, vibrant urban neighbourhoods teeming with knowledge workers and international students who cycle to work or ride around on trams and hang out in small laneway bars is a model primarily for the inner suburbs. It tends to gloss over the considerable challenges of transforming a very low-density, car-dominated city to its preferred new urban form. In the 1970s the great South Australian urban reformer, Hugh Stretton, set out his vision for the future growth of Adelaide based around strong suburban centres capable of providing the community life and services required in the expanding suburbs and of acting as counter-magnets to excessive concentration in the Adelaide City Centre (Stretton, 1970, p. 356). This notion of a multi-centred city was endorsed in the 1992 metropolitan strategy and remained as a constant in subsequent plans, underpinned by a strictly enforced hierarchy of metropolitan centres. The latest 30-Year Update, however, in simplifying metropolitan strategy down to a handful of selective targets biased towards the CBD and inner suburbs, seems to ignore our growing understanding of the complexity and diversity of Australian suburbs and, in particular, the fine-grained patterns of disadvantage found in the outer areas of Adelaide where most people still live.

A profile of Adelaide published in the journal *Cities* in 1985 noted a number of chronic issues impacting the state capital of South Australia at that time (Bunker, 1985). These included slow population growth, an ageing population, a high level of car dependency, a recession-hit manufacturing sector, an unemployment rate higher than the national average and growing inequality. In terms of the city's economic vulnerability, it might appear that not a lot has changed since then. As this chapter has shown, however, there have been some significant shifts over this period in the approach to planning espoused by state governments. South Australia's long tradition of public enterprise and active government involvement in the acquisition and servicing of land for urban development and in the provision of public housing was still important in the 1990s and underpinned the joint public-private development of new large, well-planned suburbs north and south of a multi-centred city, endorsed by the Bannon Government's planning review. Little of that approach now survives and Bunker and Hutchings (1996, p. 56) have described the Bannon review as 'the last gasp of the visionary tradition'.

The more recent history of planning in South Australia has seen a gradual convergence with the experience of other states. In concert with neoliberal reform agendas, Commonwealth encouragement to harmonize state planning systems, the influence of the development industry, and the hollowing-out of state planning agencies, there has been a continuing quest for simpler, standardized approval processes.

However, neoliberalism in South Australia has not led simply to a 'rolling back' of the state government's involvement in all aspects of planning. The Rann Government's early rhetoric had elements redolent of the 'Third Way' notions that gained currency in the UK in the 1990s (see Allmendinger and Haughton, 2013, p. 12). The state government was committed to being highly interventionist in support of its economic goals and also, on occasion, its social and environmental priorities. The Weatherill Government's planning reforms have maintained and, in some respects, strengthened this interventionist approach. Where interventionist planning in South Australia was once supportive of public housing, metropolitan centres and land development in the community interest, it now seems to be directed primarily towards reducing the role of local government in planning, concentrating power in the hands of the state government and using that power to weaken planning policies and controls so as to facilitate private development. There is an apparent belief that almost *any* investment – even in nuclear waste dumps – is desirable in the current, very challenging economic climate. While the state's economic prospects seemed brighter for a while in the first decade of the twenty-first century, the structural shifts since then have reinforced the fundamental weakness and high vulnerability of the South Australian economy. A consequence has been that there have been few challenges to the political discourse that perceived that regulatory obstacles to development need to be removed and objections to recent radical planning reforms have been surprisingly muted in a state once known as the 'Paradise of Dissent' (Pike, 1957).

References

ABS (Australian Bureau of Statistics) (2006) *Quickstats*. Canberra: Australian Bureau of Statistics. Available at: http://www.censusdata.abs.gov.au/census_services/getproduct/census/2001/quickstat/405?opendocument&navpos=220.

ABS (2013a) *Australian Social Trends*, July. Canberra: Australian Bureau of Statistics. Available at: http://www.abs.gov.au/AUSSTATS/abs@.nsf/Lookup/4102.0Main+Features40July+2013.

ABS (2013b) *Quickstats* Canberra: Australian Bureau of Statistics. Available at: http://www.censusdata.abs.gov.au/census_services/getproduct/census/2011/quickstat/4GADE?opendocument&navpos=220.

ABS (2013c) *Population Projections Series B*. Cat 3222.0. Canberra: Australian Bureau of Statistics. Available at: http://www.abs.gov.au/ausstats/abs@.nsf/Latestproducts/3222.0Main%20Features102012%20%28base%29%20to%202101?opendocument&tabname=Summary&prodno=3222.0&issue=2012%20%28base%29%20to%202101&num=&view.

ABS (2016a) *Regional Population Growth, Australia, 2014–2015*. Cat 3218.0 (issued 30 March). Canberra: Australian Bureau of Statistics. Available at: http://www.abs.gov.au/AUSSTATS/abs@.nsf/mf/3218.0.

ABS (2016b) *Labour Force*. Cat 6202.0 (issued 15 December). Canberra: Australian Bureau of Statistics. Available at: http://www.abs.gov.au/AUSSTATS/abs@.nsf/Lookup/6202.0Main+Features1Nov%202016?OpenDocument.

Allmendinger, P. and Haughton, G. (2013) The evolution and trajectories of English neoliberal spatial governance: 'neoliberal' episodes in planning. *Planning Practice and Research*, **28**, pp. 6–26.

Badcock, B. (1986) Land and housing provision, in Sheridan, K. (ed.) *The State as Developer: Public Enterprise in South Australia*. Adelaide: Wakefield Press.

Beer, A. and Paris, C. (2005) Sustainable housing paradigms? The impact of reforms on the social housing sector in South Australia and Northern Ireland. *South Australian Geographical Journal*, **104**, pp. 38–50.

Bellette, K. (2003) Metamorphosis – 2020 Vision 10 years on. Proceedings of the Planning Institute of Australia National Congress, Adelaide, 31 March–2 April.

Bunker, R. (1985) Adelaide. *Cities*, **2**(4), pp. 307–313.

Bunker, R. (2015) Can we plan too much? – the case of the 2010 metropolitan strategy for Adelaide. *Australian Journal of Public Administration*, **74**(3), pp. 381–389.

Bunker, R. and Hutchings, A. (1996) South Australia in the 1990s: A Review of Urban Development, Planning and Policy. *South Australian Planning Papers,* No.6. Adelaide: Planning Education Foundation/University of South Australia.

COAG Reform Council (2012) *Review of Capital City Strategic Planning Systems*. Report to the Council of Australian Governments. Sydney: COAG Reform Council.

Coffee, N.T., Lange, J. and Baker, E. (2016) Visualising 30 years of population density change in Australia's major capital cities. *Australian Geographer*, **(47)**4, pp. 511–525.

Dodson, J. (2009) The 'infrastructure turn' in Australian metropolitan spatial planning. *International Planning Studies*, **14**(2), pp. 109–123.

Dodson, J. (2016) Suburbia in Australian urban policy. *Built Environment*, **42**(1), pp. 23–36.

DPLG (Department of Planning and Local Government) (2009a) *Planning The Adelaide We All Want.* Adelaide: Department of Planning and Local Government.

DPLG (2009b) *Background Technical Report: The Plan for Greater Adelaide.* Adelaide: Department of Planning and Local Government.

DPLG (2010) *The 30-Year Plan for Greater Adelaide.* Adelaide: Department of Planning and Local Government.

DPTI (Department of Planning, Transport and Infrastructure) (2013a) *Planning Strategy for South Australia: Annual Report Card.* Adelaide: Department of Planning, Transport and Infrastructure.

DPTI (2013b) *2004–2010 Residential Demolition and Subdivision Report.* Adelaide: Department of Planning, Transport and Infrastructure.

DPTI (2015) *Renewing Our Retail Policy.* Adelaide: Department of Planning, Transport and Infrastructure.

DTUPA (Department for Transport, Urban Planning and the Arts) (2002) *Urban Growth Boundary: Plan Amendment Report by the Minister.* Adelaide: Department for Transport, Urban Planning and the Arts.

EDB (Economic Development Board) (2003) *A Framework for Economic Development in South Australia.* Adelaide: Department of Trade and Economic Development.

Expert Panel on Planning Reform (2014) *The Planning System We Want.* Adelaide: Government of South Australia.

Fagan, R. and O'Neill, P. (2015) *Work, Places and People in Western Sydney: Changing Suburban Labor Markets 2001–2014.* Sydney: University of Western Sydney.

Forster, C. (2006) The challenge of change: Australia cities and urban planning in the new millennium. *Geographical Research*, **44**(2), pp.174–183.

Forster, C. and McCaskill, M. (2007) The modern period: managing metropolitan Adelaide in Hutchings, A. (ed.) *With Conscious Purpose: A History of Town Planning in South Australia*, 2nd ed. Adelaide: Planning Institute of Australia.

Giannakodakis, G. (2013) *Urban Infill versus Greenfield Development: A Review of Economic Benefits and Costs for Adelaide.* Adelaide: InfraPlan.

Government of South Australia (2004a) *Prosperity through People – A Population Policy for South Australia.* Adelaide: Government of South Australia.

Government of South Australia (2004b) *South Australia's Strategic Plan.* Adelaide: Government of South Australia.

Government of South Australia (2005) *Planning Strategy for Metropolitan Adelaide.* Draft for Public Consultation (April). Adelaide: Government of South Australia.

Government of South Australia (2006) *Planning Strategy for Metropolitan Adelaide.* Adelaide: Government of South Australia.

Government of South Australia (2007a) *Planning Strategy for Metropolitan Adelaide.* Adelaide: Government of South Australia.

Government of South Australia (2007b) *Tackling Climate Change: South Australia's Greenhouse Strategy 2007–2020.* Adelaide: Government of South Australia.

Government of South Australia (2012) *Budget Papers.* Adelaide: Department of Treasury and Finance. Available at: http://www.treasury.sa.gov.au/__data/assets/pdf_file/0004/2200/bp1_budget_overview 2012-13.pdf.

Government of South Australia (2015) *South Australia's Climate Change Strategy 2015–2050: Towards a Low Carbon Economy.* Adelaide: Government of South Australia.

Government of South Australia (2016a) *30-Year Plan for Greater Adelaide 2016 Update: Draft for Consultation.* Adelaide: Department of Planning, Transport and Infrastructure.

Government of South Australia (2016b) *Population Estimates, June Quarter, 2016.* Adelaide: Department of Premier and Cabinet.

Hamilton, C. and Kellett, J. (2017) Cost comparison of infrastructure on greenfield and infill sites. *Urban Policy and Research.* Published online on 9 January http://dx.doi.org/10.1080/08111146.201 6.1274257.

Hamnett, S. (2000) The late 1990s: competitive versus sustainable cities, in Hamnett, S. and Freestone, R. (eds.) *The Australian Metropolis: A Planning History.* Sydney: Allen and Unwin.

Hamnett, S. and Hutchings, A. (2009) Urban development and planning, in Spoehr, J. (ed.) *State of South Australia: From Crisis to Prosperity?* Adelaide: Wakefield Press, pp. 265–285.

Hamnett, S. and Kellett, J. (2016) Recent South Australian Planning Reforms in Comparative Perspective. Paper to the Australasian Conference of Planning and Environment Courts and Tribunals, Adelaide.

Hampton, T., Birch, C. and Gelber, F. (2013) Economy, in Spoehr, J. (ed) *State of South Australia: Turbulent Times.* Adelaide: Wakefield Press, pp. 9–29.

Hansard (2007) *Statement by the Minister for Urban Development and Planning on 'Urban Boundary Realignment'.* Parliament of South Australia, Legislative Council, 25 July, pp. 455–456.

Hansard (2010) *Population Targets (Minister for Urban Development and Planning)* Legislative Council Question Time, 23 November, p. 1554.

Howe, R. (2000) A new paradigm: planning and reconstruction in the 1940s, in Hamnett, S. and Freestone, R. (eds.) *The Australian Metropolis: A Planning History.* Sydney: Allen and Unwin, pp. 80–97.

Hugo, G. (2008) Australia's state specific and regional migration scheme: an assessment of its impacts in South Australia. *Journal of International Migration and Integration,* **9**(2), pp.125–145.

Hutchings, A. (ed.) (2007) *With Conscious Purpose: A History of Town Planning in South Australia,* 2nd ed. Adelaide: Planning Institute of Australia.

Hutchings, A. and Bunker, R. (1986) *With Conscious Purpose: A History of Town Planning in South Australia.* Adelaide: Wakefield Press.

Hutchings, A. and Kellett, J. (2013) Urban development and planning, in Spoehr, J. (ed.) *State of South Australia: Turbulent Times.* Adelaide: Wakefield Press, pp. 371–386.

Landry, C. (2004) *Rethinking Adelaide – Capturing Imagination.* Government of South Australia/Adelaide Thinkers in Residence program: Department of Premier and Cabinet.

Lennon, M. (2000) The revival of metropolitan planning, in Hamnett, S. and Freestone, R. (eds.) *The Australian Metropolis: A Planning History.* Sydney: Allen and Unwin, pp. 149–167.

Marsden, S. (2011) *Business, Charity and Sentiment: Part Two: The South Australian Housing Trust 1987–2011.* Adelaide: Wakefield Press.

Mees, P. (2010) *Transport for Suburbia: Beyond the Automobile Age.* London: Earthscan.

Mees, P. and Groenhart, L. (2012) *Transport Policy at the Crossroads: Travel to Work in Australian Capital Cities 1976–2011.* Melbourne: RMIT University.

Mill, J.S. (1834) Wakefield's The New British Province of South Australia. *The Examiner,* 20 July, available in Robson, J. (1963–1991) *The Collected Works of John Stuart Mill.* Toronto: University of Toronto Press.

Minister for Mineral Resources Development/Minister for Urban Development and Planning (2011) *Assessment Report – Environmental Impact Statement Olympic Dam Expansion.* Adelaide: Government of South Australia. Available at: www.olympicdameis.sa.gov.au/html/AssessmentReport/ODX AssessmentReport-web.pdf.

Minister for Planning and Minister for Transport (2013) *Draft Integrated Transport and Land Use Plan.* Adelaide: Government of South Australia.

Minister for Planning and Minister for Transport (2015) *Integrated Transport and Land Use Plan.* Adelaide: Government of South Australia.

Nuclear Fuel Cycle Royal Commission (2016) *Report.* Adelaide: Government of South Australia.

O'Leary, K. (2005) Get the public more involved in planning or fail. *Adelaide Review,* 22 July, p. 12.

Office for Infrastructure Development (2005) *The Strategic Infrastructure Plan for South Australia 2005/6–2014/15.* Adelaide: Government of South Australia.

Ombudsman SA (2013) *Investigation into the Growth Investigation Areas Report Procurement.* Final Report, March. Adelaide: Ombudsman SA.

PIA (Planning Institute of Australia) (2005) *Submission on the Metropolitan Adelaide Planning Strategy,* 31 July. Adelaide: Planning Institute of South Australia.

PIA (2009) *Submission on the Draft 30-Year Plan for Greater Adelaide.* September. Adelaide: Planning Institute of South Australia.

Pike, D. (1957) *Paradise of Dissent: South Australia, 1829–1857.* London: Longman, Green & Co.

Planning, Development and Infrastructure Act (2016) Adelaide: Parliament of South Australia. Available at: https://www.legislation.sa.gov.au/LZ/C/A/Planning%20Development%20and%20 Infrastructure%20Act%202016.aspx.

Planning and Development Review Steering Committee (2008) *Report to the Minister for Urban Development and Planning*. Adelaide: Government of South Australia.

Planning Review (1992*a*) 2020 *Vision – Final Report: A Planning System*. Adelaide: Department of Environment and Planning.

Planning Review (1992*b*) *2020 Vision – Planning Strategy for Metropolitan Adelaide*. Adelaide: Department of Environment and Planning.

Premier of South Australia (1998) *Planning Strategy: Metropolitan Adelaide*. Adelaide: Planning SA.

Premier of South Australia (2003) *Planning Strategy for Metropolitan Adelaide*. Adelaide: Department of Transport and Urban Planning.

Productivity Commission (2011) *Performance Benchmarking of Australian Business Regulation: Planning, Zoning and Development Assessments*. Research Report (2 vols). Melbourne: Commonwealth of Australia.

Property Council (SA) (2016) Council amalgamations to deliver $500m to State. *Media Release*. Available at: http://www.propertycouncil.com.au/Web/Content/Media_Release/SA/2016/Council _amalgamations_to_deliver__500m_to_state.aspx.

Stretton, H. (1970) *Ideas for Australian Cities*. Melbourne: Georgian House.

South Australia's Strategic Plan Audit Committee (2012) *South Australia's Strategic Plan: Progress Report 2012*. Adelaide: Department of Premier and Cabinet.

Transport SA (2002) *Adelaide Travel Patterns: An Overview* (Research Summary TP 02/8). Adelaide: Transport SA.

UDIA (Urban Development Institute of Australia) (South Australia) 2016 *Submission on the 30-Year Plan Update*. Adelaide: UDIA(SA). Available at: http://udiasa.com.au/uploads/Submission%20 30%20Year%20Plan%20UDIA211016.pdf.

Waldhuter, L. (2017) Adelaide's Frome Road separated bikeway to be ripped up to help peak-hour traffic flow. ABC On-line News, 8 March. Available at: http://www.abc.net.au/news/2017-03-08/ adelaides-frome-street-separated-bike-way-to-be-ripped-up/8333630.

Acknowledgements

The authors are grateful for helpful and perceptive comments on drafts of this chapter provided by Raymond Bunker, Donna Ferretti and Peter Houston. Needless to say, however, the opinions expressed are entirely those of the authors.

Chapter 6

Perth:
From 'Large Provincial City'
to 'Globalizing City'

Paul J. Maginn and *Neil Foley*

Perth is often proclaimed to be one of the world's most remote capital cities. Yet despite its remoteness, Perth found itself at the epicentre of a global resources boom in the early 2000s and enjoyed one of the 'most rapid economic expansion[s] in Australia's post-Federation history' (Tonts *et al.*, 2016, p. 174). As the economy expanded so too did the population, with Western Australia (WA) experiencing the highest rate of population growth of any state (26 per cent) between 2001 and 2011. Most of this growth was concentrated in the Perth metropolitan region and was largely underpinned by overseas migration (Maginn and Hamnett, 2016). This level of economic and population growth has posed planning challenges for metropolitan Perth. The general consumer preference for single dwellings on individual lots, fuelled by a development industry dominated by large WA-based developers specializing in suburban subdivisions and by project home builders, has perpetuated low-density spread as a key policy concern since the 1950s (Maginn, 2016). Relatedly, as the economic boom continued and population growth outstripped the supply of accommodation, housing affordability within the homeowner and rental sectors has also become a major problem.

The first two decades of the new millennium saw a series of state elections (2001, 2005, 2008, 2013 and 2017) which produced governments from the Australian Labor Party (2001–2008 and 2017) and the Liberal/National Parties (2008–2017). These decades also witnessed two metropolitan planning strategies and the beginning of significant reforms to the planning system. This chapter is concerned with tracing the rapid transformation of metropolitan Perth from a 'large provincial city' at the end of the twentieth century to a 'globalizing city' and the somewhat paradoxical role of strategic metropolitan planning in trying to manage sustainable urban growth while also facilitating economic development. First, changes in the physical, demographic, social and economic character of metropolitan Perth since 2000 are outlined. Next, a brief historical overview of

Perth provides a broader evolutionary context to the growth of the metropolitan region. Third, the overall character and central aims of the two metropolitan strategies developed under different state governments – *Network City* (2004) and *Directions 2031 and Beyond* (2010) – are explored. Despite the different ideological perspectives of these administrations, there was a strong sense of continuity in strategic vision and objectives. Finally, the challenges of implementing and realizing the key objectives of *Directions 2031* are considered.

From 'Large Provincial City' to 'Globalizing City'

Perth has long tended to be perceived as more of a 'large provincial city' than a 'real' city because of its comparatively smaller population base and economy, isolation and low-density suburban landscape. Yet in population terms, Perth ranks as the fourth largest city in Australia. In 2011 the Greater Perth capital city statistical area, which comprises the Perth Metropolitan Region and the urbanized portion of the Peel Region to its south, had a population of 1,704,935 people – up from 1,379,532 (23.58 per cent) in 2001 (ABS, 2012). Greater Perth was the fastest growing Australian metropolitan region over the period 2001–2011 (see table 6.1).

Despite the significant population growth in Perth over the past decade, it remains a low-density suburban city stretching for approximately 150 kilometres north–south along the coastline. As shown in table 6.1, gross population density in 2011 stood at just 266 persons per square kilometre, although this was up by 23.6 per cent from 215 persons in 2001. Of the major capital city regions, only Greater Brisbane had a lower gross population density. Detached houses accounted for 77.7 per cent of Greater Perth's total housing stock in 2001 and 2011.

Population growth in Perth was slow during the early decades after initial settlement in 1829. From the mid-nineteenth century the population expanded as a result of, first, WA becoming a penal colony in 1850; and, second, the gold rushes from the 1880s. By the early twentieth century politicians and citizens

Table 6.1. Population change and density, metropolitan Australia, 2001–2011.

Capital City City Region	Area (km²) 2011	Population 2001–2011	Population 2011 Change	Population Change No. (%)	Gross Density 2001 (persons per km²)	Gross Density 2011 (persons per km²)
Perth	6417.9	1,379,532	1,704,935	325,403 (23.6%)	214.9	265.6
Adelaide	3257.7	1,110,240	1,214,674	104,434 (9.4%)	340.8	372.8
Melbourne	9990.5	3,385,053	3,976,061	591,008 (17.5%)	338.8	397.9
Sydney	12367.7	3,948,015	4,378,456	430,441 (10.9%)	319.2	354.0
Brisbane	15825.9	1,669,559	2,058,627	389,068 (23.3%)	105.4	130.0

Source: ABS, 2012.

became concerned about rapid population growth and haphazard un-serviced land subdivision and development (Hedgcock and Yiftachel, 1992; Stokes and Hill, 1992). These concerns were addressed by the introduction of the Town Planning and Development Act 1928 which centralized land subdivision control and allowed for local government planning schemes to be approved by the Minister. The Metropolitan Town Planning Commission produced the first metropolitan planning report in 1930 (Boas, 1930). However, it was not until 1955 that the first *bona fide* metropolitan plan, the so-called Stephenson-Hepburn Plan, was produced (Stephenson and Hepburn, 1955). This plan designated significant tracts of land to accommodate suburban expansion, freeway development, two new railway lines and provision for regional parks. The 1955 Plan 'strongly advocated that a firm line should be drawn as a limit to the lateral expansion of the main built-up area' (Stephenson and Hepburn 1955, p. 7). In other words, Perth needed an urban growth boundary. The designated urban footprint of the 1955 Plan was considered sufficient to accommodate a population of 1.4 million by the year 2000, an extra million people. Notably, however, when the population eventually reached this level, the built-up area of the metropolitan region was virtually double the size of the 1955 planned footprint.

Although WA has the most centralized statutory planning system in Australia, with the Western Australian Planning Commission (WAPC), an independent planning authority, responsible for the Metropolitan Region Scheme since 1963 and for land subdivision controls since 1928, state policy-makers have fought a long-running battle in trying to manage the outward urban expansion of Perth. Even as urban consolidation, new urbanism and sustainable development came to dominate Australian planning thinking and practice from the late 1980s, planners still had to contend with people's preferences for the 'great Australian dream' of owning a home on its own block (Troy, 1996). Over the same period, there has been a general fear of the amenity impacts of higher density housing on local neighbourhoods and communities, with private multi-storey residential dwellings generally considered an inferior form of housing.

Perth is not a city renowned for high-density housing. Data from the Australian Bureau of Statistics (2012) show that 'flats/units/apartments' accounted for only 42,413 dwellings or 7.9 per cent of total housing stock in Greater Perth in 2001. Most of this housing was only one or two storeys (54.3 per cent) with three-storey and four or more storey housing accounting for 24.4 per cent and 21.2 per cent of the stock, respectively. By 2011, however, the overall volume of flat/unit/apartment dwellings had increased by almost 50 per cent to 63,516 and accounted for almost 10 per cent of total housing stock. There was significant growth in the number dwellings with four or more storeys, increasing by 69.2 per cent or over 15,000 units. This growth in apartment developments has tended to be mainly in inner-city suburbs and has been fuelled by a combination of urban renewal policies, overseen by what is now the Metropolitan Redevelopment Authority (MRA), and by private sector property development and speculation stimulated by the mining and resources boom. In 2011, for example, there were five suburbs in metropolitan Perth where the majority of housing stock comprised flats/units/apartments. These were: East Perth (64.3 per cent), West Perth (61.1 per cent) and Northbridge (50.8 per cent), all located within the City of Perth and built mainly in the 1990s; Jolimont (54.3 per cent) in the City of Subiaco; and Glendalough (50.5 per cent) in the City of Stirling where much of this housing comprises one- and two-bedroom flats built in the 1960s.

The mining and resources boom during 2005–2015 played a key role in enhancing Perth's globalizing city status. For example, Tonts *et al.* (2012, p. 14) note that in 2011–2012 WA was Australia's leading exporter contributing 'a record 45.6 per cent towards Australia's merchandise export earnings worth A\$264.3 billion'. The global demand for WA's resources, especially from China, combined with a labour shortage in mining, meant that international migrants flocked to WA during the 2000s to take advantage of the economic opportunities. As a consequence Perth has one of the highest levels of overseas-born populations in metropolitan Australia (Martinus *et al.*, 2016). In broad economic terms, the impacts of the resources boom can be seen in the changing employment distribution since the turn of the century. The number of people employed in Greater Perth in the mining sector increased by 212 per cent between 2001 and 2011, up from 11,323 to 35,306 people. The mining sector's share of employment duly increased from 1.8 per cent to 4.2 per cent. Relatedly, as the mining industry was mainly in the construction phase of its economic development cycle, the construction sector also experienced significant employment growth. The number of people employed in construction grew by 82 per cent from 45,110 to 82,050. Other industry sectors to experience major growth as a result of the mining boom included professional, scientific and technical services – up from 45,182 to 70,370 (56 per cent), and public administration and safety – up from 35,952 to 54,550 (52 per cent).

With this growth came policy concerns about the health and social wellbeing of metropolitan-based 'fly-in/fly-out' (FIFO) workers and their families, as well as the impacts of FIFO employment on the economic well-being of regional towns (Haslam McKenzie, 2011; Lawrie *et al.,* 2011; Education and Health Standing Committee, 2015).

The broader economic impacts of the resources boom were also reflected in changes in household incomes and in the inflationary impacts these had on housing costs. Median total household weekly income increased in Greater Perth by 83 per cent from A\$795 to A\$1,455 between 2001 and 2011. In comparison, the increase at the national level was from A\$784 to A\$1,203 or 56.8 per cent. While median monthly mortgage repayments at the national level increased by 107.6 per cent over the same period, in Perth the increase was an elevated 130.7 per cent. Similarly, while median weekly rents at the national level almost doubled, increasing by 96.5 per cent from A\$145 to A\$285 between 2001 and 2011, rents in Perth rose from A\$135 to A\$320 per week, an increase of 137 per cent. At the height of the resources boom, vacancy rates in the residential rental sector fell as low as 1–2 per cent, making it extremely difficult for low-income households to gain entry to the rental market.

The housing market in Greater Perth experienced exceptional growth over the period 2000–2015 with median house prices increasing by almost 250 per cent. Data from the Urban Development Institute (WA) (2013) and REIWA (2017), covering the periods 2000–2012 and 2013–2015 respectively, show that median house price increases were particularly pronounced (see figure 6.1). Whilst house prices increased by 60 per cent between 2000 and 2004, they almost doubled again (92 per cent) between 2004 and 2008. The significant increases in the latter period occurred during the rapid expansion phases of the resources boom. Housing affordability inevitably became a major policy issue within not only metropolitan Perth but also regional WA (Haslam McKenzie and Rowley, 2013). The dip in house prices between 2008 and 2009 (–6.3 per cent) was a result of market volatility and uncertainty as a consequence of the global financial crisis (GFC) but, as evident in figure 6.1, median house prices continued to increase in overall terms between 2008 and 2015, albeit at a slower rate of 13.5 per cent. Median house prices peaked in 2014, reaching A$550,500, but had slipped to A$520,000 by September 2016 (REIWA, 2017).

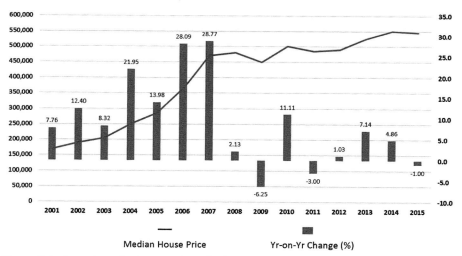

Figure 6.1. Annual median house prices, Perth, 2000-2015. (*Source:* Derived from Real Estate Institute of Western Australia (2017) *Perth Suburbs Price Data*)

Planning Metropolitan Perth: Some Historical Context

Perth has a long tradition of metropolitan planning which can be traced back to the Metropolitan Town Planning Commission (1928–1931) and then to the 1955 Plan, which has been the cornerstone of metropolitan planning ever since. This plan is responsible for the enduring urban form comprising Perth as the primary and Fremantle as the secondary centre, supplemented by a series of district centres, industrial hubs and regional parks dispersed in an orderly spatial manner along major road and rail corridors. Over time and with subsequent metropolitan strategies, the number of major sub-regional centres has increased, thus giving rise to a hierarchical network which has been incorporated into official policy (WAPC, 2010e). Other enduring legacies of the 1955 Plan have included: the establishment in 1960 of what eventually became the Western Australian Planning Commission; the implementation of a supra-strategic statutory zoning and land reservation plan, the Metropolitan Region Scheme (MRS) in 1963, to which all local government planning schemes must adhere; and the introduction of a hypothecated Metropolitan Region Improvement Tax (MRIT) that provides the WAPC with direct revenue so that it can reserve and purchase private land for future strategic planning purposes such as roads, railways or regional open spaces (Maginn and Foley, 2014; Foley and Williams, 2016).

The 1955 Plan came about because of concerns about 'the rapid outward expansion of the metropolis and growing congestion in the centres of Perth and Fremantle' (Stephenson and Hepburn, 1955, p. 1). These concerns have been an enduring aspect of all subsequent metropolitan strategic plans – *Corridor Plan for Perth* (Metropolitan Region Planning Authority, 1970); *Metroplan* (DPUD, 1990); *Network City* (WAPC, 2004); and *Directions 2031* (WAPC, 2010a) – but with varying degrees of policy commitment. It was not until the 1980s and 1990s, with the rise of sustainable development within planning theory and practice, that containing urban expansion became a more explicit strategic objective of metropolitan planning in *Metroplan* (DPUD, 1990). Paradoxically, however, *Metroplan* only provided for a relatively small share (20 per cent) of future growth to be urban infill, with most still earmarked for outer suburban greenfield locations. This policy position changed following the development of the next metropolitan strategy, *Network City* (WAPC, 2004), which explicitly called for the majority of all new residential development to be urban infill.

Network City:
An Exercise in Deliberative and Sustainable Planning?

Network City was released for public comment by the WAPC in 2004 under a Labor state government. When Labor came to office in 2001, Premier Geoff Gallop quickly set about establishing his policy interests in environmental sustainability and participatory democracy by establishing two specialist units, the Sustainability Policy Unit (SPU) and the Civics and Citizens Unit (CCU), within the Department of Premier and Cabinet (DPC). The CCU published two policy documents that championed deeper and more innovative approaches to civic engagement in decision-making processes (CCU, 2002; 2003), while the SPU published a State Sustainability Strategy (SSS) (Government of Western Australia, 2003). This was the first state-level document of its kind in Australia. The SSS emphasized the need to contain urban growth and suggested that a growth boundary be introduced for Perth. In addition, it also recommended that greater policy efforts be made to encourage more brownfield redevelopment to increase residential densities to the level required to support public transit. In order to help realize this proposal, it was recommended that a specialist department, the Revitalisation Directorate, be set up. Moreover, the SSS stressed that a heightened collaborative policy approach was needed in order to realize successful outcomes.

This policy commitment to sustainability and participatory democracy was exemplified in the extensive community consultation process that preceded the release of the *Network City* planning strategy. It is worth noting that a review of the previous *Metroplan* strategy had actually been initiated by the former Liberal state government (1993–2001) in 1999 (WAPC, 1999). In a public consultation document, *Towards a Vision for Perth in 2029* (Ministry for Planning, 2000), the then Minister for Planning stated that the WAPC was preparing a new strategic plan, provisionally titled *Future Perth*. This new plan was underpinned by three key themes – living, working and enjoying – and spoke to the overarching idea of the triple-bottom line of sustainability. In November 2000 the state government released a detailed update on its review of *Metroplan*. This update, *Scenarios of Our Future – Challenges for Western Australian Society* (WAPC, 2000), made explicit that the government, despite its conservative standpoint, was committed to the idea of sustainable development.

As part of the decision-making process underpinning the *Future Perth* initiative, a participatory scenario planning approach was adopted by the WAPC (Hopkins and Zapata, 2007). This entailed interviewing and bringing together a range of key institutional stakeholders from state and local government, the private sector and non-governmental organizations (NGOs) to consider a fundamental question: what is the future sustainability of the Perth Metropolitan Region and the South West? This process generated a scenario framework which explored key driving forces (e.g. globalization, social inequities and energy security) and potential outcomes under different conditions. Ultimately, this scenario-based approach to strategic planning was not about predicting the future but rather about identifying the major future sustainability challenges facing Perth and the South West Region. The *Scenarios of Our Future* document did not provide any explicit indications of the government's preferred scenario. Ultimately, as a result of losing the state election in February 2001, the Liberal government failed to complete its new planning strategy.

Despite the change in government, the WAPC continued with its work on the *Future Perth* initiative and, in August 2001, released the *Metropolitan Development Options Workshop (Final Report)* which concluded that there was a 'need for a new approach to regional planning' (WAPC, 2001, p. 4.1). This report reinforced a commitment to the ideals of sustainable planning which were reflected in a number of key strategic planning aspirations for the metropolitan region – namely a green, efficient, equitable, liveable and creative city. These planning aspirations were all evident in the Labor government's new metropolitan strategy, which was originally to be called *Greater Perth* (WAPC, 2003) but was subsequently renamed *Network City: Community Planning Strategy for Perth and Peel* (WAPC, 2004).

This 'new' approach to regional planning manifested itself in the *Network City* metropolitan plan which was presented as a community planning strategy. The community dimension of the new plan was premised on the extensive consultative and participatory decision-making process that preceded publication. Specifically, the consultation process was premised on deliberative democratic theory (Hartz-Karp, 2005) and involved the deployment of a range of consultation and participation techniques under the banner of 'dialogue with the city'. These included a large-scale survey of some 8,000 households; a series of issues papers on different aspects of strategic planning; a televised debate about future scenarios for Perth; an interactive website; and listening sessions with under-represented groups – youth and people from indigenous and culturally and linguistically diverse backgrounds.

The dialogue process culminated in a large-scale town hall-style community forum with over 1,000 participants (Hopkins, 2007, 2010*a*; 2010*b*). The community forum was underpinned by another preferred scenario planning approach to decision-making (Hopkins and Zapata, 2007). Community forum participants were presented with a number of possibilities for the future urban structure of Perth: dispersed city; compact city; multi-centred city; and connected network city. While the whole dialogue initiative was an impressive consultative and participatory exercise in planning decision-making, the assertion that the community forum was a *genuine* example of deliberative democracy in action has been questioned. In particular, it has been argued that the government had already decided what type of metropolitan plan and urban structure it wanted and steered community participants towards this preferred outcome (Maginn, 2007). This was achieved by giving the illusion of choice in relation to future urban scenarios for Perth when, in fact, there was strong opposition from the government to one of the scenarios (dispersed city). There was also no likelihood of realizing the compact city scenario, given Perth's extensive suburban character. The inherent opposition to the dispersed city model was made clear in the various keynote addresses during the community forum by the Premier, the Minister for Planning and Infrastructure and several international experts who all championed the virtues of sustainable development and transit-oriented development and warned against the disastrous effects of continued suburban sprawl (Maginn, 2007).

Fundamentally, *Network City* was an urban growth management strategy underpinned by a commitment to the ideals of sustainability while simultaneously trying to ensure that the metropolitan region enjoyed continued economic growth and emerged as a vibrant globalized city. The principal aspirations of the plan and its underlying values are summarized in table 6.2.

The major planning dilemma at the heart of *Network City* (as for all metropolitan strategies since 1955) was demographic. Perth's population was projected to increase from 1.46 million in 2001 to 1.99 million by 2021 and then to 2.22 million by 2031. Relatedly, the number of dwellings was expected to increase from 580,000 (2001) to 840,000 by 2021 and then to 950,000 by 2031. All of this begged the questions

Table 6.2. Network City Planning Strategy: vision, values, principles and objectives.

Planning Visions	'... by 2030 Perth people will have created a world-class sustainable city: vibrant, more compact and accessible, with a unique sense of place' (WAPC, 2004, p. 4)
Planning Values	(i) Sustainability; (ii) Inclusiveness; (iii) Innovation & Creativity; (iv) Sense of Place; (v) Equity
Principles	(i) Enhance efficiency of urban land use and infrastructure; (ii) Protect/rehabilitate the environment, improve resource efficiency & energy use; (iii) Enhance community vitality and cohesiveness
Key Objectives	(i) Ensure urban growth management within a networked pattern; (ii) Integrate transport/land-use planning to optimize accessibility and amenity; (iii) Protect/enhance natural environments, open spaces and heritage; (iv) Enhance quality of life for all citizens; (v) Plan with local communities; (vi) Create employment in activity centres; (vii) Deliver a city with creativity and cultural vitality; (viii) Ensure plan implementability and planning certainty

Source: WAPC, 2004.

of where and how the additional 760,000 people and 370,000 dwellings projected by 2031 would be accommodated. The *Network City* strategy report indicated that the solution to these challenges lay in the creation of a hierarchical network of activity centres and activity corridors serviced by high frequency public transport (bus) services. Moreover, in order to generate the necessary demand to support these activity centres and activity corridors, the strategy proposed a 60:40 dwelling target, whereby 60 per cent (222,000 dwellings) of all new residential development would take place within existing urban areas within the inner, middle and outer suburban rings, with the remaining 40 per cent (148,000) on new greenfield sites. In population terms, based on an average household size of 2.6 at the 2001 Census, this would translate into nearly 600,000 people or 76 per cent of the projected total population growth by 2031 living in existing urban areas.

In terms of the volume and type of dwellings approved over the course of the last decade or so, the single detached home remained the dominant form of housing between 2001–2002 and 2013–2014, accounting for almost 80 per cent of all approvals during this period (table 6.3). The share of approvals for houses fell quite significantly from 83.5 per cent in 2005–2006 to 69.2 per cent in 2007–2008. Simultaneously, the housing market in Perth experienced an increase in apartments as a share of total dwelling approvals, as discussed earlier. The housing market quickly corrected itself, however, with approvals for houses returning to around 80 per cent while apartment approvals fell to about 6 per cent between 2008–2009 and 2013–2014. In other words, the 'suburban way of life' still prevailed within Perth despite the policy aspirations of *Network City* to encourage greater densification.

A closer look at the geographical distribution of dwelling approvals over the period between 2001–2002 and 2013–2014 under both *Network City* (2004–2009)

Table 6.3. Dwelling approvals by type, Greater Perth, 2001/02–2013/14.

Financial Year	Houses	Terrace/ Townhouses	Flats and Units	Apartments	Total Dwellings
2001/02	13,890	1,684	559	283	16,416
2002/03	14,823	1,851	600	768	18,042
2003/04	15,742	1,698	781	1,018	19,239
2004/05	14,783	2,008	584	1,392	18,767
2005/06	17,100	1,863	643	873	20,479
2006/07	14,852	2,161	633	1,830	19,476
2007/08	12,819	2,345	507	2,861	18,532
2008/09	11,937	1,677	227	856	14,697
2009/10	15,520	2,529	480	997	19,526
2010/11	13,224	1,870	572	338	16,004
2011/12	12,116	1,006	441	1,132	14,695
2012/13	14,774	1,983	872	1,410	19,039
2013/14	4,864	504	205	544	6,117
All Years	176,444	23,179	7,104	14,302	221,029

Source: Urban Development Institute of Australia (WA) *Development Approval Tool* (www.udiawa. com.au).

and *Directions 2031* (2009–present) reveals that the development process was not meeting the objectives of the metropolitan strategies of managing and containing urban sprawl. Table 6.4 shows that the number and share of total approvals were significantly higher in the predominantly outer-suburban North West Statistical Area (SA4) and in the South East and South West metropolitan corridors. (SA4 refers to the Australian Bureau of Statistics geographical classification system and denotes sub-regional areas comprising between 300–500,000 people in metropolitan areas.) Together these three sub-regions accounted for almost three-quarters (72.3 per cent) of all approvals. This increases to 92 per cent when Mandurah (in Peel) and the North East are added. The majority (60.7 per cent) of all apartment approvals were concentrated in the Perth – Inner SA4 region. There are signs that other forms of higher density dwellings – terrace/townhouses and flats/units – were more common outside the Perth – Inner region. As seen in table 6.4, terrace/townhouses were the most popular form of dwelling after houses with some 23,179 approvals between 2001–2002 and 2013–2014, with well over half (59.7 per cent) of these approvals in the North West (33.1 per cent) and South East (26.6 per cent) corridors.

Crucially, the vast majority of approvals for all SA4 regions (except for Perth – Inner) were for houses, accounting for 80.6 per cent to 86 per cent of each region's total approvals (see table 6.4). Despite the relatively large increase in the number of approvals for apartments, this type of dwelling was mainly concentrated in the Perth CBD and surrounding suburbs. Terrace/townhouse style housing, accounting for just over 10 per cent of all approvals, tends to be concentrated in inner-middle ring suburban areas along the major metropolitan transport corridors.

The apparent inability of the policy framework provided by *Network City* to meet its urban containment and densification objectives can be partly explained by two factors. First, the release of the *Network City* strategy coincided with rapid demographic growth as a result of the resources boom. Between 2005 and 2008 the

Table 6.4. Dwelling approvals by housing type (SA4), Greater Perth, 2001/02–2013/14.

Region (SA4)	Houses		Terrace/ Townhouses		Flats/Units		Apartments		Total Dwellings	
	No	%	No	%	No	%	No	%	No	%
Perth – Inner	6,281	3.6	1,351	5.8	1,456	20.5	8,685	60.7	17,773	8.0
Perth – North-East	21,304	12.1	2,578	11.1	649	9.1	335	2.3	24,866	11.3
Perth – North-West	51,922	29.4	7,661	33.1	1,330	18.7	810	5.7	61,723	27.9
Perth – South-East	42,084	23.9	6,177	26.6	1,637	23.0	1,835	12.8	51,733	23.4
Perth – South-West	39,917	22.6	3,127	13.5	1,398	19.7	1,968	13.8	46,410	21.0
Mandurah	14,936	8.5	2,285	9.9	634	8.9	669	4.7	18,524	8.4
Total	176,444	100.0	23,179	100.0	7,104	100.0	14,302	100.0	221,029	100.0

Source: Urban Development Institute of Australia (WA) *Development Approval Tool* (www.udiawa. com.au).

estimated resident population in Greater Perth grew from 1,549,231 to 1,687,175 people – an increase of 137,944 people in just 3 years. *Network City* had predicted that the metropolitan population would reach 1.99 million by 2021, but this figure was surpassed by 2014 when the estimated resident population reached 2,012,876 people (ABS, 2016). Furthermore, *Network City* predicted that the population would reach 2.22 million by 2031. However, given the average annual growth rate (2.9 per cent) of the estimated resident population in Greater Perth for the period 2005–2015, the population is now expected to reach 2.2 million by 2018 (ABS, 2016).

Second, *Network City* was never formalized as the Government's metropolitan strategy. Whilst the 2004 Network City report issued for public comment had been listed as a regional strategy in the WAPC's State Planning Policy (SPP) No.1 *State Planning Framework Policy* (WAPC, 2006b), the WAPC initiated steps to clarify that *Network City* was to replace *Metroplan* (DPUD, 1990) by issuing a draft SPP for public comment specifically for *Network City* (WAPC, 2006a). An SPP is the highest level of planning policy control and guidance in WA and thus carries considerable political and policy authority, although it would not have conferred statutory status on *Network City*. Ultimately, however, the draft SPP was never finalized. As Maginn *et al.* (2017) have noted, changes in government tend to provoke planning policy reforms. In late 2008 a new Liberal/National state government was elected and, as it had indicated when in opposition, quickly set about implementing a 'new' planning policy agenda that included major reforms to the planning system and the development of a 'new' metropolitan planning strategy. The new government, while in opposition, had expressed concerns, in particular, about the high urban infill targets in *Network City*.

From 'Planning is the Problem' to 'Planning Makes it Happen'

Table 6.5 below provides an overview of the major strategic plans – state, metropolitan and transport – and some of the key planning reforms introduced over the course of the Liberal/National parties' two terms in office, 2008–2013 and

2013–2017. The proposed changes to the planning system and the aspirations of the new metropolitan strategy were all underpinned by a neoliberalist philosophy and narrative that privileged economic development. In overall terms, the new government's approach to planning exhibited aspects of what Peck and Tickell (2002, p. 389) term 'roll-out' (i.e. 'new forms of institution-building and governmental intervention' such as Development Assessment Panels and the Metropolitan Redevelopment Authority) and 'roll-back' neoliberalism (i.e. the deregulation and dismantling of state apparatus). This is clearly reflected, for example, in the government's key planning reform document, *Planning Makes it Happen: A Blueprint for Planning Reform,* in which the Minister for Planning stated that:

> … for Western Australia to continue as Australia's most successful economy, the planning system has to be supportive of economic development and job creation while offering lifestyle choice, urban amenity and a sustainable future for a growing population. (Department of Planning, 2009*b*, p. i)

After only six months in office the government released a consultation paper, *Building a Better Planning System* (Department of Planning, 2009*a*), outlining its policy agenda on reforming the WA planning system. While the consultation paper noted that the planning system was 'fundamentally sound', it was simultaneously framed as problematic and in need of repair. The system was portrayed as being overly bureaucratic and unable to deal with the demands being put upon it as a result of economic and population growth. Moreover, it was also claimed that there was a lack of public and business confidence in the system. Proposed new governance structures would remove some planning powers from local councils and even the WAPC (Maginn and Foley, 2014). The state government also attempted (unsuccessfully) to amalgamate local governments within the Perth metropolitan region, mainly in order to reduce perceived inefficiencies in the local government sector. The Metropolitan Local Government Review Panel (2012, p. 9) found local planning to be 'fragmented … [and] unnecessarily complicated, uncoordinated and lacking in strategic focus'.

The central tenets of the government's planning reform agenda included 'cutting red tape'; standardizing key planning instruments such as structure plans; focusing more on strategic planning outcomes rather than statutory planning processes; and creating a more streamlined institutional and governance framework. A second wave of proposed planning reforms in 2013–2014 gave emphasis to specific matters: improving strategic statutory planning processes by means including a review of the long-established Metropolitan Region Scheme so that it conformed and complemented the newer Peel Region Scheme; improving amendment processes for region planning schemes; applying the Metropolitan Region Improvement Tax model to the Peel and Greater Bunbury regions; and improving local planning scheme review and amendment processes. Other proposed reforms included introducing a new electronic development application system and further examination of governance structures such as Development Assessment Panels, the Infrastructure Co-ordination Committee and the WAPC itself (Department of Planning, 2013; 2014). Some of these proposals have been implemented by legislative amendments and other processes.

Directions 2031 and Beyond

As table 6.5 shows, there was a flurry of policy activity in relation to strategic planning, with a draft metropolitan strategy *Directions 2031: Draft Spatial Framework for Perth and Peel* (*Directions 2031*) and associated documents (WAPC, 2009*a*; 2009*b*; 2009*c*; 2009*d*). The draft metropolitan strategy was somewhat critical of its predecessor, highlighting that this was 'not a traditional plan that can be used to inform and guide future growth of the region' and was nothing more than a 'diagrammatic representation of urban growth principles'. Despite these criticisms, the draft plan acknowledged that it 'builds on many of the aspirational themes identified in Network City' (WAPC, 2009*a*, p.1). A final strategy, *Directions 2031 and Beyond: Metropolitan Planning Beyond the Horizon* (WAPC, 2010*a*) (*Directions 2031+*), was released in August 2010 and was accompanied by two draft sub-regional strategies and a final Activity Centres SPP for Perth and Peel (WAPC, 2010*b*; 2010*c*; 2010*d*; 2010*e*).

A series of 'Delivering Directions 2031 Report Cards' indicating the progress of implementation of *Directions 2031+*, was published over the next few years (WAPC, 2012*b*; 2013; 2014*a*) while Urban Growth Monitor reports continued to document land supply and other data relevant to planning implementation (e.g. WAPC, 2009*e*; 2016*a*). Strategic studies identifying land for non-heavy industry for the long-term were also completed as part of implementing *Directions 2031* (WAPC, 2009*f*; 2012*a*). As required under the *Planning and Development Act* 2005, the high level 1997 *State Planning Strategy* was also reviewed (WAPC, 2012*c*; 2014*b*). Work to refine and implement the metropolitan strategy subsequently saw the release of the *Draft Perth and Peel @ 3.5 Million* report plus a suite of draft sub-regional frameworks (WAPC, 2015*a*; 2015*b*; 2015*c*; 2015*d*; 2015*e*).

Directions 2031 put forward a series of urban growth scenarios similar to those used in *Network City*. The key difference, however, was a change in terminology to describe the alternatives which became 'linear city'; 'connected city'; and 'compact city'. The new strategy opted for the connected city model with an urban infill target of 47 per cent, down from the 60 per cent sought by *Network City*.

When *Directions 2031+* was released it was confirmed as the new metropolitan strategy for Perth and Peel, thereby officially replacing *Network City* and *Metroplan* – the latter actually being Perth's official metropolitan plan with *Network City*, as previously noted, never formally adopted. The planning vision of *Directions 2031+* was to create 'a world class liveable city; green, vibrant, more compact and accessible with a unique sense of place' (WAPC, 2010*a*, p. 2). This vision was underscored

Table 6.5. Metropolitan plans and planning reforms, 2008–2015.

STRATEGIC PLANS AND POLICIES Metropolitan Planning Strategies	KEY PLANNING REFORMS Planning & Governance Reforms

1. *Directions 2031: Draft Spatial Framework for Perth and Peel* (WAPC, 2009a)
 	
  (i) *Southern Metropolitan and Peel Sub-Regional Structure Plan* (WAPC, 2009d)
 	
2. *Directions 2031 and Beyond: Metropolitan Planning Beyond the Horizon* (WAPC, 2010a)
 	
  (i) *Central Metropolitan Perth Sub-Regional Strategy* (WAPC, 2010c)
 	
  (ii) *Outer Metropolitan Perth and Peel Sub-Regional Strategy* (WAPC, 2010d)
 	
3. *Draft Perth and Peel @ 3.5 Million (WAPC 2015a)*
 	
  (i) *Draft Central Sub-Regional Planning Framework* (WAPC 2015b)
 	
  (ii) *Draft North West Sub-Regional Planning Framework* (WAPC 2015c)
 	
  (iii) *Draft North East Sub-Regional Planning Framework* (WAPC 2015d)
 	
  (iv) *Draft Southern Metropolitan Peel Sub-Regional Planning Framework* (WAPC 2015e)
 	
Other Strategic Plans/Policies
 	
4. *Draft SPP Activity Centres for Perth and Peel* (WAPC, 2009b)
 	
5. *SPP 4.2 Activity Centres for Perth and Peel* (WAPC, 2010e)
 	
6. *Public Transport for Perth in 2031: Mapping Out the Future for Perth's Public Transport Network* (Department of Transport, 2011)
 	
7. *Draft Industrial Land Strategy Perth and Peel* (WAPC, 2009f)
 	
8. *Economic Employment Lands Strategy: Non-heavy Industrial Perth and Peel* (WAPC, 2012a)
 	
9. *State Planning Strategy 2050* (WAPC, 2014b)
 	
10. *Perth and Peel Green Growth Plan for 3.5 Million* (Government of Western Australia, 2015)
 	
11. *Transport @ 3.5 Million: Perth and Peel Transport Plan* (Department of Transport, 2016)
	1. *Building a Better Planning System – Consultation Paper* (Department of Planning, 2009a)
	
	2. *Planning Makes it Happen: A Blueprint for Planning Reform* (Department of Planning, 2009b)
	
	3. *Implementing Development Assessment Panels in Western Australia* (Department of Planning, 2009c)
	
	4. *The Planning and Development (Development Assessment Panels) Regulations (DAP Regulations)* (Government of Western Australia, 2011a)
	
	5. *Metropolitan Redevelopment Authority Act* (Government of Western Australia, 2011b)
	
	6. *Planning Makes it Happen Phase 2: Discussion Paper on Planning Reform* (Department of Planning, 2013)
	
	7. *Review of the Development Assessment Panels – Planning Makes it Happen Phase 2* (Department of Planning, 2013)
	
	8. *Planning Makes it Happen Phase 2: Blueprint for Planning Reform* (Department of Planning, 2014)

Sources: Various Western Australia Planning Commission, WA Department of Transport and Government of Western Australia publications.

by several strategic objectives that would see Perth transformed into a liveable, prosperous, accessible, sustainable and responsible city. Notably, the objective of making Perth an equitable city in the draft *Directions 2031* plan was omitted from the final plan.

In terms of making Perth an accessible city, the Liberal/National state government's draft public transport plan (Department of Transport, 2011) was informed by the demographic issues underpinning *Directions 2031* and the need to develop a more robust public transport system to cope with increased population. The draft strategy gave emphasis to three key initiatives: increasing the capacity of the existing transit network (i.e. investing in new rolling stock and buses, upgrading key bus interchange stations, constructing new train stations); expanding the current network via new priority bus lanes, constructing a new rail link to the airport and extending the Joondalup rail line to Yanchep in the outer northern metropolitan region; and developing a new light rail system to service suburbs in the northern middle ring suburbs and connecting the specialist centres of Curtin University, University of Western Australia and the QEII Hospital complex in the western suburbs. These same broad priorities are reflected in the most recent transport strategy (Department of Transport, 2016). That said, the Liberal/National government did not seem to show a strong commitment to light rail and abandoned the proposed northern suburbs MAX Light Rail project in 2016 (O'Connor, 2016). The Liberal/National government also invested heavily in road infrastructure over the course of its time in office with, for example, A$1 billion spent on the Gateway WA project near Perth Airport (Gateway WA, 2017). There was considerable political debate on transport in the run-up to the March 2017 state election with the incumbent Liberal/National government pressing ahead with the controversial Roe 8 road project in the south-eastern suburbs whilst the Labor Party championed its suburban rail proposal, METRONET. As Bunker and Troy (2015, p. 26) have noted '[t]he most important challenge [for Perth] is to put in place an adequate transport policy, central to the idea of a connected city'. The new Labor state government ordered an immediate stop of all construction work on the Roe 8 project after taking political office. The Labor state government's determination to press ahead with its METRONET project finally paid off with the Federal government agreeing to provide A$700m of a total A$1.2b budget for this project (Government of Western Australia, 2017).

As part of the overarching strategy to encourage development and consolidation within existing urban areas, a hierarchy of activity centres was outlined in *Directions 2031+* (figure 6.2a). Moreover, in order to strengthen this polycentric objective, the government also issued *SPP 4.2 Activity Centres for Perth and Peel* (WAPC, 2010e). This SPP identified just over 100 activity centres across an eight-point typology – (*i*) capital city; (*ii*) specialized centres; (*iii*) primary centres; (*iv*) strategic metropolitan centres; (*v*) secondary centres; (*vi*) district centres; (*vii*) neighbourhood centres; and (*viii*) local centres – that reflected varying degrees of intensity and diversity in terms of land-use functions as well as the nature and extent of transport services, connectivity and accessibility. *Directions 2031+* was accompanied by two draft sub-regional strategies for the Central Metropolitan Perth planning region, an area encompassing nineteen local governments; and the Outer Metropolitan Perth and Peel region which embraced four metropolitan sub-regional planning areas (North-West, North-East, South-West, South-East) and the Peel sub-region,

Figure 6.2a. Activity centre hierarchy. (*Source*: WAPC, 2010a, p. 34)

encompassing fourteen local government areas (figure 6.2b). These strategies set out housing and employment targets at the sub-regional level.

In pursuit of urban consolidation, table 6.6 shows the spatial distribution of the housing stock in 2008 and additional dwellings required by 2031. In overall terms, it was anticipated that the Central Perth sub-region would have the largest increase (121,000) in dwellings by 2031, equating to a 38 per cent increase in the dwelling stock. Despite this increase, however, the Central sub-region's overall share of the dwelling stock would decrease from 46.7 per cent to 43.5 per cent. In other words, the outer suburban sub-regions would see an increase in their overall share of the projected metropolitan housing stock from 53.3 per cent to 56.5 per cent, again raising questions about the ongoing challenge of managing suburban growth.

Interestingly, only the Central Perth draft sub-regional strategy provided details on the spatial distribution of housing targets at the local government area level (figure 6.3). In absolute terms, the City of Stirling, the largest local government in WA in terms of population, was assigned the highest housing target with 31,000 new dwellings, an increase of 36 per cent on the existing housing stock. Elsewhere, other large absolute increases in housing were set for Perth (12,600, 145 per cent); Victoria Park (11,200, 73 per cent); Melville (11,000, 27.5 per cent); Canning (9,000, 27.7 per cent); and Bayswater (8,500, 32 per cent). Although lower absolute dwelling targets were set for local governments in the high-income

140 • PLANNING METROPOLITAN AUSTRALIA

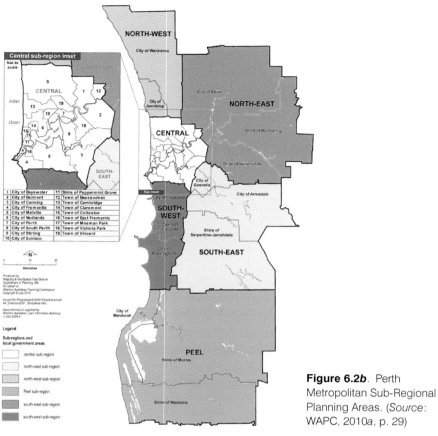

Figure 6.2b. Perth Metropolitan Sub-Regional Planning Areas. (*Source:* WAPC, 2010a, p. 29)

Table 6.6. Directions 2031 Dwelling Targets by Metropolitan Sub-Region.

Sub-Region	2008 Dwellings	% Share 2008 Dwelling Stock	Target Dwellings by 2031	% Share of Additional Dwellings	Total Dwellings by 2031	% Change in Dwelling Stock	% Share 2031 Dwelling Stock
Central	319,400	46.7	121,000	36.9	440,400	37.9	43.5
North-West	106,700	15.6	65,000	19.8	171,700	60.9	17.0
North-East	73,400	10.7	40,000	12.2	113,400	54.5	11.2
South-East	64,800	9.5	35,000	10.7	99,800	54.0	9.9
South-West	82,000	12.0	41,000	12.5	123,000	50.0	12.1
Peel	38,200	5.6	26,000	7.9	64,200	68.1	6.3
Total	684,500	100	328,000	100	1,012,500	47.9	100

Source: WAPC, 2010c, p.17.

western suburbs, these were significant in terms of the proportional change to the local dwelling stock. Most western suburbs councils are relatively small in area and population but they are characterized as having well-planned suburbs with generous space standards and access to quality public open space and other amenity features, most notably the Swan River. A generally conservative and NIMBY culture tends to prevail within many of these wealthy suburbs to a greater degree than elsewhere and densification has often been vociferously opposed by elected members and local community members (see figure 6.4).

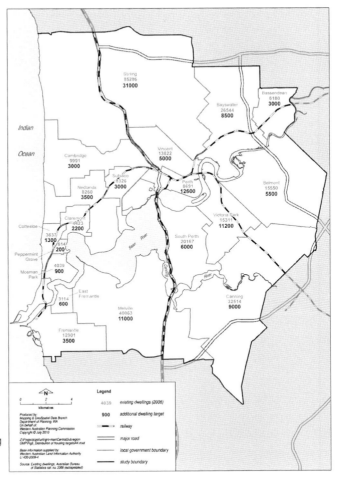

Figure 6.3. Local government area dwelling targets. (*Source*: WAPC, 2010c, p. 17)

Figure 6.4. Local community opposition to densification in Dalkeith, City of Nedlands. (*Source*: Photo courtesy of Nick Middleton, NJM Spatial, Esperance, WA)

In many respects *Directions 2031+* and SPP 4.2 seem to be informed by central place theory (Christaller, 1933) in that both policy instruments seek to create an optimal settlement pattern for metropolitan Perth. Furthermore, they also seek to provide a greater degree of certainty within the planning system, assuring developers that planners are supportive of particular types and scales of development within different activity centres and corridors. The establishment of independent Development Assessment Panels as part of the government's planning reform agenda may be seen as another means of instilling greater certainty into the planning system (Department of Planning, 2009*b*) by seeking to depoliticize the development assessment and approval process at the local government level.

Towards Implementing *Directions 2031+*

In May 2015 the WA government released the draft *Perth and Peel @ 3.5 Million* suite of strategic land-use planning documents (WAPC 2015*a*; 2015*b*; 2015*c*; 2015*d*; 2015*e*). This suite of documents included an overarching report that: (*i*) reasserted the need to put sustainable development at the heart of strategic planning; (*ii*) redefined the strategic vision of *Directions 2031+* such that Perth is now to be an 'innovative 21st century city delivering distinctive western Australian lifestyle choices and global opportunities' (WAPC, 2015*a*, p. 4); and (*iii*) refined the strategic objectives, such that the metropolitan strategy intends to create a city that is liveable, prosperous, connected, sustainable and collaborative. Notably, the overarching aim of Perth becoming a 'global city', as stated in the draft *Directions 2031* strategy, was dropped and replaced with becoming an innovative twenty-first century city.

The major components of this latest suite of documents were the four draft sub-regional planning frameworks covering the Central, North-West, North-East, and South Metropolitan and Peel sub-regions. These planning frameworks were intended to facilitate implementation of *Directions 2031+* through more detailed structure planning and the statutory planning process. They had been under preparation since 2011 but had been held up by a strategic assessment of vegetation being prepared jointly by the Commonwealth and the WA governments to ensure land identified for development would not be constrained by the Commonwealth's *Environment Protection and Biodiversity Conservation Act* 1999. This strategic assessment was still in draft form in 2015 (Government of Western Australia, 2015) and remains so at the time of writing.

The new *Perth and Peel @ 3.5 Million* documents 'aim to establish a long-term integrated planning framework for land use and infrastructure' (WAPC, 2015*b*, p. 5). Moreover, they represent a crucial step in implementing the strategic visions, aims and objectives outlined in *Directions 2031+* by providing 'guidance in relation to anticipated timeframes and sequencing for the delivery of urban development sites and key infrastructure' (WAPC, 2015*a*, p. 15). Furthermore, they aim to provide a sense of planning certainty by establishing urban infill dwelling targets across *all* local government areas up to and beyond 2031. The WAPC's most recent report card on progress being made in relation to the urban infill housing targets in *Directions 2031+* stated that 'there would have to be significant increase in residential infill development over the next three years if short term infill targets are going to be met' (WAPC, 2014*a*, p. 24).

Ultimately, the draft frameworks are to be converted into sub-regional structure plans and will be incorporated into *SPP 1: State Planning Framework Policy (Variation No. 2),* thereby affording them considerable policy authority. That said, if history is any measure of future policy outcomes, then *Directions 2031+* faces a major challenge in realizing its urban consolidation objectives – a feat that no previous metropolitan strategy has successfully achieved. Although the *Perth and Peel @ 3.5 Million* sub-regional frameworks provide detailed guidelines and are designed to translate the strategic vision and aims of the metropolitan strategy into real planning outputs and outcomes, an implementation gap is likely to persist. As Taylor (1998, p. 126) observes, planning systems in liberal democratic societies do 'not themselves provide development, but rather [regulate] and [control] it'. Although the state government has some direct responsibility for implementation through the Metropolitan Redevelopment Authority and Landcorp, its land development agency, the responsibility for implementation rests mainly with the investment decisions of property developers and investors who are in turn responding to individual, household and institutional consumer preferences and demands. Now that the resources boom in WA has passed, many aspects of *Directions 2031+* can be expected to suffer from an implementation gap for the foreseeable future.

Conclusion

WA has a long history of formal metropolitan planning strategies that dates back to the mid-1950s. It also has the most centralized planning system in Australia, but the advantages afforded by the powers held by the WAPC have not resulted in the full realization of the urban growth management objectives of successive non-statutory metropolitan plans. That said, these strategic statutory planning instruments have arguably resulted in the creation of 'less-worse' planning outcomes than would otherwise have been produced. Despite the best intentions of state governments since the 1950s, metropolitan planning has had to contend with a complex mix of political and economic forces – capitalism, neoliberalism and globalization – and has had to address people's continued preferences for single detached homes. Although the average size of lots has been decreasing and 'new' cultural and market preferences for higher density forms of housing have emerged, especially over the last decade, the WAPC's most recent report card (2014*a*) on the extent of progress towards the urban infill and housing targets set out in *Directions 2031+* indicates that considerable work still needs to be done. The current downturn in the economy only serves to exacerbate this challenge. In order to improve design outcomes in new residential developments, the WAPC released a series of documents under the banner *Design WA* including a draft SPP, a draft Apartment Design Policy, a draft Design Review Guide and a draft Design Skills Discussion Paper, aimed in part at lessening community resistance to higher density development (WAPC, 2016*b*; 2016*c*; 2016*d*; 2016*e*).

Strategic planning's efforts to make sense of, manage and create socio-spatial order within the Perth metropolitan system will face profoundly new challenges – *disruptive urbanisms* – as the so-called sharing economy continues to evolve. The rise of increased online retailing (Drechsler, 2014), the 'uber-ization' of services, driverless vehicles and hyper-flexible labour markets suggest that planners will need to move beyond looking at metropolitan Perth through a traditional physical land use lens (Davidson and Infranca, 2016). The state Labor government, elected in March 2017, has indicated a commitment to sustainability, public transport and greater community consultation and participation in planning matters (ALP WA, 2015). At this stage the new government has yet to provide much detail of its planning policy agenda. It will be interesting to see when and how, if at all, the new government will introduce its own planning reform agenda, and, more crucially, a new metropolitan strategy that reflects its particular policy priorities and political philosophy.

References

ALP WA (2015) *WA Labour Platform 2015*. Perth: ALP WA. Available at: https://www.walabor.org.au/platform.

ABS (Australian Bureau of Statistics) (2012) *Census of Population and Housing 2011 – Time Series Profile* (CAT 2003.0). Canberra: Australian Bureau of Statistics. Available at: http://www.abs.gov.au/AUSSTATS/abs@.nsf/Lookup/2003.0Main+Features12011%20Second%20Release?OpenDocument.

ABS (2016) *Regional Population Growth, Australia*, CAT 3218.0. Canberra: ABS. Available at: http://www.abs.gov.au/AUSSTATS/abs@.nsf/DetailsPage/3218.02014-15?OpenDocument.

Boas, H. (1930) *Report of the Metropolitan Town Planning Commission Perth, Western Australia. December 1930*. Perth: Government Printer.

Bunker, R. and Troy, L. (2015) The Changing Political Economy of the Compact City and Higher Density Urban Renewal in Perth. Planning in a Market Economy: ARC Discovery Project Working Paper No. 2. Sydney: UNSW/City Futures Research Centre.

CCU (Citizens and Civics Unit) (2002) *Consulting Citizens: A Resource Guide*. Perth: CCU/DPC.

CCU (2003) *Consulting Citizens: Planning for Success*. Perth: CCU/DPC.

Christaller, W. (1933) *Die zentralen Orte in Süddeutschland*. Jena: Gustav Fischer. (Translated in part by Carlisle W. Baskin (1966) as *Central Places in Southern Germany*. Englewood Cliffs, NJ: Prentice Hall).

Davidson, N.M. and Infranca, J.J. (2016) The sharing economy as an urban phenomenon. *Yale Law & Policy Review*, **34**(2), pp. 216–279. Available at: http://digitalcommons.law.yale.edu/ylpr/vol34/iss2/1.

Department of Planning (2009*a*) *Building a Better Planning System Consultation Paper*. Perth: DoP.

Department of Planning (2009*b*) *Planning Makes It Happen – A Blueprint for Reform*. Perth: DoP.

Department of Planning (2009*c*) *Implementing Development Assessment Panels in Western Australia*. Perth: DoP.

Department of Planning (2013) *Planning Makes It Happen: Phase Two – Discussion Paper on Planning Reform*. Perth: DoP.

Department of Planning (2014) *Planning Makes It Happen: Phase Two – A Blueprint for Reform*. Perth: DoP.

Department of Transport (2011) *Public Transport Plan for Perth in 2031: Mapping Out the Future for Perth's Public Transport Network. Draft for Consultation*. Perth: Department of Transport.

Department of Transport (2016) *Transport @ 3.5 Million: Perth and Peel Transport Plan*. Perth: Department of Transport.

DPUD (Department for Planning and Urban Development) (1990) *Metroplan: A Planning Strategy for the Perth Metropolitan Region*. Prepared for State Planning Commission. Perth: DPUD.

Drechsler P. (2014) Metropolitan activity centre planning in Australia: implications of millennial consumption practices. *Urban Policy and Research*, **32**(3), pp. 271–287.

Education and Health Standing Committee (2015) *The Impact of FIFO Work Practices on Mental Health – Final Report*. Perth: Legislative Assembly, Parliament of Western Australia, Available at: http://www.parliament.wa.gov.au/Parliament/commit.nsf/(Report+Lookup+by+Com+ID)/2E970A7A4934026448257E67002BF9D1/$file/20150617%20-%20Final%20Report%20w%20signature%20for%20website.pdf.

Foley, N. and Williams, P. (2016) Funding and governance of regional public land in Perth and Sydney. *Urban Policy and Research*, **34**(3), pp. 199–211.

Gateway WA (2017) *Perth has a New Front Door*. Available at: http://gatewaywa.com.au/.

Government of Western Australia (2003) *Hope for the Future: The Western Australian State Sustainability Strategy – A Vision for Quality of Life in Western Australia*. Perth: Government of Western Australia.

Government of Western Australia (2011*a*) *The Planning and Development (Development Assessment Panels) Regulations.* Perth: Government of Western Australia.

Government of Western Australia (2011*b*) *Metropolitan Redevelopment Authority Act.* Perth: Government of Western Australia

Government of Western Australia (2015) *Perth and Peel Green Growth Plan for 3.5 Million. Summary*. Perth: Department of the Premier and Cabinet (December).

Government of Western Australia (2017) *$2.3 Billion Jobs and Infrastructure Boost for Western Australia*. Joint Media Statement, 7 May. Available at: https://www.mediastatements.wa.gov.au/Pages/McGowan/2017/Joint-media-statement-2-point-3-billion-dollars-jobs-and-infrastructure-boost-for-Western-Australia.aspx.

Hartz-Karp, J. (2005) A case study in deliberative democracy: dialogue with the city. *Journal of Public Deliberation*, **1**(1), Article 6. Available at: http://www.publicdeliberation.net/cgi/viewcontent.cgi?article=1002&context=jpd.

Haslam McKenzie, F.M. (2011) Fly-in fly-out: the challenges of transient populations in rural landscapes, in Luck, G., Race, D. and Black, R. (eds.) *Demographic Change in Rural Landscapes: What does it mean for Society and the Environment?* London: Springer, pp. 353–374.

Haslam McKenzie, F.M. and Rowley, S. (2013) Housing market failure in a booming economy. *Housing Studies*, **28**(3), pp. 373–388.

Hedgcock, D. and Yiftachel, O. (eds.) (1992) *Urban and Regional Planning in Western Australia*. Perth: Paradigm Press.

Hopkins, D. (2007) 'Heads I Win, Tails You Lose': Information, Power, and the Illusion of Choice in Participatory Planning. Paper presented to the Australian and New Zealand Association of Planning Schools (ANZAPS) Conference, University of Otago.

Hopkins, D. (2010*a*) Planning metropolitan Perth through 'dialogue': participatory democracy or manufactured consent? in Alexander, I., Hedgcock, D. and Greive, S. (eds.) *Planning Issues and Challenges for Western Australia: A Reader in Theory and Practice*. Perth: Fremantle Arts Press.

Hopkins, D. (2010*b*) Planning a city through 'dialogue': deliberative policy-making in action in Western Australia. *Urban Policy and Research*, **28**, pp. 261–276.

Hopkins, L.D. and Zapata, M (2007) *Engaging the Future: Forecasts, Scenarios, Plans and Projects*. Cambridge, MA: Lincoln Land Institute.

Lawrie, M., Tonts, P. and Plummer, P. (2011) Boomtowns, resource dependence and socio-economic well-being. *Australian Geographer*, **42**(2), pp. 139–164.

Maginn, P.J. (2007) Deliberative democracy or discursively biased? Perth's dialogue with the city initiative. *Space and Polity*, **11**(3), pp. 331–352.

Maginn, P.J. 2016) The triumph of suburbia? The (in)ability of planning to contain the 'Great Australian Dream', in Biermann, S., Olaru, D. and Paul, V. (eds.) *Planning Boomtown and Beyond*. Perth: UWA Press, pp. 158–188.

Maginn, P.J. and Foley, N. (2014) From a centralised to a 'diffused centralised' planning system: planning reforms in Western Australia. *Australian Planner*, **51**(2), pp. 151–162.

Maginn, P. J. and Hamnett, S. (2016) Multiculturalism and metropolitan Australia: demographic change and implications for strategic planning. *Built Environment*, **42**(1), pp. 181–205.

Maginn, P.J., Goodman, R., Gurran, N. and Ruming, K. (2017) What is so strategic about Australian metropolitan plans and planning reform? The case of Melbourne, Perth and Sydney, in Albrechts, L., Balducci, A. and Hillier, J. (eds.) *Situated Practices of Strategic Planning: An International Perspective*. London: Routledge, pp. 135–157.

Martinus, K., Tonts, M., Myat, P., Fulker, M., Davis, G., Harford-Mills, G., Maginn, P. and Atkins, M. (2016) *Committee for Perth: A Decade of Positive Impact*. A FACTBase Special Report. Perth: The University of Western Australia and Committee for Perth. Available at: https://www.committeeforperth.com.au/assets/documents/FACTBase-Special-Report-a-decade-of-positive-impact.pdf.

Metropolitan Local Government Review Panel (2012) *Final Report of the Independent Panel*. Perth: Government of Western Australia. Available at: http://www.parliament.wa.gov.au/publications/tabledpapers.nsf/displaypaper/3815506ab06573e0bcb5ffbb48257aa300037750/$file/5506.pdf.

Metropolitan Region Planning Authority (1970) *The Corridor Plan for Perth*. Perth: MRPA.

Ministry for Planning (2000) *Towards a Vision for Perth in 2029*. Perth: Ministry for Planning (brochure).

O'Connor, A. (2016) Perth MAX light rail promise abandoned by WA Government in long-term transport plan. *ABC News*, 21 June. Available at: http://www.abc.net.au/news/2016-06-21/government-confirms-max-light-rail-abandoned/7529756.

Peck, J. and Tickell, A. (2002) Neoliberalizing Space. *Antipode*, **34**(3), pp. 380–403.

REIWA (Real Estate Institute of Western Australia) (2017) *Perth Suburbs Price Data*. Available at: http://reiwa.com.au/the-wa-market/perth-metro/.

Stephenson, G. and Hepburn, J.A. (1955) *Plan for the Metropolitan Region: Perth and Fremantle*. Report and separate Atlas of Maps. Perth: Government of Western Australia.

Stokes, R. and Hill, R. (1992) The evolution of metropolitan planning in Western Australia, in Hedgcock, D. and Yiftachel, O. (eds.) (1992) *Urban and Regional Planning in Western Australia*. Perth: Paradigm Press, pp. 111–130.

Taylor, N. (1998) *Urban Planning Theory Since 1945*. London: Sage.

Tonts, M., Huddleston, V., Maginn, P.J., Huddleston, P. and Wetzstein, S. (2012) *Perth as a Global Minerals and Energy Resources Hub*. A Factbase Special Report. Perth: The University of Western Australia and Committee for Perth. Available at: https://www.committeeforperth.com.au/events/perth-as-a-global-minerals-and-energy-resources-hub.

Tonts, M., Haslam McKenzie, F.M. and Plummer, P. (2016) The resource 'super-cycle' and Australia's remote cities. *Built Environment*, **42**(1), pp. 174–188.

Troy, P. (1996) *The Perils of Urban Consolidation*. Annandale: Federation Press.

Urban Development Institute of Australia (WA) (2013) *View 40 Years of House Price Data in Perth*. Available at: http://blog.udiawa.com.au/article/median-house-price-perth.

Urban Development Institute of Australia (WA) (nd) *Dwelling Approval Tool*. Available at: www.udiawa.com.au.

WAPC (Western Australia Planning Commission) (1999) *Future Perth*. Perth: Western Australian Planning Commission (brochure).

WAPC (2000) *Scenarios of Our Future: Challenges for Western Australian Society*. Perth: Western Australian Planning Commission.

WAPC (2001) *Metropolitan Development Options Workshop (Final Report)*. Perth: Western Australian Planning Commission.

WAPC (2003) *Greater Perth Discussion Papers 1–9*. Perth: Western Australian Planning Commission (Compact Disc).

WAPC (2004) *Network City: Community Planning Strategy for Perth and Peel: For Public Comment*. Perth: Western Australian Planning Commission.

WAPC (2006a) *Draft State Planning Policy: Network City*. Perth: Western Australian Planning Commission.

WAPC (2006*b*) *State Planning Policy No. 1: State Planning Framework Policy (Variation No. 2)*. Perth: WA Government Gazette, 3 February.

WAPC (2009*a*) *Directions 2031: Draft Spatial Framework for Perth and Peel*. Perth: Western Australian Planning Commission.

WAPC (2009*b*) *Draft State Planning Policy: Activity Centres for Perth and Peel*. Perth: Western Australian Planning Commission.

WAPC (2009*c*) *Planning Activity Centres for Communities and Economic Growth: Discussion Paper*. Perth: Western Australian Planning Commission.

WAPC (2009d) *Southern Metropolitan and Peel Sub-Regional Structure Plan: For Public Comment*. Perth: Western Australian Planning Commission.

WAPC (2009e) *Urban Growth Monitor: Perth Metropolitan and Peel Regions: Urban Development Program*. Perth: Western Australian Planning Commission.

WAPC (2009*f*) *Draft Industrial Land Strategy 2009 Perth and Peel.* Perth: Western Australian Planning Commission.

WAPC (2010*a*) *Directions 2031 and Beyond: Metropolitan Planning Beyond the Horizon.* Perth: Western Australian Planning Commission.

WAPC (2010*b*) *What Was Said about Directions 2031 Draft Spatial Framework for Perth and Peel*. Perth: Western Australian Planning Commission.

WAPC (2010*c*) *Central Metropolitan Perth Sub-Regional Strategy.* Perth: Western Australian Planning Commission.

WAPC (2010*d*) *Outer Metropolitan Perth and Peel Sub-Regional Strategy.* Perth: Western Australian Planning Commission.

WAPC (2010*e*) *State Planning Policy 4.2: Activity Centres for Perth and Peel*. Perth: WA Government Gazette, 31 August.

WAPC (2012*a*) *Economic and Employment Lands Strategy: Non-heavy Industrial – Perth Metropolitan and Peel Regions.* Perth: Western Australian Planning Commission.

WAPC (2012*b*) *Delivering Directions 2031: Annual Report Card 2012.* Perth: Western Australian Planning Commission.

WAPC (2012*c*) *State Planning Strategy: Planning for Sustained Growth and Prosperity – Draft for Public Comment.* Perth: Western Australian Planning Commission.

WAPC (2013) *Delivering Directions 2031: Annual Report Card 2013.* Perth: Western Australian Planning Commission.

WAPC (2014*a*) *Delivering Directions 2031: Annual Report Card 2014.* Perth: Western Australian Planning Commission.

WAPC (2014*b*) *State Planning Strategy 2050: Planning for Sustained Growth and Prosperity.* Perth: Western Australian Planning Commission.

WAPC (2015a) *Draft Perth and Peel @ 3.5 Million.* Perth: Western Australian Planning Commission.

WAPC (2015*b*) *Draft Central Sub-Regional Planning Framework: Towards Perth and Peel @ 3.5 Million.* Perth: Western Australian Planning Commission.

WAPC (2015*c*) *Draft North-West Sub-Regional Planning Framework: Towards Perth and Peel @ 3.5 Million.* Perth: Western Australian Planning Commission.

WAPC (2015*d*) *Draft North-East Sub-Regional Planning Framework: Towards Perth and Peel @ 3.5 Million.* Perth: Western Australian Planning Commission.

WAPC (2015*e*) *Draft Southern Metropolitan Peel Sub-Regional Planning Framework: Towards Perth and Peel @ 3.5 Million.* Perth: Western Australian Planning Commission.

WAPC (2016*a*) *Urban Growth Monitor: Perth Metropolitan, Peel and Greater Bunbury Regions.* Perth: Western Australian Planning Commission.

WAPC (2016*b*) *Draft State Planning Policy No.7: Design of the Built Environment*. Perth: Western Australian Planning Commission.

WAPC (2016*c*) *Draft Apartment Design Policy*. Perth: Western Australian Planning Commission.

WAPC (2016*d*) *Draft Design Review Guide.* Perth: Western Australian Planning Commission.

WAPC (2016*e*) *Draft Design Skills Discussion Paper.* Perth: Western Australian Planning Commission.

Chapter 7

South East Queensland: Change and Continuity in Planning

Paul Burton

Of all the metropolitan regions of Australia, South East Queensland (SEQ) is the most paradoxical. On the one hand it is presented as something of an exception, not simply because its very name avoids reference to the capital city at its core but because it reflects also the fact that Brisbane as the state capital is less dominant than in other states and territories, accommodating less than half of the state's population (Burton, 2010; Gleeson and Steele, 2010). On the other hand, as one of the fastest growing regions in Australia for much of the last half century, it is seen to epitomize the challenges facing metropolitan regions in general and to serve as a test bed for urban planning and growth management policies (Savery, 2010). As Gleeson and Steele also note, this corner of Queensland has come to be seen as an 'increasingly important crucible of change that captures and reflects many of the growth management dilemmas and opportunities facing the Australian settlement system ... at the metropolitan level' (Gleeson and Steele, 2010, p14).

With people drawn from elsewhere in Australia and, indeed, the rest of the world, by its congenial climate, the proximity of beaches and other high-quality environmental attractions and by a variety of campaigns promoting these and other benefits, the scale and pace of this population growth has presented substantial challenges to planners and politicians. In trying to ensure that employment opportunities are available to the newcomers, that public services and infrastructure keep pace with population growth and that the environmental attractions of the region are not substantially damaged in the process of growth, plans for the region must deal with conflicting pressures and expectations. The regional plans produced over the last decades have been recognized in many quarters for their strategic and integrated approaches to growth management (Margerum, 2002; Abbott, 2009; Gleeson *et al.*, 2012), but as growth continues and new social, economic and environmental pressures emerge so do the challenges associated with developing and implementing effective regional plans. While focusing on metropolitan and regional planning in SEQ over the last 16 or so years, this chapter considers also how planning at this scale might develop in the coming years.

The chapter, which is in four sections, begins by describing briefly the growth of SEQ since 2000 before charting chronologically the various attempts since the beginning of this century to meet the challenges of growth management through processes of metropolitan and regional planning. It goes on to identify the main features of these plans and to offer a critical assessment of their successes and failures. The concluding section focuses on the political and institutional pressures and problems associated with developing collaborative arrangements between state and local governments and considers the consequences of a shifting balance of power and responsibility between these levels over the last 16 years.

Growth and Change since 2000

Since 2000 the region has continued to follow a similar pattern to its growth over the preceding decades. In the first decade of the new century, it grew by approximately 700,000 people to reach 3.18 million at an average annual growth rate of 2.5 per cent, consistent with the average annual growth rate since 1980. The coastal cities of Brisbane, the Gold Coast and the Sunshine Coast remained the focal points of population growth within the region, while the more western settlements of Ipswich, Toowoomba and Beaudesert experienced more modest increases in total population. Patterns of growth within these major urban areas and cities were also varied and typically clustered around particular nodes. Brisbane, for example, saw growth and increases in density concentrated within its inner, middle and outer suburbs but areas beyond about 50 kilometres from the centre remained stable or even declined in the decade to 2011 (Coffee *et al.*, 2016). Within the City of Gold Coast, growth has typically been greatest within its coastal strip on the eastern edge of the city, but significant concentrations of new housing continue to be developed west of the Pacific Motorway in the north of the city. A similar pattern is seen on the Sunshine Coast, where growth has been concentrated in the coastal regions of Maroochydore and Caloundra with little significant population growth in the inland and western regions.

Much of the population growth of SEQ is the product of inter-state and international migration, driven by the pursuit of an attractive lifestyle. Writing about the sustained growth of the Gold Coast, Bernard Salt (2015, p. 6) has spoken of the city being 'willed into existence because of the fundamental demand for leisure and lifestyle'. While this partly reflects the hyperbole of popular demography, it captures a widely held view that the growth of the whole region has continued to be built upon factors not directly associated with economic growth, but with more nebulous lifestyle attractions (Guhathakurta and Stimson, 2007). In other words, the initial decision to move to SEQ often reflects a desire for an attractive lifestyle, while more specific locational decisions take additional account of the accessibility of the dominant labour market of Brisbane.

Figure 7.1. Local government boundaries in SEQ. (*Source:* Reproduced with permission of Queensland Department of Infrastructure, Local Government and Planning)

The components of this growing population reflect a combination of net overseas migration, net interstate migration and a slightly positive rate of natural increase. Net overseas migration into Queensland has always been a function of the national profile, with the state typically receiving a share of migrants commensurate with its share of the total population of Australia. However, net overseas migration to Australia has varied considerably over the years, ranging from low points of around 20,000 per annum in the mid-1970s and mid-1990s to around 300,000 by the late 2000s. These variations are primarily policy-driven and reflect changing attitudes to the need for key workers, family reunification and the obligations of humanitarian settlement. Net interstate migration has also fluctuated considerably although, in the last two decades of the twentieth century, there was an average annual net gain of 30,000 people moving to Queensland from interstate. Fertility and mortality rates across the state have also changed, but are much less volatile, leading to a rate of natural increase that continues to rise slowly but surely and which currently accounts for over half of the total population growth of the state (Queensland Government Statistician's Office, 2016). Bell *et al.* (2010) have explored possible population futures for SEQ, including the consequences of setting population targets or caps in the name of sustainable development.

They conclude that, in order to limit overall growth to 2010 levels, almost 10,000 people per annum would be required to leave the region, simply to offset the rate of natural increase.

Recent population data reveal some interesting new developments that would not have been part of the assumptions that underpinned previous metropolitan plans and appear to have had only a marginal impact on the latest draft strategy. While neither the continued growth of the state's population nor the relatively slow rate of growth is surprising, the increasing significance of natural increase as the driver of growth is noteworthy. Although net interstate migration remains positive, the impact of overseas migration is of greater significance as these migrants typically have a younger age profile and are serving to slow the overall ageing of the population. In other words, much of the population growth of SEQ and some of its major cities such as the Gold Coast has, in the past, been due to the interstate migration of older people accelerating the ageing of the total population, whereas the growing significance recently of younger, international migrants has slowed this process.

Of course, the ageing of the population as a whole continues and in the future there may be social challenges in caring for an increasingly ethnically diverse population of older people as well as demand for new types of housing, different patterns of public services, especially in health and social care, and continuing pressures to preserve the environmental amenities that have been hallmarks of the attractiveness of the region.

State-wide trends are also reflected in the relationship between SEQ and the rest of Queensland. Annual growth in SEQ has outpaced the rest of the state over the past 20 years and eight out of the ten most populous local government areas are located in SEQ, with only two of the ten, Townsville and Cairns, located outside the region. Following the end of the recent resources boom, migration to these centres of mining and processing in regional towns has declined while migration to the more diverse economies of SEQ cities continues.

Chronology of Plans

The Twentieth-Century Foundations of Regional Planning in SEQ

Regional planning in Queensland and SEQ took firm hold in the early years of the twenty-first century, but the foundations were laid in the later years of the twentieth century. Queensland became exceptional in grasping the political nettle of enforcing local government amalgamation on its capital city in 1925, enabling the Greater Brisbane Council to play, in theory at least, a more prominent and proactive role in planning and managing the rapid growth of the city and served also to deflect for a time political pressures for the Queensland Government to become more involved in planning for the wider region. By the 1970s, concern for regional scale planning in the south-east corner of the state saw the creation of the Moreton Regional Coordination Council (MRCC) with a remit to prepare a regional growth strategy for the area covered by Brisbane City and sixteen surrounding municipalities. Although the MRCC was abolished in the mid-1970s in the face of a shared anti-planning disposition by state Premier Joh Bjelke-Petersen and Prime Minister Malcolm Fraser, it continued to meet as the Moreton Regional Organisation of Councils (MROC), reflecting the recognition by all seventeen local authorities that some degree of planning and coordination among themselves was mutually beneficial.

By the 1990s this recognition had spread to the state government, in particular through the support of Tom Burns, Local Government Minister in the newly elected Goss Labor Government. John Abbott (2012) describes this period as one of initial voluntary growth management, in which relations between the local governments of the region and the state government were reasonably cordial, but underlain by a sense of suspicion, certainly on the part of the local councils.

While these arrangements were seen in a very positive light and indeed as something of a model outside Queensland, within the state government tensions were emerging around the development and implementation of a number of related but more focused plans. In particular, a Regional Open Space System plan, designed to limit the loss of open space and manage the remaining stock more effectively, was subject to review in 1996 by a new National-Liberal coalition government led by Premier Rob Borbidge and became a source of public concern around regional planning processes, and for the Labor Government of Peter Beattie, elected in 1998. Less visible to the public at large, but nonetheless significant in laying the foundation for a regional planning system, sectoral plans and strategies were prepared, covering transport, air quality, water, economic development, and nature conservation. While each was valuable, there was minimal collaborative planning across these substantive areas, which typically reflected departmental silos within the state government. Despite considerable efforts by government officials to collaborate and coordinate their efforts, a plethora of only occasionally interconnected sectoral strategies emerged and continue to this day (James and Burton, 2016).

From Voluntary to Statutory Regional Planning

Following the re-election of the Beattie Government in 2001, the process of strengthening the statutory basis of regional planning in SEQ gained momentum. A major evaluation of the economic performance of the region (DLGP, 2002) found some positive trends (strong residential and employment growth in Brisbane's CBD) and some negative (lack of employment growth in other designated growth areas), but the report's greatest significance lay in preparing the ground for what was to become the 2005 South East Queensland Regional Plan (SEQRP). While identifying areas and issues for new policy work, the report also flagged eight issues that were already deemed important, but which appeared to be struggling in their implementation. Most of these areas fell under the broad heading of environmental policy, including biodiversity conservation, coastal management, water and air quality, and water supply.

Part of this implementation problem lay in the relationship between regional plans and the local planning schemes prepared in accordance with Queensland's Integrated Planning Act introduced in 1997, through which regional objectives were to be realized. The local governments of SEQ were struggling to prepare planning schemes that could effectively manage the consequences of rapid population growth in the absence of a statutory regional plan, although Planning Minister Nita Cunningham appeared to see the problem differently in suggesting that any sensible regional plan would simply be the sum of all local plans (Abbott, 2012, p. 38).

At this point a disparate coalition of forces began to emerge to give public expression to the need for a new regional plan with more statutory power. The Queensland divisions of the Planning Institute of Australia and the Urban Development Institute of Australia and, importantly, the local media began to campaign for change, alongside the Brisbane Institute under the leadership of urban historian Peter Spearritt. The challenge was taken up by the South East Queensland Regional Organisation of Councils which, following a summit of SEQ mayors held at the end of 2003, agreed to press for a new statutory approach to regional planning. This was in turn accepted by the Beattie Government, re-elected in February 2004, and led by Minister Mackenroth from his position as chair of the SEQ Regional Coordination Committee. This planning process was overseen by yet another state-level committee, the Urban Management and Infrastructure Coordination Committee (UMICC), which recommended the creation of an Office of Urban Management (OUM) to lead regional planning in SEQ.

Among the more significant responsibilities of the OUM, established in March 2004, were the inclusion of open space and landscape planning in the statutory framework and the preparation of regional infrastructure plans as part of the annual budget process. The Executive Director of the OUM, Michael Kerry, seconded from his role as head of Urban Management at Brisbane City Council, set about preparing a draft SEQRP for public consultation by October 2004. This proved to be a relatively popular process by the standards of regional planning consultation, with over 8,000 formal submissions received following thirteen public meetings and an extensive advertising campaign in the local media.

The SEQRP, 2005–2026

The SEQRP was published in June 2005 (OUM, 2005*b*) and received widespread support from the public, from the development industry and from other levels of government.

This first statutory SEQRP was designed primarily to manage anticipated population growth and its consequences over a 20-year period, trying to reconcile the benefits of growth with a desire to protect the quality of life. It was prepared under the auspices of an amended Integrated Planning Act, 1997, which required a degree of public consultation over draft proposals, and, during plan preparation, with the Regional Consultative Committee, first established in 1994 as a joint venture between the state and local governments. The SEQRP for the first time had the weight of being a state planning instrument and took precedence over all local planning policies and regulations. Planning schemes prepared by local authorities within the region were expected to be consistent with the SEQRP, and those already in existence had to be amended within a reasonable period if they were not.

The main elements of what was essentially an indicative spatial plan included the identification of suitable land for future development to accommodate a growing population; the provision of infrastructure to service this population; a preference for more compact urban forms through urban infill and a limited number of new major development areas; diversification of the regional economy; and the protection of natural environments and biodiversity. Of course, some of these elements were in conflict, not least the desire to identify suitable greenfield land for new housing while at the same time trying to protect native vegetation and

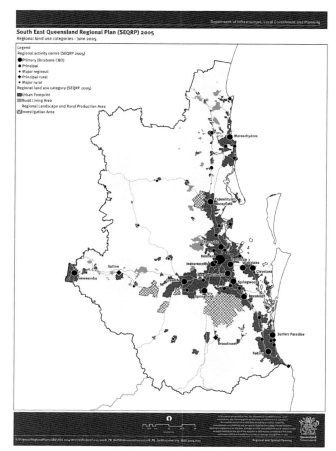

Figure 7.2. SEQRP 2005: land uses and major centre. (*Source:* South East Queensland Regional Plan, 2005; reproduced with permission of Queensland Department of Infrastructure, Local Government and Planning)

maintain biodiversity. One of the most visible and significant components of the new plan was the definition of an 'urban footprint' with statutory effect that sought to limit the location of major new development.

The desire for a more compact urban form has been a feature of all the strategic plans for SEQ, but its definition has typically lacked precision (Searle, 2010). Spencer *et al.*'s (2015) comparative analysis of population density in Australia's three largest cities reveals that in Brisbane, while 89 per cent of the population live within parts of the city that might be called 'urban' with a gross density of four or more people per hectare, this is limited to only 6 per cent of the total land area of the city (compared to, say, London where 99 per cent of the population live in urban areas which cover 80 per cent of the city). In other words, there appears to be considerable scope to increase densities to achieve a more compact urban form and, indeed, the first SEQRP proposed that 50 per cent of new residential dwellings should be built within the existing urban footprint.

The SEQRP also anticipated the preparation of a number of other plans, including growth management strategies and structure plans relating to local government areas. Local Growth Management Strategies (LGMS) were to be produced by each of the (then) eighteen local governments in the region to identify major development areas that would require subsequent structure planning. This process recognized that it would take some time for local planning schemes to be amended and brought into line with the SEQRP. The LGMS were expected to perform a dual and potentially conflicting role in reflecting the strategic intent of the SEQRP at the local level while, at the same time, identifying and assessing possible new major growth areas not yet reflected in the plan.

Just as previous voluntary regional planning frameworks had struggled in some areas with implementation, so the governance arrangements associated with the new statutory SEQRP were criticized for failing to clarify problematic relationships between state and local government planning policies (Ireland, 2006). In particular, there remained some ongoing lack of clarity about the incorporation of local structure plans into amended versions of the SEQRP. This proved an especially difficult political challenge as it exposed different stances between some local councils and the state in the location of emerging and potential new growth areas. These tensions often played out in the regional leadership forums established in the years leading up to the publication of the first SEQRP. While important preparatory work had been carried out by SEQROC, in late 2005 this body was reformed into the Council of Mayors SEQ (COMSEQ) under the leadership of Campbell Newman, Liberal Mayor of the City of Brisbane who came to office in 2004. While the focus of COMSEQ was more on the implementation of what was in the first version of the SEQRP rather than on getting new elements included, its capacity to manage conflicting local views on growth location remained limited.

Because of the imperative to avoid delays in publishing the first draft of the SEQRP, a number of 'pipeline' growth areas were already under consideration but were not able to be included. Hence, the plan was subject to almost immediate review through an investigation of the development potential of what was known as the Mt Lindsay/North Beaudesert Study Area. This was formalized as Amendment 1 and came into effect in September 2006, identifying major activity centres at Flagstone, Yarrabilba, Jimboomba and Park Ridge. This illustrates that the plan's content remained subject to constant pressure for revision from the outset, which in turn complicated the already complex processes of implementation. Another significant complicating factor was the relationship of its spatial components with the planning of infrastructure investment.

The SEQ Infrastructure Plan and Program, 2005–2026

One of the distinctive and valued aspects of the first statutory regional plan for SEQ was the Infrastructure Plan and Program (SEQIPP) that accompanied it. In their foreword, Premier Beattie and Deputy Premier Mackenroth pointed out that 'for the first time in history, the Queensland government is making a ten year commitment to fund the necessary infrastructure that supports growth in SEQ'. This 10-year investment commitment was indeed novel as most forward commitments extended no further than 4 years and previous attempts at regional planning in Queensland had been bedevilled by a persistent failure to integrate infrastructure and regional planning processes (Minnery and Low Choy, 2010). As both the SEQRP and the SEQIPP were prepared by the Office of Urban Management, there was initial optimism that a degree of integration would be achieved in practice and, indeed, the SEQIPP was designed to show where a variety of critical state infrastructure investments were planned to support the spatial planning ambitions expressed in the SEQRP. While some criticized this 'infrastructure turn' for its apparent subordination of spatial planning to project-based investment planning (Dodson, 2009; Gleeson and Steele, 2009), in SEQ the more pertinent criticism has been that the various iterations of the SEQIPP have not, in the face of financial dependency on Federal partners and the impact of the global financial crises, actually delivered all of the promised infrastructure (Regan and Bajracharya, 2010).

The SEQRP, 2009–2031

By 2008 many of the growth management issues that lay at the heart of the 2005 plan were not only continuing, but becoming ever more pressing. High population growth, housing unaffordability, transport congestion and the need for employment generation persisted, but were joined by a new recognition that the impacts of climate change would exacerbate all these problems. A new Draft SEQRP 2009–31 was published for public consultation in December 2008 and, in the light of submissions, a final version was prepared in consultation with the Regional Coordination Council, coming into effect in July 2009. This new plan (DIP, 2009a) set out a number of new and emphatic strategic directions. Perhaps

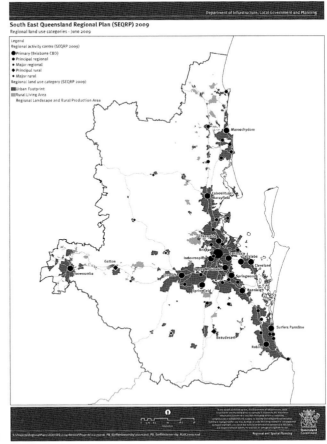

Figure 7.3. SEQRP 2009: land uses and major centres. (*Source:* South East Queensland Regional Plan, 2009; reproduced with permission of Queensland Department of Infrastructure, Local Government and Planning)

the most significant new emphasis was given to the impacts of climate change and oil vulnerability. The plan spoke of the need to mitigate climate change by reducing greenhouse gas emissions and to adapt to unavoidable impacts by protecting areas at risk, in particular from sea level rise. It also recognized the state's increasing vulnerability to rising oil prices and the consequent desire to reduce car dependency through a more compact urban form, although an analysis of travel in SEQ between 1992 and 2009 by Queensland's Department of Transport and Main Roads showed that, despite this policy objective, private car use had remained fairly constant over this period at around 80 per cent for all trips (DTMR, 2012). Greater emphasis was also given to protecting the regional landscape and biodiversity as well as supporting rural production. The overall strategic vision for the region was one of inter-connected communities that were more self-contained in terms of services and employment than in the past and which, therefore, would generate less demand for travel in private vehicles between residential and employment centres.

The new plan was prepared not by the OUM, which had been abolished in April 2008, but by the new Department of Infrastructure and Planning (DIP), and a related SEQIPP for the period 2009–2026 was published alongside this new SEQRP. While departmental reorganizations are nothing new in state or federal governments, the abolition of the OUM was seen to have led to a loss of focus on integrated regional planning within the Queensland State Government and to a weakening of productive relations with other sectors, including the development industry and community representatives (Abbott, 2012, p. 54).

The period since the adoption of the 2009 SEQRP has been one of considerable political change, with the Bligh Labor Government replaced by the Newman Liberal-National Party Government in March 2012, which was replaced in turn by the Palaszczuk Labor Government in February 2015. Nevertheless, regional planning continued both in practice and as a process of monitoring, evaluation and review. In March 2010 a Growth Management Summit was held to consider, yet again, the challenges of planning for a rapidly growing population in SEQ and to propose new priorities for future iterations of the SEQRP. One consequence of the Summit was the establishment of the SEQ Growth Management Program (SEQGMP), designed to 'inform and help prioritize state and local government planning actions and infrastructure investment' (Growth Management Queensland, 2011, p. 2).

Intended to deliver annual progress reports, the SEQGMP was concerned principally with availability of land for housing and industrial development and aimed to ensure a minimum of 10 years planned supply within local planning schemes and any relevant state government plans.

The election of the Newman Government saw a pronounced shift in emphasis from earlier periods and earlier versions of the SEQRP, even though Newman, as Lord Mayor of Brisbane, had endorsed both the 2005 and 2009 versions. As Premier he brought a renewed focus on the stimulation of economic growth and a commitment to reduce what he often described as growth-stunting green and red tape regulatory burdens (see, for example, Newman, 2012). This manifested itself most vividly in a series of battles with the Federal Government over its use of the Environment Protection and Biodiversity Conservation Act, 1999 to review and block a number of major project proposals in Queensland. At the same time, however, the Newman Government embarked on the preparation of an ambitious plan for the whole of the state. Following what was described as 'the largest state-wide community engagement activity of its kind ever undertaken in Queensland, with more than 80,000 people contributing to the process' (Queensland Government, 2014), the Queensland Plan was published in 2014, setting out a comprehensive array of policies and programmes for all aspects of future growth. It included policies on environmental protection, infrastructure investment and regional development but, perhaps in recognition of criticism that state governments tended to be Brisbane-centric, it emphasized the importance of supporting population and economic growth outside SEQ, especially in the cities of north Queensland. The election of a new government only one year later meant that the Queensland Plan had little time to serve as the foundation for more detailed planning or indeed for the re-shaping of the 2009 SEQRP. The Palaszczuk Labor Government elected in 2015 made a commitment to review many policy commitments and a review of the SEQRP was announced before the end of its first year in office.

2016 Draft SEQRP: Shaping SEQ

The motivations and ambitions of the latest SEQRP, released in draft form in late 2016 (DILGP, 2016b), are very familiar: the population of SEQ is expected to continue to grow by approximately 2 million over the next 25 years if current trends continue and the consequences of this growth must be managed sensibly and sustainably. The plan aims to capitalize on the region's climatic location in making SEQ 'a world leading model of sub-tropical living' and, in her introduction to the draft plan, Deputy Premier Jackie Trad (who at the time was both Minister for Infrastructure, Local Government and Planning and also Minister for Trade and Investment) set great store on the breadth and depth of community consultation that went into its preparation and on its focus on those issues that the community at large said were important. These included affordable housing, protection of the natural environment and the unique lifestyle offered by living in the region. In emphasizing the importance of basing the plan on an extensive programme

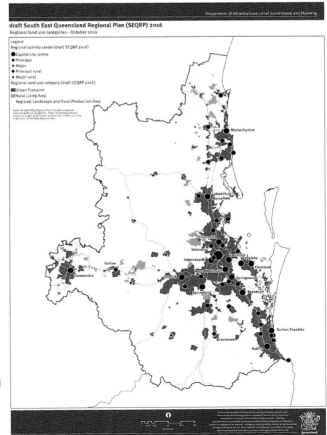

Figure 7.4. SEQRP 2016: land uses and major centres. (*Source:* Draft South East Queensland Regional Plan 2016 (ShapingSEQ); reproduced with permission of Queensland Department of Infrastructure, Local Government and Planning)

Figure 7.5. Brisbane tropical living. (*Source:* Shutterstock; purchased under licence)

of consultation, especially with the local councils and their mayors, the Deputy Premier was maintaining a tradition of engagement while making a claim to be doing it better than ever before.

While a 50-year vision for the region is offered in response to a set of so-called mega-trends (Hajkowicz *et al.*, 2012), the plan itself focuses only on the next 25 years and, if past practice is repeated, will be reviewed in 5–6 years' time. As with previous plans, the delivery of many of the plan's objectives will be achieved (or not) through the development and implementation of local planning schemes and the action of other state government departments and agencies, such as Economic Development Queensland and the office of the Queensland Government Architect.

In consultation events held around the region, officials from the Department of Infrastructure, Local Government and Planning (DILGP) – established in 2015 by the Palaszczuk Labor Government – have set out the key elements of the plan and what distinguishes it from its predecessors. The principal element is the expansion of the urban footprint by 21,800 hectares, which includes 13,600 hectares of land over and above the 2009 plan and 8,200 hectares of 'new future urban land'. One major new development area is proposed at Beerwah East and eleven future growth areas are identified throughout the region. The plan provides indicative net residential densities for some of its regional activity centres, including 150–500 dwellings per hectare in capital city and principal regional activity centres, such as Beenleigh, Southport and Toowoomba, and 80–200 dwellings per hectare in major activity centres, such as Coolangatta, Noosa and Yarrabilba. Density guidelines at smaller spatial scales and in other areas are to be determined by local governments through their local planning processes.

Figure 7.6. Yarrabilba street scene. (*Photo*: Paul Burton)

The plan also presents a set of major aspirations including:

◆ building a globally competitive regional economy by identifying and facilitating areas of high value and export-oriented business;

◆ focusing more development in existing urban areas to accommodate SEQ's projected population and employment growth;

◆ placing greater emphasis on public and active transport to move people around the region;

◆ maximizing the use of existing facilities before building new infrastructure and identifying new 'region-shaping' infrastructure only where needed to increase accessibility and productivity to support the settlement pattern and economic policies;

◆ increasing emphasis on protecting and sustainably using SEQ's regional landscapes and natural assets; and

◆ identifying and mapping regional biodiversity corridors and values to support the protection of these values.

While there is much continuity between the current draft and previous plans, there are also some significant differences, including:

- ◆ using employment planning benchmarks to ensure land and infrastructure are planned for and delivered locally to meet growth projections;

- ◆ explicitly valuing good design, through the work of the Queensland Government Architect and the Urban Design and Places Panel, as a way to create greater housing choice and more memorable and liveable urban places and spaces to benefit communities socially, economically and environmentally;

- ◆ working in parallel with the State Infrastructure Plan to ensure a coordinated approach to ongoing infrastructure and service delivery;

- ◆ developing a more sophisticated (although as yet unspecified) approach to determining urban land supply, as well as improving ways to monitor supply and development activity, and the plan's performance over time;

- ◆ delivering the plan by specific actions, including through City Deal partnerships with the Australian Government and SEQ local governments.

The draft plan claims to be clearer and more concise than its predecessors and to provide a greater emphasis on delivery and implementation. This remains to be seen, but the public reception has so far been positive and, even within the development industry, there appears to be cautious optimism. The consultation period on the draft plan closes in March 2017 ahead of a further round of community conversations as well as preliminary analysis of submissions.

Distinctive Features, Achievements and Criticisms of SEQ Metropolitan Plans and Strategies

Over the last two decades, the plans, both voluntary and statutory, for SEQ have shown a high degree of consistency in their main aims and objectives and, indeed, these are not dissimilar to those expressed in the regional planning strategies of the other major cities (Hamnett and Freestone, 2016). The principal aim is to manage the consequences of anticipated population growth, rapid or otherwise, by identifying areas where that growth might be best accommodated. The second is to prepare the ground for economic development and job growth to employ this growing population. The third is to ensure that if these two forms of growth do not occur in broadly the same areas, then they are at least well connected through improved infrastructure for public and private transport. Finally, this transport infrastructure has also to connect other public service infrastructure such as schools, universities and hospitals. The achievement of these aims requires some degree of balance between different and competing pressures and imperatives, such as the promotion of population and economic growth and the protection and conservation of biodiversity, wildlife habitats and ecosystems in general. This is reflected in choices and tensions between accommodating growth through infill at higher densities or through new development on so-called 'greenfield' sites. One final common thread to the various SEQ regional plans and strategies lies in an enduring concern with their implementation; this is not to say that implementation has always been successful, but rather that an explicit concern with implementation has persisted over the years and across various strategies. Each of the major planning aims described above is elaborated below.

Growth Areas and Urban Footprints

Each of the regional plans has attempted to manage growth by restricting it to certain designated areas, typically the existing built up areas around the major cities but also to a number of smaller growth centres in more rural areas. The definition of these growth boundaries draws on information contained in the State Government's Digital Cadastral Database and provides a more precise delineation than previously. This delineation has considerable political and economic significance as it helps determine the development potential and hence the value of land. While the certainty provided by such boundaries is broadly welcomed, the limitations they impose on development outside the footprint are subject to constant criticism from the development sector and its political representatives (e.g. Vit, 2016). Although these boundaries are supposed to reflect a supply of land sufficient to meet the need for new housing over the coming decades, this calculation is itself subject to constant challenge in the face of changing expectations of house and lot sizes, the acceptance of higher density development and the enduring problem of

Figure 7.7. Brisbane medium density infill. (*Source:* Shutterstock; purchased under licence)

assembling land in fragmented ownership. The latest plan proposes a new balance in the assessment of areas of growth potential and future land supply, with a shift in favour of more infill development within the urban footprint.

This represents the continuation of a long-term trend, with the 2005 plan proposing an infill target of 40 per cent, the 2009 plan a 50 per cent target and the current plan a 60 per cent target. While these are relatively modest in comparison with other state targets, many in the Queensland development industry remain sceptical about their achievement, pointing to the lack of large parcels of land, the often high costs of site assembly and higher construction costs, all of which, it predicts, will lead to higher prices for new developments and an ongoing problem of housing affordability.

Economic Development as the Foundation for Growth

Regional plans produced under the auspices of state governments led by different political parties have typically placed more or less emphasis on the fundamental need to stimulate economic growth as well as accommodating population growth. The latest draft plan proposes new employment planning benchmarks, but these appear to simply take the sectoral estimates of job growth produced by the Treasury and allocate them formulaically to local governments in the region. Thus, the City of Gold Coast is expected to identify sufficient land to accommodate precisely 433,432 new jobs in the period to 2041, although it is not clear what assumptions these estimates make about the relationship between economic growth and job growth in the light of anticipated but unspecified technological changes. To be sure, the current plan also identifies areas where new growth might be based on the proximity of R&D functions in a number of 'knowledge precincts', and is committed to promoting better connections between residential and employment areas. Nevertheless, the plan remains unavoidably focused on the spatial distribution of economic growth rather than being a detailed prospectus for generating that growth.

Connectivity through Transport Infrastructure

Improved connectivity is, rightly, seen as one of the most significant ways in which growth can be managed in a sustainable way and the lifestyle attractions of the region preserved or even enhanced. One notable feature of the new plan, however, is that it is not accompanied by a dedicated infrastructure plan. This was held to be one of the strengths of the previous two plans, but is considered unnecessary as the state now relies on one consolidated and integrated State Infrastructure Plan (DILGP, 2016a) which includes an analysis of the specific needs and opportunities within the SEQ region. While motorway upgrades and new rail services are planned, there is also a belief that urban consolidation and focused growth will over time reduce the considerable costs of congestion already experienced.

Figure 7.8. Public transport infrastructure, Gold Coast. (*Source:* Shutterstock; purchased under licence)

Keeping Pace with Public Services

In addition to large-scale transport infrastructure in the form of roads and railways, tunnels and bridges, a growing population also needs community-based services such as schools and hospitals. The location of these facilities presents significant challenges for regional planners as low-density, dispersed populations generate considerable traffic flows with residents typically travelling to schools and health services by car. Within existing urban areas, where challenging infill targets have been set in the latest SEQRP, finding the space for new schools, hospitals and other health care facilities is going to become increasingly difficult.

Growth and Conservation

The various plans for SEQ have always included a commitment to protecting and preserving native vegetation and ecosystems beyond and within the urban footprint and to conserving designated open space. While threats to the survival of flora and fauna in the region are becoming increasingly apparent, there is also growing recognition of the beneficial effects of greenspaces and vegetation within cities (Matthews *et al.*, 2015). However, development pressures continue and the latest plan, like its predecessors, will no doubt struggle to strike a balance between growth and conservation that satisfies all parties.

Implementation

Although recognized by many as a series of laudable regional plans and strategies (Gleeson and Steele, 2010; Minnery and Low Choy, 2010), the various SEQ regional plans have also been subject to criticism, not least because of their failure to deliver their strategic visions in practice. The representative bodies of the development industry have, unsurprisingly, been among the staunchest critics. For example, the Property Council of Australia (PCA) has set out a series of criticisms and weaknesses of past SEQ regional plans, which they say should be addressed in the latest version (Property Council of Australia, 2016).

First, they claim that many planning schemes prepared by local governments do not properly reflect the intent of the regional plans. This criticism is almost entirely based on their perception that local planning schemes have not released sufficient greenfield land for new residential development or have been insufficiently accommodating in their assessment of development proposals within the urban footprint. There is, however, little empirical evidence to support this claim (Gurran *et al.*, 2013) which continues to be part of the litany of the PCA.

Second, and more tellingly, they claim that there has been a failure to integrate other environmental plans and policies produced by both state and local governments in the region with the SEQ regional plans. This is part of a more widespread perception of what is often referred to as a lack of 'joined up government'. A recent review of the integration of spatial and sectoral strategies in Queensland (James and Burton, 2016) found some evidence to support this criticism, with many plans prepared by Queensland government departments and agencies having little or no explicit connection with each other, although the integration of spatial planning and infrastructure investment was more evident than in other fields.

The third criticism is that, while state governments of different political persuasions have increasingly put economic growth and job creation at the heart of their broader political programmes, there is a lack of attention paid to the detail of how and where new jobs will be created in the region. While there are more specific policy measures, including R&D support schemes and employment incentives, one of the leading policy measures is the designation of State Development Areas with planning regimes supportive of growth and in which infrastructure investment is focused. The nine current SDAs are dominated by mining and related activities, a sector that employs only 2.7 per cent of the workforce and is moving into a period of employment decline.

Overall, while the institutional arrangements of intergovernmental collaboration are well established and can reasonably be expected to continue to work satisfactorily into the future, there remains a legitimate ongoing concern with the translation of the regional strategy into local plans with the capacity to deliver local outcomes. This is, of course, a wider problem of planning that will be returned to in the concluding section.

Conclusion

The most significant feature of metropolitan planning for South East Queensland is that it has existed and endured for almost 50 years and helped manage the growth of this consistently fast growing region. Few other metropolitan regions in Australia have enjoyed such a consistent regional planning framework, perhaps because of its support from a strategic partnership of the state government and a relatively small group of local governments (albeit a partnership that has shifted from a voluntary to a statutory basis), and it is now almost impossible to imagine that regional planning in SEQ will not continue in one form or another.

The various iterations of the SEQRP have not, of course, been immune from criticism, often conflicting and contradictory. For example, the latest version has been criticized on the one hand for failing to take sufficient account of the changing circumstances caused by climate change and past environmental degradation and not adequately protecting greenspaces and other ecosystems, and on the other hand for its continuing reluctance to release sufficient greenfield land that would increase the affordability of new residential developments. There is also an ongoing debate about the capacity of multi-faceted regional plans such as SEQRP to serve as useful vehicles for integrating an array of sectoral plans and strategies. They do offer the opportunity of integration through a place-based focus, but also run the risk of becoming overburdened with policies that have no clear spatial dimension.

But perhaps the greatest threat to regional planning in SEQ at present lies in the political arena. The next state election must be held before January 2018 and it is possible that Pauline Hanson's right-wing libertarian One Nation Party will win sufficient seats to hold the balance of power in the next parliament. While there has been a high degree of cross-party consensus on the case for regional planning in SEQ and for much of the policy substance of successive plans, it is much more difficult to anticipate or predict the stance of One Nation on matters such as the need to accommodate a growing population through urban consolidation, environmental protection and 'smart growth'.

Finally regional plans, like plans for any other spatial scale, continue to confront the challenge of being able to regulate and manage, but not create growth. There will be parts of some regions, although few in SEQ, where the planning challenge is how to cope with inexorable economic and population decline, but mainly the task is to regulate growth in such a way as not to stifle it.

Regional and indeed local growth management strategies such as the SEQRP must create an environment in which growth is encouraged, but then regulated in ways that are widely accepted as reasonable and sensible. It is not always easy to strike an appropriate balance between encouragement and regulation, with the long-term consequences of not doing so including substantial loss of amenity and quality of life on the one hand and the emergence of a low-wage, low-growth economy on the other, with its attendant fiscal challenges for governments at all levels. The goals of triple (or even quadruple) bottom line sustainable development continue to underpin many regional and metropolitan planning strategies, including in SEQ, but their comprehensive achievement remains as elusive as ever.

References

Abbott, J. (2009) Planning for complex metropolitan regions: a better future or a more certain one? *Journal of Planning Education and Research*, **28**(4), pp. 503–517.

Abbott, J. (2012) *Collaborative Governance and Metropolitan Planning in South East Queensland – 1990–2010: From a Voluntary to a Statutory Model*. Sydney: Australian Centre of Excellence for Local Government, University of Technology Sydney.

Bell, M., Charles-Edwards, E., Wilson, T. and Cooper, J. (2010) Demographic futures for South East Queensland. *Australian Planner*, **47**(3), pp. 126–134.

Burton, P. (2010) Growing pains: the challenges of planning for growth in South East Queensland. *Australian Planner*, **47**(3), pp. 118–125.

Coffee, N., Lange, J. and Baker, E. (2016) Visualising 30 years of major population density change in Australia's major capital cities. *Australian Geographer*, **47** (4), pp. 511–525.

DIP (Department of Infrastructure and Planning) (2009*a*) *South East Queensland Regional Plan 2009-31*. Brisbane: The State of Queensland. Available at: http://www.dilgp.qld.gov.au/resources/plan/seq/regional-plan-2009/seq-regional-plan-2009.pdf.

DIP (2009*b*) *South East Queensland Infrastructure Plan and Program, 2009–2026*. Brisbane: The State of Queensland. Available at: https://www.cabinet.qld.gov.au/documents/2009/Jun/SEQIPP%20 2009-26/Attachments/seqipp.pdf.

DILGP (Department of Infrastructure, Local Government and Planning) (2016*a*) *State Infrastructure Plan*. Brisbane: DILGP.

DILGP (2016*b*) *Shaping SEQ: Draft South East Queensland Regional Plan*. Brisbane: DILGP.

DLGP (Department of Local Government and Planning) (2002) *South East Queensland Performance Monitoring Report 2001*. Brisbane: DLGP.

Dodson, J. (2009) The 'infrastructure turn' in Australian metropolitan spatial planning. *International Planning Studies*, **14**(2), pp.109–123.

DTMR (Department of Transport and Main Roads) (2012) *Travel in South-East Queensland: An Analysis of Travel Data from 1992 to 2009*. Brisbane: DTMR.

Gleeson, B. and Steele, W. (2009) The Bellwether Zone? Planning and Infrastructure in South-East Queensland. Paper to the 4th State of Australian Cities Conference, Perth. Available at: http://apo. org.au/node/60117.

Gleeson, B. and Steele, W. (2010) Afterword: the state of exception, in Gleeson, B. and Steele, W. (eds.) *A Climate for Growth*. Brisbane: University of Queensland Press, pp. 277–285.

Gleeson, B., Dodson, J. and Spiller, M. (2012) Governance, metropolitan planning and city-building: the case for reform, in Tomlinson, R. (ed.) *Australia's Unintended Cities: The Impact of Housing on Urban Development*. Clayton South, Vic: CSIRO Publishing, pp. 117–133.

Growth Management Queensland (2011) *South East Queensland Growth Management Program, Annual Report, 2010*. Brisbane: Department of Local Government and Planning.

Guhathakurta, S. and Stimson, R. (2007) What is driving the growth of new 'Sunbelt' metropolises? Quality of life and urban regimes in Greater Phoenix and Brisbane-South East Queensland Region. *International Planning Studies*, **12**(2), pp. 129–152.

Gurran, N., Gilbert, C. and Phibbs, P. (2013) Planning and the Housing Market: Measuring Regulatory Difference and Implications for Explaining Supply and Affordability Trends. Paper to the 7th Australasian Housing Researchers' Conference, Fremantle. Available at: http://ceebi. curtin.edu.au/local/docs/ahrc13/Planning-and-the-Housing-Market-Measuring-Regulatory-Difference-and-Implications-for-Explaining-Supply-and-Affordability-Trends.pdf.

Hajkowicz, S., Cook, H. and Littleboy, A. (2012) *Our Future World: Global Megatrends that will Change the Way We Live*. Brisbane: CSIRO.

Hamnett, S. and Freestone, R. (eds.) (2000) *The Australian Metropolis: A Planning History*. Sydney: Allen and Unwin.

Hamnett, S. and Freestone, R. (2016) The Australian Metropolis 2000–2015. Proceedings of the 17th International Planning History Society Conference, Delft, The Netherlands. Available at: http://journals.library.tudelft.nl/index.php/iphs/article/view/1324.

Ireland, J. (2006) *Local Growth Management Strategies and Structure Plans*. Brisbane: Hopgood Ganim Lawyers. Available at: http://www.hopgoodganim.com.au/icms_docs/135818_HG_Paper_SEQ_Regional_Plan_2005-2026_-_Growth_Management_Structure_Plans_-_Nov_2006.pdf.

James, B. and Burton, P. (2016) *Review of Queensland State Government Plans and Strategies*. Unpublished report available on request from Griffith University, Cities Research Institute.

Margerum, R.D. (2002) Evaluating collaborative planning. *Journal of the American Planning Association*, **68**(2), pp. 179–193.

Matthews, T., Lo, A. and Byrne, J. (2015) Reconceptualizing green infrastructure for climate change adaptation: barriers to adoption and drivers for uptake by spatial planners. *Landscape and Urban Planning,* **138**, June, pp. 155–163.

Minnery, J. and Low Choy, D. (2010) Early innovations and false starts, in Gleeson, B. and Steele, W. (eds.) *A Climate for Growth*. Brisbane: University of Queensland Press, pp. 23–38.

Newman, C. (2012) Campbell Newman makes big pitch to business. *ABC/PM transcript*, first broadcast 25 September, Available at: http://www.abc.net.au/pm/content/2012/s3597684.htm.

Office of Urban Management (2005*a*) *South East Queensland Infrastructure Plan and Program 2005–2026*. Brisbane: Queensland Government.

Office of Urban Management (2005*b*) *South East Queensland Regional Plan 2005–2026*. Brisbane: Queensland Government.

Property Council of Australia (2016) *Making the Plan a Reality: South East Queensland Regional Plan 2016 – The Industry Perspective on Achieving Best Practice Regional Planning*. Brisbane: Property Council of Australia. Available at: https://www.propertycouncil.com.au/Web/Content/News/QLD/2016/Making_the_Plan_a_Reality.aspx.

Queensland Government (2014) *The Queensland Plan*. Brisbane: The State of Queensland.

Queensland Government Statistician's Office (2016) *Population Growth Highlights and Trends, Queensland* (2016 edition). Brisbane: Queensland Treasury.

Regan, M. and Bajracharya, B. (2010) Integrating regional and infrastructure planning: lessons from South East Queensland, Australia, in Yigitcanlar, T. (ed.) *Sustainable Urban and Regional Infrastructure: Technologies, Applications and Management*. Hershey, PA: IGI Global/Information Science Reference, pp. 259–276.

Salt, B. (2015) Foreword: imagining the Gold Coast of the future, in *Beyond the Horizon*, Report for Regional Development Australia Gold Coast Inc by KPMG. Available at: http://futuregoldcoast.com.au/wp-content/uploads/2015/01/beyond-the-horizon-report-12feb2015.pdf.

Savery, N. (2010) Planning and growth in South East Queensland. *Australian Planner*, **47**(3), p. 117.

Searle, G. (2010) Too concentrated? The planned distribution of residential density in SEQ. *Australian Planner*, **47**(3), pp. 135–141.

Spencer, A., Gill, J. and Schmahmann, L. (2015) Urban or Suburban? Examining the Density of Australian Cities in a Global Context. Paper to the 7th State of Australian Cities Conference, Gold Coast. Available at: http://apo.org.au/node/63334.

Vit, M. (2016) South East Queensland Regional Plan: Letter to Stuart Moseley, DILGP. Available at: http://www.udiaqld.com.au/getmedia/c464942b-8397-4e2f-8a80-9ea3fb063733/Letter-to-Stuart-Moseley-re-UDIA-s-SEQRP-position-28-July-2016.pdf.aspx?ext=.pdf.

Chapter 8

Canberra: 'Normalization' or 'the Pride of Time'?

Karl Friedhelm Fischer and *James Weirick*

The year 2000 was pivotal in the planning history of Canberra. Eleven years after the introduction of self-government for the Australian Capital Territory (ACT), the local planning agency turned to the Paris-based OECD for help in articulating a vision for the future of the national capital. Political and administrative turbulence in the 1990s at both territory and national levels had seriously compromised the planning achievements of previous decades (Wettenhall, 2009; Fischer, 2004). The OECD study, released in 2002, confirmed a number of critical issues and, in particular, the lack of an up-to-date strategic plan for the city, a function of the complex division of planning responsibilities between the Territory and National Governments which had been created at the time of self-government (OECD, 2002). The resolution of this issue was played out over the period 2000–2016. It began with the ACT Government embarking on its own strategic planning exercise in the years 2002–2004 and ended with the disengagement of the national government from the strategic planning challenge in 2016.

This chapter focuses on the concepts, promises and realities of the major plans at national and territory level produced between 2000 and 2016. A snapshot of today's Canberra and a look at the cultural controversies that continue to determine the fate of one of the great planned capitals of the modern age precede this analysis. We conclude that Canberra is in a new phase of development, retreating from national capital aspirations and planning standards towards market-oriented 'normalization'.

A Snapshot of Canberra

Developed as a unique experiment based on the 1911 plan by the Chicago architects Walter Burley Griffin and Marion Mahony Griffin, the city passed through years of stagnation in the inter-war period before being turned into one of the great planned capitals of the modern age in the years 1957–1988. This was the achievement of the National Capital Development Commission (NCDC), an organization made up of professional planners that derived its power from political support at the national level, a large budget, public ownership of land and a high level of professional expertise (Fischer, 1984; 1989). In 1988, however, the Federal (Commonwealth) Government moved to divest itself of financial responsibility for the city beyond core national capital functions. This accelerated a process of 'normalization' of urban development for city and territory (Freestone, 2009; Brown, 2014). The details of this division and its associated economics have remained as contested as the question of what 'normalization' might mean, particularly in view of Canberra's outstanding planning history and distinctive physical form.

As a planned national capital built and managed much in the way of a government company town between its foundation in 1913 and its late attainment of self-government in 1988–1989, Canberra is 'the odd city out' amongst Australia's capital cities. Situated within its own political territory, Canberra is Australia's only inland metropolitan area. With a population of 400,000 in 2016, it is much smaller than most state capitals (ABS, 2016) while its population growth rate of 1.3 per cent in 2015–2016, was slightly less than the national average of 1.4 per cent (ABS, 2017). Moreover, the capital remains dependent on contributions from the Commonwealth, to which it exports services such as administration, education and research. At the regional level, Canberra provides services for a population of half a million. Around 20,000 commuters travel to work in the ACT each day from rural areas and a range of settlements including the town of Queanbeyan (population 42,000), across the border in New South Wales (NSW), which forms part of Canberra's urban system.

As a predominantly administrative city but with a diversifying economy, Canberra has never suffered from the consequences of significant structural change through decline of the manufacturing sector as experienced by other cities, although it is vulnerable to periodic reductions in the Federal public service. A different kind of ongoing structural change, however, began in 1988–1889 in the form of new and ever changing divisions of political and administrative arrangements with the long overdue introduction of political self-government. Tables 8.1 and 8.2 provide a lengthy but selective overview of the plans, reports and public enquiries undertaken for Canberra and the ACT over the period 2000–2015.

Canberra – Planning History and Cultural Controversies

While no city can really be understood without a grasp of its history and cultural context, this is valid in a particular way for Canberra as an internationally renowned model city – 'one of the treasures not only of Australia, but of the entire urban world' (Reps, 1997, p. 267). While cultural and political controversies are embedded in all urban development processes, the special situation in Canberra

Table 8.1. Principal plans, studies and reports for Canberra and the ACT, 2000–2016.

Organization, Agency Plans, Planning Studies and Reports

2000	NCA National Capital Authority	Parliamentary Zone Review: Outcomes Report
2001	Capitals Alliance / NCA	Forum (Ottawa 2001) and 1st Meeting (Canberra 2002)
2002	OECD	Urban Renaissance: Canberra – A Sustainable Future
2002	ACT Government	Planning and Land Act: PALM replaced by ACTPLA, LDA, Planning and Land Council
2003	ACT Government	ACTPLA established
2004	NCA	The Griffin Legacy: Canberra, The Nation's Capital in the 21st Century
2004	ACT Chief Minister's Office	The Canberra Plan: Social, Spatial, Economic
2004	ACTPLA ACT Planning & Land Authority	Canberra Spatial Plan
2004	ACTPLA	The Sustainable Transport Plan for the ACT
2006	NCA	National Capital Plan Amendment 56 – The Griffin Legacy Principles and Policies
2007	ACT Government	Planning and Development Act
2008	ACTPLA	Garden City Values and Principles: Design Considerations for Inner North and South Canberra
2008	ACT Government	The Canberra Plan: Towards Our Second Century
2008	ACT Government	New Territory Plan
2009	ACTPLA	Territory Plan Urban Principles Review
2010	ACT Government	Time to Talk – Canberra 2030 Outcomes Report
2010	ACTPLA	Urban Form Analysis: Canberra's Sustainability Performance
2011	ACT Public Service Review	Governing the City State: One ACT Government — One ACT Public Service, Final Report
2011	Alan Hawke	Canberra: A Capital Place: Report of the Independent Review of the National Capital Authority.
2011	ACT Chief Minister's Office	ACT and NSW Memorandum of Understanding for Regional Collaboration
2012	ACT Government.	ACT Planning Strategy: Planning for a Sustainable City
2012	ACT Government	Transport for Canberra
2012	ACT Government	A New Climate Change Strategy and Action Plan for the ACT
2012	COAG Reform Council	Review of Capital City Strategic Planning Systems
2014	ACT Government	The City Plan. Strategic Plan 2014 Canberra
2015	NCA	National Capital Plan Exposure Draft
2016	NCA	National Capital Plan: Amendment 86 – Revised National Capital Plan
2016	ACT Auditor-General	Certain Land Development Agency Acquisitions

Table 8.2. Principal public inquiries and consultations, Canberra and ACT planning, 2000–2015.

	Government Committee, Agency	Public Inquiries and Consultations
2001	ACTSCPE ACT Legislative Assembly Standing Committee on Planning and Environment	Inquiry into Proposals for the Gungahlin Drive Extension
2002	ACTSCPE	Inquiry into Planning and Land Bill 2002 and Associated Legislation
2004	JSCNET Australia. Parliament. Joint Standing Committee on the National Capital and External Territories	A National Capital, A Place to Live – Inquiry into the Role of the National Capital Authority
2006	ACTSCPE	Inquiry into Exposure Draft Planning and Development Bill 2006
2006	ACTSCPE	Inquiry into the ACT as a UNESCO Biosphere Reserve
2007	JSCNET	Review of the Griffin Legacy Amendments
2007	NCA National Capital Authority	Consultation, National Capital Plan Draft Amendment 53, Albert Hall Precinct
2008	JSCNET	The Way Forward: Inquiry into the Role of the National Capital Authority
2008	ACTSCPE	Draft Variation to the Territory Plan no. 281 – Molonglo and North Weston
2008	PWC Australia. Parliament. Standing Committee on Public Works	Inquiry into Bridging of Kings Avenue over Parkes Way at the Russell Roundabout, Canberra, ACT
2009	JSCNET	Inquiry into the Immigration Bridge Proposal
2009	NCA	Consultation, National Capital Plan Draft Amendment 57, Blocks 12 & 13, Section 9, Barton
2011	JSCNET	Etched in Stone – Inquiry into the Administration of the National Memorials Ordinance 1928
2013	JSCNET	Inquiry into the Provision of Amenity within the Parliamentary Triangle
2015	ACTSCPE	Inquiry into Draft Variation to the Territory Plan no.327 – Capital Metro, Light Rail Stage 1, Gungahlin to Civic
2015	NCA	Consultation, National Capital Plan Exposure Draft

is that cultural debates about the nature and even the very necessity of the capital have always played an existential role. They shaped the metropolitan planning process in 1900 as much as in the period between 2000 and 2015.

From the beginning, Canberra's mission was to be more than an administrative capital. It was to become the prestigious symbol of a young federation, 'the finest Capital City in the World – the Pride of Time' in the words of King O'Malley (Harrison, 1995, p. 6). Yet its very creation amidst the competition between Sydney and Melbourne was influenced by the 'haggling of provincialisms' (Hancock,

1930, p. 278). This dialectic of pride and parochialism has persisted over long periods. During the twenty-first century, affirmations of the national commitment to the capital, culminating in the centennial celebrations in 2013, have contrasted with crippling budget cuts, political statements of disdain and eventually with plans for the transfer of national agency staff to smaller provincial cities in the electorates of responsible ministers (*Canberra Times*, 2016). In 2017, Deputy Prime Minister Barnaby Joyce declared 'moving public servants out of Canberra [was] core business for the Turnbull government' (Massola and Towell, 2017).

Torn between advocates of the capital and 'Canberra bashers' (the term was even added to the Oxford Australian National Dictionary in 2013), the city has nonetheless won international acclaim as a planned capital of the twentieth century. The template provided by the Griffin plan received the greatest praise. While transformed over time, the skilful use of space as a design element (Bacon, 1968, p. 625) and the integration of landscape features with the disposition of activity centres that has prevailed to this day give the city its distinctive character. Emerging from this, a number of overlapping cultural discourses have emphasized specific aspects contributing to the identity of Canberra as a garden city (ACTPLA, 2008); the 'bush capital' (Pegrum, 1983); 'a city in the landscape' (Taylor, 2006); and a city of 'democratic symbolism' (Weirick 1988, pp. 7–11; 1998, pp. 62–68).

In the lead-up to Canberra's centennial celebrations, research on the Griffin plan intensified (Reid, 2002; Vernon, 2002; Headon, 2003; NCA, 2004; Weirick, 2012; Fischer, 2013). While appreciation for the plan has grown, the Griffin plan remains exposed to a remarkable mixture of iconic reverence, ridicule and crude exploitation as a real estate branding device (e.g. Stockland Corporation, 2005; UDIA, 2008, p. 79). In the discussion about 'normalizing' Canberra's urban development, even its planning minister dismissed the Griffin plan as quirky and old-fashioned (Barr, 2010; Wensing, 2013).

The significance of Canberra for planning history is, however, not restricted to the realized elements of the Griffin plan. From the beginning of the National Capital Development Commission (NCDC) era in the late 1950s, Canberra took its orientation from international planning models, adapting them in the light of Australian values. Like an 'open air museum of modernist planning' (Freestone, 2009), the morphology of today's Canberra displays important developments from a century of planning ideas (Fischer, 1984; 1989; 2013).

Knowledge of the principles of metropolitan planning from the NCDC era, however, seems to have dissipated (Mees, 2014, p. 28). During the 2013 celebrations for the centenary of Canberra, the NCDC received virtually no mention (Fischer and Weirick, 2013). Nevertheless, the NCDC era is notable for the evolution of metropolitan structure planning, now partly forgotten but with important implications for the twenty-first century. The first major post-war plan – *The Future Canberra* (NCDC, 1965) with its radial-concentric configuration of districts – had been inspired by Ebenezer Howard's 'Social City' (Howard, 1898, p. 130). However, modelling of traffic flows converging on the city centre from a corona of satellite districts (De Leuw Cather, 1963) was already warning that the freeways required for congestion-free traffic would have drowned the city centre in a vast sea of asphalt (Fischer, 1989, p.178; Reid, 2002, p. 259).

Two important conclusions were drawn on the basis of a subsequent land-use transportation study (Voorhees, 1967). First, instead of developing a conventional CBD, a significant share of the retail functions and offices would have to be decentralized into the satellite 'New Towns' – a term chosen in order to indicate that a high level of self-containment was intended. Second, the new districts had to be stretched into the form of a linear city with the urban districts of the Griffin plan at its core, connected by peripheral freeways and a central public transport spine that would allow for the introduction of rapid transit once the 500,000 population level was reached. Dividing the city into two branches for its northern extension was intended to make public transport more effective. The frame of this 'Y-plan' was fitted out with housing and shopping centres, community facilities and streets organized into perfect hierarchies.

The Canberra of this era might have been called 'the perfectionist garden city metropolis' (Fischer, 2013, p. ix). It was certainly more than 'the world's biggest Garden City' (Hall, 1988, p. 196). There is no other city in which Howard's Garden City principles have been implemented so comprehensively, ranging from a (moderately) revenue-producing land leasehold system to a set of rather autonomous 'self-contained satellites', separated by green belts and connected to a 'central city' with a green core. There are many more characteristics established in this period which have made Canberra a unique city. Among them is the strategy of conceiving the capital city as a whole instead of splitting attention between a carefully designed capital district and an 'ordinary' urban area left to spread as typical Australian suburbia. This was also reflected in the introduction of a 'National Capital Open Space System' (NCOSS), which designated areas to be kept free of urban development including, significantly, the greenbelts between the satellite districts (NCDC, 1984, p. 173).

One of the most obvious problems associated with the Y-Plan is its extreme orientation to the motorcar. Not surprisingly, the predominantly low-density urban form has ensured very high dependence on private automobilies during most post-war history. While the very generous provision of freeways poses overwhelming competition for public transport, the linear shape of the city nevertheless holds a promise that is often overlooked, with the potential of the public transport spine connecting the sub-centres. Significantly, between the 1970s and mid-1980s, 'changes introduced by a reformist Federal Government saw public transport usage rates double … while car usage stopped growing' (Mees, 2014, p. 1). By 1985, at the highpoint of suburban office decentralization, Canberra's public transport usage rate was the second highest in Australia after Sydney (Mees, 2014, p. 15). Since then, however, public transport usage has been falling.

While surveys indicated reasonable levels of 'self-containment' well into the era of self-government (ACTPLA, 2009a), questions about whether 'effective centres [are] a planning dream' (Quirk, 2007) and about what is required to make them effective are complex. An essential challenge lies in the extent to which the allocation of jobs in the town centres depends on government policy. This has shifted dramatically with the emergence of neoliberalism in Australia and its assumption that 'markets and money can always ... deliver better outcomes than states and bureaucracies' (Pusey, 1992, p. 65).

Neoliberalism and Privatizing the Government Office Market in the 1970s and 1980s

Fundamental changes towards a neoliberal agenda began as early as 1970 when, in the fever of a Canberra by-election, the leasehold system was emasculated by replacing land rent with municipal rates, thereby transforming property in the ACT from leasehold to virtual freehold tenure (Brennan, 1971). This provided a windfall benefit to the property sector and shifted the ethos of Canberra's development from the 'common wealth' to conventional property speculation.

The year of the dismissal of the Federal Whitlam Labor Government – 1975 – was another major turning point. At the level of government office policy, the succeeding conservative Fraser Government ended the 'company town' practice of building and owning its own office complexes, creating instead a market for private commercial development underpinned by long-term leases from government departments. The privatization of office accommodation led in due course to the creation of powerful development interests – ostensibly market-driven but in reality, 'as subsidised as a military brothel' (Waterford, 1987) – which successfully lobbied to concentrate office development in the central city at the expense of the New Towns. By the 1980s, the planning culture of the city had shifted to a corporatist mode in tune with the aspirations of the private sector and the phenomenon of planning agencies supporting development contrary to their own plans emerged (Gilchrist, 1988, p. 36; Wensing, 1994). These changes were part of the broader shift to economic rationalism in the Australian public service. The public sector was considered 'riddled with inefficiencies' and the private sector 'self-evidently superior' (Whitwell, 1990, p. 124). 'Rationalisation became a euphemism for shutting down as much of the public sector as possible' (Pusey, 1992, p. 64). In this intellectual climate, Federal Government surrender of responsibility for the planning and construction of Canberra was a logical move. It also aligned with the fact that the introduction of self-government was a step long overdue in a democratic society.

The Introduction of Self-Government: Two Authorities, Two Plans 1988–1989

The Australian Capital Territory (Planning and Land Management) Act (1988) was the core piece of planning legislation created at the time of self-government.

This set in place a 'highly complex and sometimes confusing' dual planning system (JSCNET, 2008, p. 1) in which two bodies took over the baton from the NCDC: a statutory authority with reduced powers at the national level, the National Capital Planning Authority (NCPA); and a municipal-style planning department at the territory level, the Planning and Land Management Agency (PALM). The NCPA was charged with responsibility for an overall National Capital Plan (NCPA, 1990) and given specific control of areas of national importance in and beyond the parliamentary zone around Lake Burley Griffin, the artificial lake in the centre of Canberra. These areas included the principal approach roads, the hills and ridges, the buffer zones between the New Towns and other landscape features safeguarding the character of the capital. A subservient Territory Plan was 'to ensure, in a manner not inconsistent with the National Capital Plan, the planning and development of the Territory' (Australian Capital Territory [Planning and Land Management] Act, 1988, Section 25/2).

In its conception, the new system included serious defects. At the legal level, the 1988 Act failed to define adequately the scope and content of each planning jurisdiction (Powell, 2012). This led to conflicting policies and overlapping control mechanisms including the introduction of 'no fewer than nine instruments for implementing land use controls' (Wensing, 1992, p. 63). Both plans replaced the policies embodied in the Y-Plan with a zoning system which lacked strategic content. The National Capital Plan became, in effect, a statutory land-use plan rather than a metropolitan strategy plan. The Territory Plan emerged as a land-use zoning plan granting development rights to property owners and, as such, subject to predictable pressures which have ensnared the Territory Government in development controversies for decades.

At the economic level, a 'city-state' (ACTPS, 2011) like the ACT without a productive hinterland could not operate in the same way as other states raising revenue from mining, manufacturing and industry. Furthermore, in a system set up with the intention of minimizing Federal funding, grants proved to be a continuing bone of contention. As a consequence, the ACT Government has to finance a significant part of its revenue through the sale of its principal asset, greenfield land (Corbell, 2005; ACT Government, 2005; Sansom, 2009). This approach is unsustainable, given the limited extent of developable land in the ACT. It has also reversed what had once been managed as a viable method of providing leasehold land at reasonable cost for the homes of average citizens. The ACT Office of Asset Management, founded in 1988, focused on maximizing land values and immediate returns (Fischer, 2004) 'irrespective of environmental or planning considerations' (Powell, 2012, p. 7). The exigency of raising revenue for the day-to-day requirements of the Territory budget increased the pressure to achieve rapid returns from greenfield development and weakened the ACT Government's negotiating power with the development industry.

Towards Private-Led Development

The Draft National Capital Plan attempted to retain a balanced distribution of employment in the dispersed town centres. In 1990, however, these essential features of the metropolitan strategy were removed on the grounds that little office space would be built by the private sector outside central Canberra (Peake, 2016). With this decision, decades of technocratic planning were overturned by 'market forces'. In 1996, Federal departments were granted the liberty to decide their own location. They could also decide whether to continue owning their accommodation or to pursue short-term financial gains by selling their office buildings and leasing commercial space from the private sector. By 2000, the cost of private office space leased to the Federal Government approached 500 million dollars annually and the government had lost control of employment distribution in Canberra. The erosion of planning powers – symbolized by the elimination of the letter 'P' from the NCPA's acronym in 1996 – was exacerbated by the abolition of the post of National Capital Plan Director between 2003 and 2015, rendering the National Capital Authority (NCA) incapable of carrying out its statutory obligations to monitor and update the National Capital Plan. Meanwhile, the ACT Government took the initiative for strategic planning, with the NCA merely acquiescing in the Territory's push for more greenfield development. The Territory Plan, despite its lack of strategic planning powers, thus became the cuckoo in the nest that threw out the overarching role of the National Capital Plan.

The significance of the National Capital Plan further declined when Canberra Airport was privatized in 1998 in the context of a nationwide policy of divestment by the Federal Government. Situated on 'designated' national land, the airport was originally subject to the National Capital Plan. But this requirement 'was seen as cumbersome and at odds with the "level playing field" ethos embodied in national competition policy' (Freestone and Wiesel, 2015, p. 46) and was removed by 2007. Subject only to Commonwealth legislation and outside ACT jurisdiction, Canberra Airport thus became a 'free enterprise zone' with 'potentially unfettered commercial development opportunity' (JSCNET, 2008, pp. 98–103). Its owners seized the opportunity to transform a modest aviation facility into 'a world-class small airport city' (Freestone and Wiesel, 2015, p. 51). While Canberra Airport boasts high design standards in buildings, utilizes advanced environmental technology and incorporates progressive site planning, the dimensions of the commercial and retail hub are fundamentally in conflict with existing metropolitan planning policies. Some 50,000 square metres of malls and factory outlet centres, plus an IKEA store and two business parks with office space exceeding 200,000 square metres in 2015, have been 'tugging at the centre of gravity' of the city (Brown, 2014, p. 235). With Federal departments taking up long-term leases, the viability of the business parks was guaranteed, while the out-competed, distant employment centres of the New Towns were threatened by decline. In the absence of an effective strategic plan, the fragmented planning system encountered difficulties in responding to structurally new developments.

Great Expectations at the Turn of the Millennium

It was in this context that the Territory planning organization (PALM) invited the OECD to evaluate Canberra as part of its studies of sustainable urban development in selected cities worldwide. The OECD's recommendations in 2002 led to a range of new initiatives at Territory and Federal levels, for which political changes in the ACT provided a catalyst.

The election of a local Labor-Greens coalition in 2001 enabled the Territory Government to embark on an ambitious programme that responded to the OECD report and incorporated many of the planning principles discussed internationally since the 1990s. Social inclusion; increased sustainability through higher usage of public transport, including the introduction of a light-rail system; urban consolidation; a more compact urban form; and innovative ways to engage the different actors in new patterns of public-private partnership arrangements were to be pursued by three integrated plans. Under the summary heading of 'The Canberra Plan', a spatial plan, a social plan and an economic white paper were developed in a consultative process between the Territory Government and the community (CMD, 2004; Fenton-Menzies, 2004). These elements promised to add up to a strategic development concept for orientation and action that had not existed in Canberra since the all-encompassing modernist development plans of the NCDC – not as a simple repetition, however, but as a new hybrid approach which we might call 'modernism re-loaded' (Fischer, 2007). Aimed at overcoming the weaknesses of modernist planning and integrating its strengths with perspectives of planning for a more sustainable city, the catalogue of aspirations looked as if it had been compiled from contemporary textbook notions of planning (Fischer, 2013, p. vii).

In parallel with the new start made at Territory level, the NCA initiated a 'new urbanist' study of the symbolic centre of the National Capital, proposing large-scale commercial and residential development. Drawing on an intensive re-examination of the original Canberra plan, including previously unknown documents, the NCA's 'Griffin Legacy' proposals dovetailed with the Territory's ideas for a compact urban form. In December 2004, a lavishly produced publication presented the 'Griffin Legacy' to the public (NCA, 2004). The concept promised to re-instate the Griffins' vision of grand boulevards of cosmopolitan splendour in the national central area and to transform the vast empty lawns around the lake into prime real estate of immense value. As a self-funding project, the transformation of 1,845,000 square metres (Maunsell, 2006, p. 14) of parkland and highway cloverleaf junctions into a new urbanist network of street-defining buildings was expected to deliver 'revenues from land sales in the order of $1 billion' (Lloyd, 2004). The scheme was presented as 'a blueprint … directing public and private investment in core areas of the capital' (NCA, 2006, p. 8) and was swiftly forged into amendments to the National Capital Plan in 2006, prior to a parliamentary enquiry. The time frame only allowed for fragmentary studies into engineering and heritage assessments and for limited public discussion. Broad concerns about the planning implications of the proposals (JSCNET, 2007) and the 'Darling Harbour-esque' aspects of the lakefront vision (Vernon, 2007, p. 40) had little influence on the procedure. Community resistance, however, stopped several development projects that threatened heritage values (Doherty, 2010; Raggatt, 2016). In 2008 substantial cuts to the NCA's budget seemed to signal the death of the project. Nevertheless, the basic ideas continued to reverberate in projects around the lake.

The Canberra Spatial Plan (2004) and its Metamorphoses

If the NCA's Griffin Legacy remained a fragmentary exercise, so did the promising Canberra Plan process, initiated by the Territory Government in a context of turbulent administrative reform aimed at putting planning matters at 'arms-length' from local politics. New Territory legislation – the Planning and Land Act 2002 (ACT Government, 2002) – replaced PALM with the ACT Planning and Land Authority (ACTPLA) and the Office of Asset Management with the Land

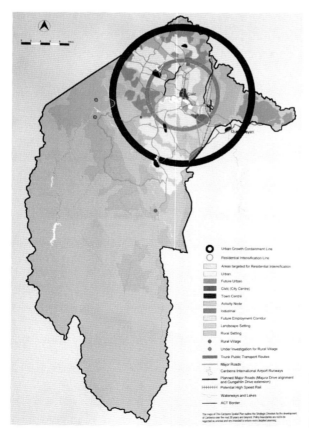

Figure 8.1. The Spatial Plan (2004). (*Source*: ACTPLA, 2004. Image courtesy of ACTPLA data bank)

Development Authority (LDA), but in the process the metropolitan planning team was disbanded and 'the program was aborted' (Powell, 2012, p. 19).

The 'strategic direction' of the Spatial Plan envisaged 'a more compact city' (ACTPLA, 2004, p. 15). The principles to achieve this were expressed in the key map (figure 8.1) of the Plan featuring two concentric circles – an 'urban growth containment line' and a 'residential intensification line' – as its graphically most striking elements. Convincing at first sight, a closer look reveals that the containment line coincides largely with the boundaries of the ACT and in places transgresses them to incorporate lands beyond the ACT's jurisdiction. In other places it coincides with steep mountainous terrain with limited potential for urban development, rendering the line somewhat tokenistic. In the east of the ACT, the line is even negated by a large site for greenfield development which extends beyond it on to the Kowen Plateau. In the west, an area of grazing country and land devastated in the major bushfires of 2003 is identified for the new satellite district of Molonglo (population 50,000), incorporating notions of sustainable design. These sites form part of a ring of new urban districts around the city centre reminiscent of the NCDC's first attempt at a metropolitan strategy (NCDC, 1965), abandoned due to its traffic impact on central Canberra as noted previously. The principle of strong functional decentralization was now rejected and the city centre was to be built up as a conventional CBD, to be complemented by suburban town centres and other activity nodes like a 'normal' big Australian city (ACTPLA, 2004, p. i). This rationalized the integration of the 'airport city' as part of the new growth concept – the very antithesis of sustainability in terms of employment location and transportation demands.

By massively extending the market for greenfield land – partly beyond the urban growth containment line – and by incorporating the office and retail market at the airport and other locations, thus weakening the position of the designated town centres, the plan displayed a continuing radical market-orientation at the expense of the rational planning that had informed the Y-plan. Ignoring the lessons of the transportation studies of the 1960s, it rejected the guiding idea of the linear city. There is no evidence that the earlier analyses by the NCDC and its consultants (De Leuw Cather, 1963) had been re-considered. The consequences of an east–west development corridor are highly problematic.

From Y-plan to H-Plan?

Among the likely consequences of the Spatial Plan, therefore, is a traffic tsunami breaking its way along the lake shore from the new residential district in the west, past the CBD to the 'airport city' with its competing interests of passengers, office workers and shopping mall visitors. While this prediction may amuse observers of today's quiet traffic scene, the calamity is already taking shape in the expanding highway infrastructure culminating in the space-eating Kings Avenue/Parkes Way overpass (Public Works Committee, 2008). In effect, the Y-plan was changed to an

H-Plan, with Parkes Way, the east–west motorway following the northern shoreline of Lake Burley Griffin, forming the bar of the H cutting through the symbolic centre of the national capital. The problem was exacerbated by construction of a vast building for the Australian Security Intelligence Organization (ASIO) on this route. The sheer bulk of the ASIO complex sits in the proposed urban fabric of the NCA's Griffin Legacy like an embolus – far too big in terms of block size and outright deadly for urban life in terms of its single-use and security requirements. Such developments are destroying the Griffin concept as a manifestation of good urban form. One of the key sites identified by the NCA for an urban renaissance under the 'Griffin Legacy' study was thus developed in a way contrary to the very principles of this study. With custodianship of development sites vested in departments rather than in the NCA, the successful push by the Defence Department to build the ASIO headquarters on 'its land', regardless of the NCA's plans for fine-grained, mixed-use urban development in this location, highlighted the conflict between the self-interest of individual departments on the one hand and the ambition to reach an overall satisfying urban design outcome on the other.

Territory Plan (2008) and 'Canberra Plan: Towards Our Second Century' (2008)

The strategic principles of the Spatial Plan were incorporated into the Territory Plan (2008) following the Planning and Development Act 2007 (ACT Government, 2007) and further reviewed in a follow-up publication in 2008, *The Canberra Plan: Towards Our Second Century*. This last document did not in fact present a new plan; rather it was designed to be 'a launching pad for serious and thorough community conversations about issues that go to the heart of who we are as a city – conversations about future urban form and sustainable transport, conversations about reducing our ecological footprint, and conversations about the implications of our shifting demographic' (ACT Government, 2008, p. 1). Following this, a series of promising studies and consultation exercises emerged in the context of a three-year Sustainable Future Program. They included projects exploring urban forms and principles (ACTPLA, 2009*b*; 2010), which measured and compared the social and environmental performance of case study areas in Canberra suburbs as well as benchmarked showcases for sustainability from Germany and Canada.

In parallel, a series of workshops explored strategies for increasing Canberra's sustainability (ACTPLA, 2009*c*), preparing the ground for a new climate change strategy (ESDD, 2012) and an ambitious strategic consultation exercise under the heading of 'Time to Talk, Canberra 2030' (ACT Government, 2010), intended to go beyond the usual engagement mechanisms. For the first time in Canberra, the Territory Government applied online engagement techniques, demonstrating the potential usefulness of technology in complementing traditional methods. The interpretations of the outcome of the exercise range from 'overall community endorsement for a compact … globalised city' (Norman and Sinclair, 2014, p. 182) to 'evidence that the ACT Government was intent on using Time to Talk as a mechanism for legitimizing its existing planning approach' (Stewart and Lithgow, 2015, p. 29). Furthermore, an analysis by the Productivity Commission observed that the survey 'contained loaded questions' and could have given participants the impression that some key decisions had already been taken (Productivity Commission, 2011, pp. 437–438).

At the same time, an independent review of the ACT public service replaced the residual autonomy of ACTPLA with direct ministerial control under the Environmental and Sustainable Development Directorate (ESDD). Although politicized, this created an entity with strategic planning capacity previously lacking at the Territory level (ACTPS, 2011). A parallel inquiry at the national level by the same author, Alan Hawke, recommended abdication of national responsibility for strategic planning (Hawke, 2011).

The Planning Strategy (2012)

The ACTPLA Sustainable Future Program and the public service review studies contributed to the development of a new Planning Strategy for metropolitan Canberra and the ACT (ACT Government, 2012a) which had to meet the criteria formulated for Australia's capital cities by the Council of Australian Governments (COAG, 2009; COAG Reform Council, 2012). The strategy continued and indeed magnified the dual trends of the Spatial Plan towards the radial expansion

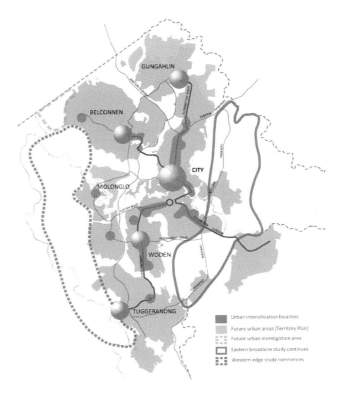

Figure 8.2. ACT Planning Strategy (2012). (*Source*: ACT Government, 2012a)

of the urban area through opening up substantially larger greenfield areas while intensifying development in the city centre. A new Draft City Plan (ESDD, 2013) 'slipped in' 'City' as a new name for the area traditionally known as 'Civic' (Troy, 2013).

The 2012 Planning Strategy removed the 2004 urban containment boundary and replaced the 'residential intensification line' with 'urban intensification locations' along the transportation corridors. The concept of transit-oriented development with higher densities along the transportation corridors had already featured in the 2004 Spatial Plan. Complementing the centres' hierarchy, it now became a dominant element in the key map of the Planning Strategy (figure 8.2) which called for 'urban intensification ... for town and key group centres plus corridors along rapid public transit ways' (ACT Government, 2012*b*, p. 46). This approach was further visualized in a set of district master plans indicating urban consolidation along major arterials, while leaving issues such as the merits of high-density housing along arterials to 'detail review' (ACT Government, 2012*b*, p. 46). Simultaneously, the map identified three 'study and investigation areas' on the outskirts of the city. These explored urban expansion right to the borders of the ACT, raising significant issues of infrastructure connection and cross-border integration. A Memorandum of Understanding on Regional Cooperation with NSW (CMD, 2011) and the creation of a new portfolio for the ACT Chief Minister as Minister for Regional Development are expressions of a new interest in cross-border cooperation, following the production of a plethora of studies without practical consequences (Norman and Steffen, 2014).

The 'Way Forward'

While the Canberra Plan and its translation into the Territory Plan went through several iterations in the twenty-first century, only piecemeal amendments had been made to the National Capital Plan, and the conflicts between the two plans – relating to inner-city development, the linear vs. radial urban form, greenfield sites and transportation corridors – were becoming increasingly obvious. Therefore, the Joint Standing Committee on the National Capital of the Federal Parliament (JSCNET) undertook an inquiry into the role of the NCA in 2008. The Committee called for reconciliation of the National Capital Plan with the Territory's statutory plan based on 'clear geographic boundaries between the two plans' and the 'objective that, where possible, land administration be aligned with planning jurisdictions' (JSCNET, 2008, pp. xxi and 179).

The National Capital Plan 2016 – Withdrawal of the Federal Government

Although the Committee's recommendation was endorsed by the Federal Government in December 2008 (Minister for Home Affairs, 2008), the review of the National Capital Plan – the first since 1990 – was not completed until May 2016. In essence, the revised National Capital Plan (NCA, 2016) legitimized the *de facto* actions of the Territory Government since 2004. The plan reduces the extent of Federal influence on metropolitan planning in the ACT and focuses instead on the designated areas of the national capital area (figure 8.3*a*), including parts of the city area as well as on Territory land subject to special requirements – in particular the approach routes and a small selection of other sites of national interest (figure 8.3*b*), including significantly reduced elements of the National Capital Open Space System (NCOSS). For these areas, it provides detailed guidance, but most of the 'special requirements' contained in the forerunner plan (figure 8.3c) have been removed and control over the location of employment has been abandoned.

The contradictions between the Territory and National Capital plans are thus diffused by 'turning the tables', i.e. through subjugating what should have been the overarching plan designed to safeguard national interests in the ACT to the Territory Plan and to local development interests. A comparison of the Metropolitan Canberra plans in the National Capital Plans of 1990 and 2016 (figures 8.4*a* and 8.4*b*) reveals progressive loss of the greenbelt separating and surrounding the New Towns (NCPA, 1990; NCA, 2016). Obstacles to the urbanization of this previously protected land of the National Capital Open Space System have

Figure 8.3*a*. National Capital Plan: Designated Areas.
(*Source*: NCA, 2016, p. 14)

186 • PLANNING METROPOLITAN AUSTRALIA

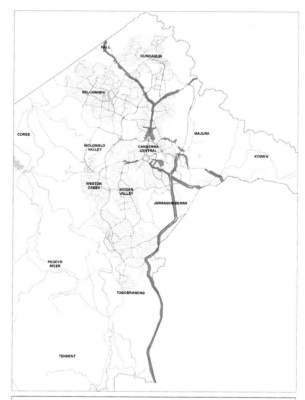

Figure 8.3b. National Capital Plan: land subject to special requirements as revised in 2016. (*Source*: NCA, 2016, p. 231)

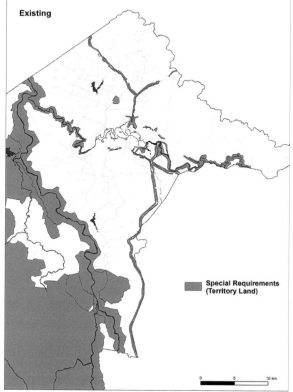

Figure 8.3c. National Capital Plan: land subject to special requirements in 2015. (*Source*: NCA, 2015)

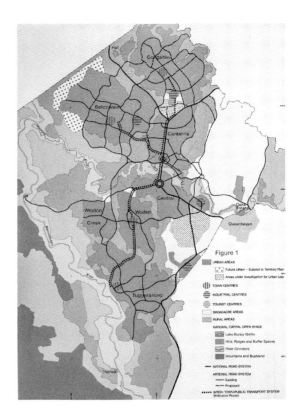

Figure 8.4a. Metropolitan Canberra 1990. (*Source*: NCPA, 1990, p. 14)

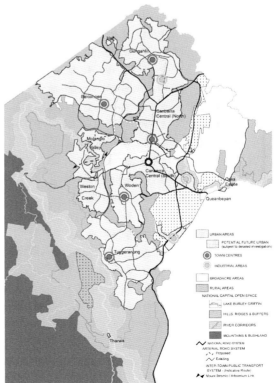

Figure 8.4b. Metropolitan Canberra 2016. (*Source*: NCA 2016, p. 22)

been removed in response to pressure to develop the greenbelt between North Canberra and Gungahlin; to re-activate plans to urbanize both banks of the major river of the region – the Murrumbidgee – which had been rejected in the 1970s on environmental grounds; and to extend urban development in the New Town of Belconnen to the far north-west border of the ACT and beyond to rural land in the adjoining state of NSW, held by property interests who have campaigned for just this result. The last-named project – a new urban district of 30,000 residents – is a joint venture initiated with the Land Development Authority, in which the ACT Government is proponent, developer and approval agency while in partnership with private developers, guaranteeing extension of ACT infrastructure beyond the border to enable conversion of speculative landholdings in NSW to urban land uses.

These developments are part of a significant expansion of greenfield development sites. Since new land release areas have been identified 'without any narrative as to whether the land has the capability of delivering the development, or how this land will be developed', the revised National Capital Plan has been termed 'not a plan at all' (Sinclair and Straw, 2016, p. 196). The neoliberal turn, which began to subjugate national capital planning to market forces in the 1970s, has thus reached its apotheosis.

Light Rail and Urban Renewal

At the same time, positive aspects of the ACT Government's plans for urban consolidation proposed in the Canberra Spatial Plan in 2004 have begun to be realized. A new City Plan (ESDD, 2013) embraced a package of interventions focused on the city centre. This included the first stage of a light-rail system to connect Gungahlin with the central city, with most of the funding coming from selling assets such as public housing stock. An ambitious 'City to the Lake' project, based on the NCA's 'Griffin Legacy' proposals for the West Basin of the lake and intended by the ACT Government to activate the city waterfront, has also been under way since 2004 (Weirick, 2013). However, in contrast to a waterfront redevelopment in the suburb of Kingston that has been realized since the 1990s, the 'City to the Lake' project has not progressed beyond construction of a boardwalk and fragmented 'Griffin Legacy' realization in spot developments at New Acton. Mixed-use developments on the edge of the central city – upmarket ventures by the private sector and a student housing precinct fostered by the Australian National University – have begun to bring life to the notoriously dead heart of the national capital. Flexible planning controls for the former trade uses zone of Braddon have succeeded in generating the seductive appeal of 'unregulated space' with pop-up stores and restaurants appearing.

A dramatic upzoning of lands along Northbourne Avenue has been proposed in the Gateway Project (ESDD, 2016) aimed at value capture along the Gungahlin–Civic Light Rail route. In the New Towns of Woden, Belconnen and Gungahlin, 'normalization' of urban development is seeing a plethora of residential tower schemes up to thirty storeys high. Canberra is on the verge of dramatic change, but the fact that in 2015 even the light rail project was threatened with cancellation (subject to the outcome of the ACT elections) reveals a highly volatile situation fraught with serious political and administrative challenges.

The spectres challenging Canberra in the middle of the second decade of the twenty-first century include the threat of decentralization of Federal departments to regional locations and the further relocation of departments remaining in Canberra from the New Towns to the city centre and the airport office park. Apart from exacerbating congestion in the centre, this will undermine the self-containment of the New Towns, reducing them to car-dependent dormitory suburbs and destroying vitality in the New Town centres. This would certainly be a most undesirable form of 'normalization' by inheriting the evils of the 'normal' Australian metropolis.

Conclusion

Through the first years of the twenty-first century Canberra has continued to be characterized by the strange dialectic of being unique and radically different from other Australian cities while, at the same time, being generic, reproducing global trends of urban development with exceptional clarity, a feature of the Australian national capital that was strongly evident in the city planning ethos of the past (Fischer, 1984; 1989; 2013). Some broad changes are evident in the years since

Figure 8.5. The isolated world of the New and Permanent Parliament House completed in 1988 – a signal to Federal politicians that the Federal Capital was itself complete. (*Source*: Photograph courtesy of John Gollings)

self-government was introduced in the ACT. The first is associated with the transformation of the city of rational comprehensive planning to a city shaped by market forces. The second is the shift from high-level political support at the Federal level during an era of prime ministerial enthusiasm for Canberra to pervasive lack of interest on the part of Federal politicians. This is popularly associated with completion of the New and Permanent Parliament House in 1988, which created the impression in the political sphere that Canberra was complete (figure 8.5). Structurally, however, Federal disengagement must be seen as a consequence of the neoliberal turn in public policy, the ideology of small government and the strategy of divestment of public assets. This in turn has led to chronic underfunding of the agencies responsible for the planning and development of the capital. As a consequence, the commitment to conceiving the capital city as a whole has ended. While the NCA is focusing on the national area, the rest of the city is expected to follow a path of 'normalization' ignoring, if not undoing, the special qualities of the city created in the twentieth century.

At the same time, the ACT Government is clearly not able to afford the city it has inherited from the Commonwealth on the basis of the revenue it can raise from rates and local taxes, and has become reliant on land sales to augment its budget, principally through greenfield development, thus further extending an already extended city and exacerbating the very costs of urban management it is seeking to defray. The fact that self-government was created at an early highpoint of neoliberalism in Australian politics, with planning arrangements that turned out to be ill-conceived, has led to endless attempts to sort out the respective powers and responsibilities of the two levels of government. The situation became critical when, as pointed out by the OECD (2002), strategic planning had to be revived. A plethora of reports and inquiries followed (tables 8.1 and 8.2) and the situation culminated in the Federal Government turning away from its historic responsibilities. A recent report by the ACT Auditor-General (2016) has revealed the planning system of the Territory Government to be alarmingly captive to development interests. Subsequently, the LDA has been abolished and will be replaced by two new organizations, a City Renewal Authority and a Suburban Land Agency (Lawson, 2017). Yet another inquiry into the Canberra planning system has also been announced (Lawson, 2016) but, on the basis of studies to date, there would appear to be little hope of new thinking.

There remains, however, the option of a more integrated Federal-Territory planning approach. In the Australian context, one model is provided by the Central Sydney Planning Committee which, although contentious at times, has achieved some balance between the interests of two levels of government. A committee of this nature in Canberra, charged with responsibility for metropolitan strategic planning and central city planning, would combine national level engagement with Territory-level local knowledge and specialized advice. This would contribute to finding ways to balance the conflicts of interest between the public and the private spheres in a way as transparent as the local culture admits. Planning would become a creative conversation between the levels of government rather than a confrontation or at best a vacuum created by the abdication of the Commonwealth. Combined with a forum for effective community consultation on the model of capitals like Washington or Berlin, such a governance structure would have the potential to help large-scale planning to transcend the current malaise and become again central to the culture of the city.

References

ABS (Australian Bureau of Statistics) (2016) *Australian Demographic Statistics*. Canberra: ABS. Available at: http://www.abs.gov.au/ausstats/abs@.nsf/mf/3101.0.

ABS (2017) *Regional Population Growth, Australia, 2015–16*. Cat 3218.0. Canberra: ABS. Available at: http://www.abs.gov.au/AUSSTATS/abs@.nsf/mf/3218.0.

ACT (Australian Capital Territory (Planning and Land Management) Act (1988) (Commonwealth). Available at: http://www.austlii.edu.au/au/legis/cth/consol_act/actalma1988526/.

ACT Auditor-General (2016) *Certain Land Development Agency Acquisitions*. Report no. 7. Canberra: ACT Audit Office.

ACT Government (2002) *Planning and Land Act* (ACT). Available at: http://www.legislation.act.gov.au/a/2002-55/20030701-3520/pdf/2002-55.pdf.

ACT Government (2005) *2005–2006 Budget: Revenue and Forward Estimates*. Budget Paper 3, Table 4.8. Canberra: ACT Government.

ACT Government (2007) *Planning and Development Act* (ACT). Available at: http://www.legislation.act.gov.au/a/2007-24/20070927-33748/pdf/2007-24.pdf.

ACT Government (2008) *The Canberra Plan: Towards our Second Century*. Canberra: ACT Government.

ACT Government (2010) *Time to Talk: Outcomes Report*. Canberra: ACT Government.

ACT Government (2012*a*) *ACT Planning Strategy: Planning for a Sustainable City*. Canberra: ACT Government. Available at: http://www.planning.act.gov.au/__data/assets/pdf_file/0008/895076/2012_Planning_Strategy.pdf.

ACT Government (2012*b*) *Towards 2030, Looking to 2060*. Canberra: ACT Government. Available at: http://www.planning.act.gov.au/__data/assets/pdf_file/0007/894967/2012_Planning_Strategy_-_Towards_2030.pdf.

ACTPLA (Australian Capital Territory Planning and Land Authority) (2004) *Canberra Spatial Plan*. Canberra: ACTPLA.

ACTPLA (2008) *Garden City Values and Principles: Design Considerations for Residential Development in Inner North and South Canberra*. Canberra: ACTPLA.

ACTPLA (2009*a*) *Employment Location in Canberra*. Canberra: ACTPLA.

ACTPLA (2009*b*) *Territory Plan Urban Principles Review*. Canberra: ACTPLA.

ACTPLA (2009*c*) *Sustainable Future Workshop Findings Report*. Canberra: ACTPLA.

ACTPLA (2010) *Urban Form Analysis: Canberra's Sustainability Performance*. Canberra: ACTPLA.

ACTPS (2011) *Governing the City State: One ACT Government – One ACT Public Service*. Final Report. Canberra: ACT Public Service Review. Available at: www.cmd.act.gov.au/__data/assets/word_doc/0005/224987/Governing_the_City_State.doc.

Bacon, E.N. (1968) Canberra as a statement of world culture. *Architecture in Australia*, **57**(4), pp. 625–626.

Barr, A. (2010) Walter Burley Griffin is dead. Available at: http://the-riotact.com/walter-burley-griffin-is-dead/30920.

Brennan, F. (1971) *Canberra in Crisis: A History of Land Tenure and Leasehold Administration*. Canberra: Dalton Publishing.

Brown, N. (2014) *A History of Canberra*. Melbourne: Cambridge University Press.

Canberra Times (2016) Editorial: Barnaby Joyce needs to rethink blatant pork barrelling move. 12 September. Available at: http://www.canberratimes.com.au/comment/ct-editorial/barnaby-joyce-needs-to-rethink-blatant-pork-barrelling-move-20160912-gre5ir.html.

CMD (Chief Minister's Department) (2004) *The Canberra Plan: Social, Spatial, Economic*, 3 vols. Canberra: ACT Chief Minister's Department.

CMD (2011) *ACT and NSW Memorandum of Understanding for Regional Collaboration*. Canberra: ACT Chief Minister's Department. Available at: http://www.cmd.act.gov.au/__data/assets/pdf_file/0004/265225/ACT-NSW-MoU-regional-collaboration.pdf.

COAG (Council of Australian Governments) (2009) *National Objective and Criteria for Future Strategic Planning of Capital Cities*. Council of Australian Governments Meeting, 7 December. Available at: https://www.coag.gov.au/meeting-outcomes/coag-meeting-communiqu%C3%A9-7-december-2009.

COAG Reform Council (2012) *Review of Capital City Strategic Planning Systems*. Report to the Council of Australian Governments. Sydney: COAG Reform Council.

Corbell, S. (2005) Media Release: Minister outlines latest land strategies. Media Release: Simon Corbell MLA, Minister for Health and Planning, 31 May. Available at: http://info.cmcd.act.gov.au/archived-media-releases/mediaf4e5.html?v=3430&s=337.

De Leuw Cather, with Rankine & Hill (1963) *Canberra Area Transportation Study. Engineering Report for the National Capital Development Commission*. Sydney: The Consultants.

Doherty, M. (2010) Money-back guarantee as Immigration Bridge abandoned. *Canberra Times*, 30 March.

ESDD (Environment and Sustainable Development Directorate) (2012) *AP2: A New Climate Change Strategy and Action Plan for the Australian Capital Territory*. Canberra: ACT Environment and Sustainable Development Directorate.

ESDD (2013) *The Draft City Plan*. Canberra: Environment and Sustainable Development Directorate – Planning.

ESDD (2016) *City and Gateway Urban Renewal Strategy*. Canberra: Environment, Planning and Sustainable Development Directorate – Planning. Available at: http://www.planning.act.gov.au/topics/current_projects/studies/City_and_Gateway_Urban_Renewal_Strategy.

Fenton-Menzies, D. (2004) The Canberra Plan: a planned city takes a fresh look for the 21st century. *Canberra Bulletin of Public Administration*, **111**, pp. 13–15.

Fischer, K.F. (1984) *Canberra: Myths and Models: Forces at Work in the Formation of the Australian Capital*. Hamburg: Institute for Asian Affairs.

Fischer, K.F. (1989) Canberra: myths and models. *Town Planning Review*, **60**(2), pp.155–194.

Fischer, K.F. (2004) Building culture, urban design culture, planning culture. Wolkenkuckucksheim, **8**(2). Available at: http://www.cloud-cuckoo.net/openarchive/wolke/eng/Subjects/032/Fischer/fischer.htm.

Fischer, K.F. (2007) Modernism reloaded: von der sozialstaatlichen Hauptstadt zur deregulierten Stadt und darüber hinaus, in Hamedinger, A., Frey, O., Dangschat, J.S. and Breitfuss, A. (eds.) *Strategieorientierte Planung im kooperativen Staat*. Hamburg: VSA, pp. 286–308.

Fischer, K.F. (2013) Canberra's centenary. *Town Planning Review*, **84**(2), pp. iii–xiv.

Fischer, K.F. and Weirick, J. (2013) Canberra 2013: planning and urban development challenges at the centenary of the National Capital, in Ruming, K., Randolph, B. and Gurran, N (eds.) *Proceeedings of the State of Australian Cities Conference, Sydney*. Available at: http://apo.org.au/node/59744.

Freestone, R. (2009) Canberra, Australia, in Hutchison, R. (ed.) *Encyclopedia of Urban Studies*. Thousand Oaks, CA: Sage, pp. 103–105.

Freestone, R. and Wiesel, I. (2015) Privatisation, property and planning: the remaking of Canberra airport. *Policy Studies*, **36**(1), pp. 35–54.

Gilchrist, J. (1988) Commercial centres in Canberra, in Schreiner, S. and Lloyd, C. (eds.) *Canberra: What Sort of City?* Canberra: Urban Research Unit, Australian National University, pp. 36–47.

Hall, P. (1988) *Cities of Tomorrow: An Intellectual History of Urban Planning and Design in the Twentieth Century*. Oxford: Blackwell.

Hancock, W.K. (1930) *Australia*. London: Benn.

Harrison, P. (edited by Robert Freestone) (1995) *Walter Burley Griffin: Landscape Architect*. Canberra: National Library of Australia.

Hawke, A. (2011) *Canberra a Capital Place: Report of the Independent Review of the National Capital*

Authority. Available at: http://www.regional.gov.au/territories/actnt/files/Canberra_A_Capital_Place.pdf.

Headon, D. (2003) *The Symbolic Role of the National Capital*. Canberra: National Capital Authority.

Howard, E. (1898) *To-Morrow: A Peaceful Path to Real Reform*. London: Swann Sonnenschein.

JSCNET (Joint Standing Committee on the National Capital and External Territories) (2007) *Review of the Griffin Legacy Amendments*. Canberra: Australian Parliament Joint Standing Committee on the National Capital and External Territories.

JSCNET (2008) *The Way Forward: Inquiry into the Role of the National Capital Authority*. Canberra: Australian Parliament Joint Standing Committee on the National Capital and External Territories.

Lawson, K. (2016) ACT Greens' Caroline Le Couteur promises planning for the community, not developers. *Canberra Times*, 13 December.

Lawson, K. (2017) New Northbourne Avenue Precinct as ACT Government details Lands Development Agency. *Canberra Times*, 8 March.

Lloyd, J. (2004) Walter Burley Griffin's new plan. Speech by Jim Lloyd, Minister for Local Government, Territories and Roads, at the launch of 'The Griffin Legacy'. Canberra: Parliament House. 8 December, typescript LS04/2004 (authors' archive).

Massola, J. and Towell, N. (2017) Moving APS is core business, and there will be more: Joyce. *The Courier*, 28 March. Available at: http://www.thecourier.com.au/story/4549219/moving-aps-is-core-business-and-there-will-be-more-joyce/?cs=8.

Maunsell AECOM (2006) *Griffin Legacy Implementation Traffic Analysis*. Canberra: NCA.

Mees, P. (2014) A centenary review of transport planning in Canberra, Australia. *Progress in Planning*, **87**, pp. 1–32.

Minister for Home Affairs (2008) Australian Government Response to JSCNET (2008) *The Way Forward: Inquiry into the Role of the National Capital Authority*. Canberra: The Minister, December 2008.

NCA (National Capital Authority) (2004) *The Griffin Legacy, Canberra, The Nation's Capital in the 21st Century*. Canberra: NCA.

NCA (2006) *National Capital Plan Amendment 56: Griffin Legacy Principles and Policies*. Canberra: NCA.

NCA (2015) National Capital Plan – Special Requirements. Available at: https://www.nationalcapital.gov.au/attachments/article/4228/Special%20Requirements.pdf.

NCA (2016) *Consolidated National Capital Plan, Incorporating Amendments May 2016*. Canberra: National Capital Authority.

NCPA (National Capital Planning Authority) (1990) *The National Capital Plan.* Canberra: NCA.

NCDC (National Capital Development Commission) (1965) *The Future Canberra*. Sydney: Angus and Robertson.

NCDC (1970*a*) *Tomorrow's Canberra: Planning for Growth and Change*. Canberra: Australian National University Press.

NCDC (1970*b*) *Development of the New Towns of Canberra*. Canberra: NCDC.

NCDC (1984) *Metropolitan Canberra: Policy Plan, Development Plan*, Canberra: NCDC.

Norman, B. and Sinclair, H. (2014) Planning reform of the Australian Capital Territory: towards a more sustainable future. *Australian Planner*, **51**(2), pp. 180–185.

Norman, B. and Steffen, W. (2014) The National Capital's place in the region. *Australian Planner*, **51**(4), pp. 318–320.

OECD (2002) *Urban Renaissance: Canberra – A Sustainable Future*. Paris: Organisation for Economic Cooperation and Development.

Peake, R. (2016) Cabinet Papers: National Capital Plan born in disagreement over office space. *Canberra Times*, 1 January.

Pegrum, R. (1983) *The Bush Capital*. Sydney: Hale and Iremonger.

Powell, A.J. (2012) *Technical Report on the Implementation of the 2009 Joint Standing Committee Recommendations on the Future Role of the National Capital Authority*. Available at: http://www.gnca.org.au/the-future-role-of-the-national-capital-authority/.

Productivity Commission (2011*) Performance Benchmarking of Australian Business Regulation: Planning,*

Zoning and Development Assessment. Research Report. Canberra: The Commission. Available at: http://www.pc.gov.au/projects/study/regulation-benchmarking/planning/report.

Public Works Committee (2008) *Inquiry into Bridging of Kings Avenue over Parkes Way at the Russell Roundabout, Canberra, ACT*. Canberra: Australian Parliament Standing Committee on Public Works.

Pusey, M. (1992) What's wrong with economic rationalism? in Horne, D. (ed.) *The Trouble with Economic Rationalism*. Newham: Scribe, pp. 63–69.

Quirk, M. (2007) Effective centres – a planning dream? *Australian Planner*, **44**(3), pp. 22–29.

Raggatt, M. (2016) Friends of the Albert Hall welcome 10-year Plan as added protection. *Canberra Times*, 11 June.

Reid, P. (2002) *Canberra Following Griffin: A Design History of Australia's National Capital*. Canberra: National Archives of Australia.

Reps, J.W. (1997) *Canberra 1912: Plans and Planners of the Australian Capital Competition*. Melbourne: Melbourne University Press.

Sansom, G. (2009) Canberra, Australia, in Slack, E. and Chattopadhyay, R. (eds.) *Finance and Governance of Capital Cities in Federal Systems*. Montreal and Kingston: McGill-Queen's University Press, pp.10–32.

Sinclair, H. and Straw, V. (2016) When is a plan not a plan: a new vision for the Nation's Capital. *Australian Environment Review*, **30**(8), pp.196–201.

Stewart, J. and Lithgow, S. (2015) Problems and prospects in community engagement in urban planning: three case studies from the Australian Capital Territory. *Policy Studies*, **36**(1), pp. 18–34.

Stockland Corporation (2005) *Advertisement flyer for The Waterfront at Kingston Foreshore, Lake Burley Griffin*. Sydney: Stockland Corporation Ltd.

Taylor, K. (2006) *Canberra: City in the Landscape*. Sydney: Halstead Press.

Troy, P. (2013) City Plan a daft proposal. *Canberra Times*, 24 May.

UDIA (Urban Development Institute of Australia) (2008) *National Awards 2008*. Sydney: UDIA. Available at: http://en.calameo.com/books/0003734956b74a8a87ba1.

Vernon, C. (2002). *A Vision Splendid: How the Griffins Imagined Australia's Capital*. Canberra: National Archives of Australia.

Vernon, C. (2007) Building the Griffin[s'] legacy. *Landscape Architecture Australia*, **113**, pp. 38–40.

Voorhees, A.M. (1967) *Canberra Land Use Transportation Study: General Plan Concept*. Prepared for the National Capital Development Commission. Canberra: NCDC.

Waterford, J. (1987) Civic is developers' bargain. *Canberra Times*, 13 December.

Weirick, J. (1988) The Griffins and modernism. *Transition*, **24**, pp. 5–13.

Weirick, J. (1998) Spirituality and symbolism in the work of the Griffins, in Watson, A. (ed.) *Beyond Architecture: Marion Mahony and Walter Burley Griffin – America, Australia, India*. Sydney: Powerhouse Museum, pp. 56–86.

Weirick, J. (2012) Griffin and the Canberra Plan. Utzon Lecture, delivered on the Centenary of the Announcement of Walter Burley Griffin as Winner of the Australian Federal Competition, 24 May 1912. Sydney: Faculty of Built Environment, University of New South Wales.

Weirick, J. (2013) *Realising the Capital in the City: The 'City Plan' & 'The City to the Lake Projects' City Centre, Canberra*. Joint Submission to the Economic Development Directorate and Environment and Sustainable Development Directorate, ACT Government, 29 May.

Wensing, E. (1992) Landlords and land use controls in the ACT: developing a new planning system. *Australian Planner*, **30**(2), pp. 63–69.

Wensing, E. (1994) Incrementalism versus strategic planning. *Australian Planner*, **32**(1), pp. 42–48.

Wensing, E. (2013) Walter Burley Griffin is dead: long live Walter Burley Griffin's planning ideals! *Urban Policy and Research*, **31**(2), pp. 226–240.

Wettenhall, R. (2009) Twenty years of ACT self-government: some governance issues. *Public Administration Today*, **18**(Jan/Mar), pp. 58–71.

Whitwell, G. (1990) The triumph of economic rationalism: the Treasury and the market. *Australian Journal of Public Administration*, **49**(2), pp. 124–140.

Chapter 9

The Metropolitan Condition

Brendan Gleeson

The Metropolitan Age

In the past decade an urban age has been declared by global institutions (UN-Habitat, 2010; OECD, 2010; World Bank, 2010) and celebrated in popular and expert commentary (e.g. Glaeser, 2011; Hollis, 2013). In contemporary Australia, this newborn discourse miscarries in two ways. First, it is nothing new; Australians have long been a highly urbanized people and may even lay claim to having forged the first suburbanized nation. Davison writes: 'Australia was born urban and quickly became suburban' (2016, p. 74). More than this, Australia has long been urbanized in a very particular way arising from high, indeed remarkable, levels of metropolitan primacy. For more than a century most Australians have lived in a handful of capital cities, albeit largely in denial of the centrality of this fact to national identity which cherished a mythic bush idyll for much of the twentieth century.

And yet, as Davison (2016, p. 57) recounts, by the late nineteenth century some local observers had already accepted that the 'metropolitan condition' (with all its worrying connotations) had arrived on the continent, so manifest was the vitality and complexity of the already sizeable principal cities. In this account 'metropolitan' was a descriptor fashioned with explicit reference to British cities; notably London, the first 'true metropolis'. A century on, as globalization took hold, the metropolitan condition referred not to these original features of British urban industrialism, but, by stark contrast, to the anonymity and internationalism of the global urban order (Davison, 2016). More and more Australians have come to accept openly the reality of their firm historical preference for metropolitan life in a world where urbanization is increasingly accepted as pivotal to the contemporary human condition. We arrive in the urban century finally acknowledging our elder status as an urban people. In Australia, we are even coming to believe that we have something to teach the world about cities as Australian urban expertise is sought through international consultancies and our metropolises are judged to be amongst the world's best in various comparative rankings.

And yet the belated dawn of the Australian urban age is darkened by the clouds of critical assessment and by rising concern amongst policy elites and in civil society about the state of our cities. This is the second way in which celebration of the urban age finds muted resonance in contemporary Australia. The preceding pages of this volume draw attention to the many problems evident in the contemporary Australian metropolis, as much as they do to their strengths and successes. In particular, they present a rather lukewarm account of the urban policy record since the publication of *The Australian Metropolis* (Hamnett and Freestone, 2000), explained largely by the relentless weakening of public institutions that has continued under the aegis of a prolonged and seemingly intractable neoliberal dispensation. The summary story is one of unremitting transition from the post-war public city of social/liberal democracy to a fluid, as yet unsettled, urban order dominated by private capital and a political ideology that continues to problematize and circumscribe the role of the state in managing cities (Gleeson and Beza, 2014). On the surface, the cities continue to function with reasonable accord and to attract international migrants in vast numbers in a troubled world. On closer inspection however, and at a level not lost to everyday commentary or increasingly to political concern, Australian cities are beset by mounting and increasingly chronic problems of housing affordability, congestion, pollution, economic dysfunction, cultural tension and manifold forms of social inequality. This volume offers a set of sober appraisals of the Australian metropolitan situation which contrasts with the exuberance of much international urban commentary.

Assessment of Australian urban, especially metropolitan, conditions remains partial. Despite its best and – important to relate – improving efforts, Australian urban studies does not provide a comprehensive account of urbanization trends and experiences. The 'evidence base' that exists remains poorly integrated with policy making; without doubt in part because urban institutions have been hollowed out by continuing neoliberal reform and therefore lack the animus and resources to undertake comprehensive policy analysis and formulation. As noted in the opening chapter, much of the work of urban and metropolitan policy crafting is now undertaken by private consultancies without recourse to publicly articulated and consistently adjudicated standards. Policy development is driven as never before by short termism, a whirl of consultant briefs, ministerial edicts and increasingly, and of great import, private lobbying and assertion. Not surprisingly, and noted in Chapter 1, Randolph maintains that metropolitan policy is 'bedevilled by a lack of understanding of how the cities planned actually work' (2013, p. 131).

Meanwhile, and in the context of this research–policy discordance, free-flowing evidence continues to demonstrate that Australia's metropolitan systems are experiencing rapid and complex changes in scale, constitution and direction. This signals a transition, still underway, from the physical and social morphology largely established by post World War Two urbanization – a time of steady strong growth – towards a different metropolitan make up, still emergent but distinctly new. In outline, the transition is from the centralized Fordist morphology of the post-war public city towards larger metropolitan regional formations that exhibit much more diverse, fluid and intensive forms. Profound and rapid sectoral changes to socio-economic conditions, cultural patterns and governance arrangements are observed. The principal forces driving these changes have been documented for some decades, usually grouped under the rubric of globalization; that is to say, transformations engendered by an increasingly fluid and connected global economy and by new patterns of migration and cultural change. Add to this, deep and increasingly disruptive transformations arising from technological and economic innovation, such as 'smart urbanism' and the 'sharing economy', have now arguably reached a point where a step change in the core urban regions may be postulated. The processes at work to effect this alteration in urban systems, from post-war public cities to polyvalent metropolitan regions, can be termed *metropolitanization*.

The idea of a step change in core metropolitan regions is observational conjecture at this stage. And yet this is a proposition surely worth considering given the testimony of the previous chapters in this book which point to rapidly unfolding and as yet poorly understood metropolitan conditions at an apparently transformational scale. What follows is an attempt to describe the process of metropolitanization whose impacts increasingly register in and disturb Australian political and social discourse. It is a thought exercise that draws lightly if suggestively from a stock of evidence that is still thin and unsystematic. After Davison (2016, p. 68), the analysis that follows is best considered at an 'imaginative distance' from its object, the contemporary Australian metropolis.

This chapter attempts that most difficult of social scientific work, theorizing contemporaneity, in this case urban change and, on the basis of this, undertakes some consideration of the Australian metropolitan prospect. The guiding assumption is that Australia should give much more priority to considering the changing course and fate of its core metropolitan regions, as well as the systems that shape and govern them.

Metropolitanization

Rising Primacy and 'Hypertrophic Urbanism'

The first thing to note about the national settlement pattern is the continuation of a long-run trend of rising metropolitan primacy, observed since the late nineteenth century and continuing with force into the new millennium. As the opening chapter noted, more than half of the national population now resides in the three major metropolitan areas of Greater Sydney, Greater Melbourne and South-East Queensland. If Greater Perth is added to this account, a picture emerges of a small core of four dynamic growth regions that are of ever increasing demographic and politico-economic centrality to the nation. The other metropolitan region of scale, Adelaide, stands somewhat apart from the core group, held back by sluggish growth that has proved entrenched and lasting in recent decades (Chapter 5). Nevertheless, its population has continued to grow, if modestly, in the past decade and the city is hardly a declining or 'rustbelt' region, especially if one considers what the concept means in North America and Europe. Canberra, in this typology, as the inland bush capital, remains preternaturally metropolitan in its refraction of the issues confronting the coastal state capitals.

The core metropolitan regions assert an ever greater centrality in national life and prospect. The metropolises have also passed size thresholds which establish them as significant 'mid-tier' regions in the world urban system – Greater Sydney and Melbourne together now contain around ten million inhabitants, approaching the population of Belgium. It would not be surprising to discover new myriad complexities in these rising conurbations as increasing scale permits, and surely engenders, changes to their fundamental constitutions and functioning.

The structure and form of the metropolitan regions continue to evolve towards larger, denser polycentric masses. Enlargement is observable at the general morphological scale, marked by larger buildings (including housing), structures and centres. The transition is well underway from a post-war low-density city, modestly housed, with a single dominant core, towards ever more extensive urban masses with dispersed, and rapidly proliferating, higher density precincts. We may perhaps describe the emerging Australian metropolitan condition as 'hypertrophic urbanism'. This new term denotes that city regions are rapidly growing under the impress of high population growth but are also experiencing internal 'cellular' enlargement (hypertrophy) as built structures and centres increase in scale and density. The extent to which urban policy is anticipating and guiding these changes is, as the preceding pages testify, a moot point at best. Market forces and demographic growth are the principal motors of change.

Hypertrophic urbanism is a broad casting of manifold changes in metropolitan systems. At a closer level of inspection, what dynamics are involved in contemporary urbanization? Two monster forces seem simultaneously at play, most particularly in Sydney and Melbourne, but also arguably present in the other capital regions.

Twin 'Monster Trends'

Metropolitanization describes two intersecting, and at times contradictory, forces at work in contemporary urbanization. They each summarize a set of churning plays that are themselves often in antagonism. First is *intensification*, meaning a variety of concentrating social and physical changes including increases in population and dwelling densities and a speeding of socio-economic and spatio-temporal rhythms. Together, these changes are making for a denser, faster urban process and experience. Second is *pluralization*, connoting an assemblage of other changes relating to cultural cosmopolitanization, migration and socio-economic polarization. This process is driven partly by more complex migrant sources and flows, including surges in certain temporary visa classes that depart from the post-war migration model. In concert, these emergent, fast changing pluralities are transforming the social constitution of Australian metropolitan regions, which less and less evoke the urban order of the post-war modernist cities they are fast replacing.

While it cannot be denied that intensification and pluralization have produced many welcome and stimulating changes in our cities, we must also register the new polarities and deprivations that have accompanied them. Complex, rapid and often countervailing change is the *leitmotif* for metropolitanization. The mix is complicated and intensified by fast moving technical and economic transformations, some of them disrupting the settled socio-technical foundations of the post-war Australian metropolis. They overlay the longer run institutional shifts evident during the past three decades (or more) of the Australian neoliberal consensus, including the segmentation, privatization and technological recasting of urban services and infrastructure.

Contemporary metropolitanization thus advances the 'splintering' of urban systems and the decline of the modern publicly-networked city noted for many Western cities since the 1980s (Graham and Marvin, 2001). In Australian terms, it is a singular process marked by strong, in some cases stark, divergences from general trends of global urban change. Not surprisingly, cultural pluralization takes unique forms, reflecting, for example, national migration priorities, but so too does physical change. Hodyl's comparative international study, for example, showed that 'high-rise apartment towers are being built in central Melbourne at four times the maximum densities allowed in Hong Kong, New York and Tokyo – some of the highest density cities in the world' (2014, p. 7). She concludes that Australian urban regulation of high-rise development is uniquely weak. This echoes other critiques which point to the feeble economic and spatial governance of Australian cities (Gleeson *et al.*, 2012). The significance and distinctiveness of the monster trends that characterize metropolitanization need to be explored in a little more detail.

Intensification

Intensification means simultaneously rising population, employment, transport and dwelling densities but in complex, sometimes contradictory, ways and roughly cast by the uneven development imposed through the neoliberal spatial economy. This economy is marked by weak market governance, rising private sector control of the public realm and disruptive innovation (Streeck, 2016). The ever extensive and intensive reach of the market is also noted, for example through its increasing penetration of the human lifeworld (hyper-consumerism) and the new temporal reach of the 'night-time economy'. Evidence of the latter is the recent decision of the Victorian Government to instate permanently 24-hour weekend public transport in Melbourne, citing in particular the commuting needs of rising numbers of night shift-workers (Tomazin, 2017).

The outcome is uneven intensification; that is to say, uneven socially as well as spatially. One small, but troubling, example is the growth of empty, high-density investor-owned dwellings in a context of acute and rising housing need, including homelessness (see, for example, Murray, 2017). Another physical manifestation is the contrast between continuing transport disadvantage and spatial entrapment in poorly serviced outer suburbs and the ever increasing traffic and mobility intensities of inner and some middle ring areas. The inner and middle rings of cities are stages for often mammoth infrastructure construction that seeks to address rising congestion and spatial friction generally – for example, privately financed and run motorways and state funded enhancements of public transport that seek to remedy worsening problems with urban circulation (see Dodson, 2009). Spatio-temporal intensification is to the fore.

Melbourne's new underground metro (due for completion in 2026) is being built to relieve pressure on an increasingly overcrowded and strained regional train system. Accordingly, its new carriages will be built so as to accommodate a '… level of crowding … comparable to that experienced in the Tokyo metro' (Carey, 2017). In planning policy and political assertion, the ever mounting threat to urban functioning raised by intensification is echoed, if indirectly, in quixotic recent declarations in favour of the '20 (or 30) minute city'. The modernist ideal of frictionless mobility remains firmly embedded in the urban policy imaginary (not least in the current enthusiasm for autonomous vehicles) but seems more and more a romantic desire in the reality of Australia's increasingly congested and fractured cities.

A principal driver for new urban intensity is net overseas migration which has been running in excess of 180,000 per annum (in some years considerably more) since 2010 (ABS, 2017). Approximately half of all new migrants are locating in Melbourne and Sydney. The intensity effect comes not, as critics allege, from land and dwelling shortages imposed by a (weak) planning system but from the sheer and inevitable frictions between rapid population growth and the time needed to effect any additions to dwelling stock. The contradictions between fluid human capital and fixed built capital are to the fore but rarely acknowledged in political discourses that continue to implicate 'supply problems' as the root cause of unaffordable housing in the face of contrary evidence.

The main disruptions to post-war urban structure include the rapid and now spatially pervasive growth in population sizes and densities of inner cities and increasingly of ageing, lower density middle rings. The modest disruption to long-run dispersion engendered earlier by gentrification has now become subsumed into a larger wave of counterurbanizations, to adapt the term to mean a structural break from the path of simple outward dispersion. Salt (2017) notes that densification, whilst prevalent, takes different forms in each of the capital cities – a rising share of households in Sydney and Melbourne exhibiting a shared preference for 'Manhattanesque lifestyles' whilst in the other cities favouring various forms of medium density infill.

Intensification and hypertrophy are two sides of the coin of change. The strategy of planned compaction (the term 'planned' is used here advisedly):

> ... has been to open up opportunities for urban renewal in inner city areas and for infill (low rise apartments and units) in established suburbia. To this end the planners have rezoned vast areas of the inner cities of Sydney and Melbourne for high-rise apartments and diminished the opportunities for municipal councils and resident action groups to oppose infill development. (Birrell and McCloskey, 2016, p. v)

Densification has thus taken two forms: smaller dwellings in high rise and ever larger dwellings in infill. In Sydney and Melbourne, and to varying extents in other cities, its most spectacular form has been a wave of inner urban hyper-densification. This 'Manhattanization' has been authorized by appeal to the compact city model which has in recent decades attracted near widespread support in Western urban thought and practice (Gleeson, 2014). It has, however, as Hodyl (2014) finds for Melbourne, authorized extreme, poor quality compaction which one might be tempted to call 'vertical sprawl'. Planning has largely been reduced to rezoning to allow redevelopment.

There is never any reason to suppose that urban trends will continue *ad infinitum*, including the process of vertical sprawl. The surge of high-rise construction, however, continues to remake the inner areas of the larger metropolitan regions, and a significant approved pipeline exists for Sydney and Melbourne, promising a further wave of densification (Birrell and McCloskey, 2016). The mismatch between supply, mostly of small apartments, and diverse housing need, including for larger, complex households (families, students, new migrants, temporary workers), is driving up dwelling densities in redevelopment areas, and producing new social intensities and tenurial relationships that are frequently injurious to wellbeing and amenity. Much of this high-density urban reformation is poorly tracked and regulated by public authorities.

Finally, in this select survey of change, what political ecological questions are raised by transition to a more intense metropolitan form and process? A growing quantum of scholarship highlights the ever more evident failures of compact urbanism to improve ecological functioning and human wellbeing in Australian cities (Gleeson, 2012; Hodyl, 2014; Thrive, 2017). Professional assessment is joining academic critique; the leading architect Kerry Clare recently commented that 'current high-rise building practices in Australia make for poor environmental performance and reduced liveability' (quoted in Lucas, 2017, p. 7).

The tendency of Australian cities to score highly on global liveability rankings masks a deeper and continuous undermining of society and ecology by market driven compaction, nowhere more evident than in the poorly designed and constructed towerscapes that have emerged through inner redevelopment (Buxton, 2016). Even the recent national *State of the Environment* report – a publication that normally resists critical editorial comment – makes a tentative finding against consolidation and intensification:

> This growth (now and in the future) of intensified urban consolidation across Australian cities provides reason for concern about the adequacy of local open space planning.

> Policies of urban consolidation have concentrated medium-density to high-density residential development in inner-ring suburbs, where green space is comparatively scarce. (Coleman, 2016, p. 92)

Market driven intensification has in many places permitted a fracturing and ransacking of urban value and amenity, and of human wellbeing, by development capital that has worn the thin robe of legitimacy provided by the compact city ideal. We might summarize this as 'urban fracking'; a new means of blasting through accumulated layers of material and symbolic value to extract profit. Lewis (1999) earlier observed that much redevelopment in Melbourne's middle ring neighbourhoods was parasitic; that is, drawing on (and thus depleting) existing amenity without adding to it. More generally, this dispossession of urban value, from public (or communal) to private, takes myriad forms: amenity and infrastructure mining through overdevelopment; transfer of public housing stock to private investors in redevelopment; the continued non-taxation of unearned land value increments; privatization of assets and services; and fast-track and favourable development approvals.

These various plunderings and injuries also potentially reduce the sustainability and resilience of our cities at a time of manifest threat, especially the 'climate emergency'. Diminution of greenspace and open space ratios in redevelopment areas raises particular risks for rapidly increasing inner-city populations. Consider that Melbourne City Council has prepared a Heatwave Response Plan which will evacuate city residents to the Melbourne Cricket Ground and Etihad Stadium and the Convention and Exhibition Centre. The Council recognizes that 82 per cent of residents now live in buildings 'without passive ventilation' (Dow, 2015): code for the air-conditioned towers that have apparently advanced the cause of consolidation and sustainability. New modelling in 2017 reveals that sea level rise from climate change is likely to flood many of the inner-city high-rise redevelopment areas in Australian cities, including the zones identified for evacuation in Melbourne's Heatwave Response Plan! The Australian Broadcasting Corporation reported recently that 'Sydney's iconic Circular Quay and Botanic Gardens, Brisbane Airport, Melbourne's Docklands and Perth's Elizabeth Quay will all be underwater in dramatic new climate modelling' (Wildie, 2017).

Although a continuous flow of new climate projections and impacts is regularly taken up in Australian media, there is little evidence that any of it is substantively informing metropolitan planning. In every major metropolitan area market-driven compaction has the potential to enhance urban heat island effects and thus expose ever denser populations to the potentially deadly vagaries of climate change. This perverse effect of intensification surely exacerbates frightening official projections of underlying climate change in all Australian urban areas through the coming century (Webb and Hennessy, 2015). The relationship between urban intensification and climate risk awaits comprehensive consideration in Australian urban policy and scholarship.

Pluralization

The primary face of metropolitanization is growth – of scale and cellular mass (hypertrophy) but also of social complexity and disparity. At the level of regional morphology, Australian metropolises not only exhibit growth and intensification everywhere, but also a rapid deepening of social plurality, including in the time-space routines of urban inhabitants; these are no longer fixed around the old Fordist choreographies but dictated by commuting, a hypercentralization of commercial and public functions and the simple dominance of automobility.

Intensity evokes also a general *hyperventilation of urban life*, of greatly speeding technological changes and of the routines of everyday life which offer new possibilities for the enabled whilst imposing new pressures on the disadvantaged and disabled. Consider the simple example of electronic ticketing and pricing in all metropolitan transport systems, hailed for convenience and efficiency for the 'average consumer' but which present new difficulties of use for many publics, including the elderly, non-English speakers and people with disabilities (Hale *et al.*, 2017).

Pluralization betokens a simultaneous cosmopolitanization and fracturing of the social fabric. The first has been largely driven by immigration in the past decade in new fluid ways that depart from the more staged pluralization of the post-war migration programmes. The forces of technological and economic globalization are driving cultural pluralization. They include the rise of a massive education services sector heavily concentrated in parts of the major cities. Immigration from Asia continues apace, maintaining an established trend of departure away from European dominance of the migration stream. Temporary visas presently account for more than half (52 per cent) of the migrant inflow (ABS, 2017) bringing new streams of workers, students and visitors into the cities which in turn engender wide scale and visible changes to retail, housing, and cultural patterns. Growth in student visas from countries outside the traditional European migration stream has been a strong force for cultural pluralization. More than half a million students are now enrolled in Australian education institutions, with a large share from China, contributing more than $A19 billion to the national economy annually (Birrell, 2017). Many of these are enrolled in the principal metropolitan universities and have a major presence in and influence on residential housing markets of inner- and middle-ring areas of cities. Undeniably, cosmopolitanization has produced much social enrichment – and vastly more entertaining, diverse, and resourced cities.

On the other side of the social ledger, the trend to increasing disparity and fracturing is manifest and undeniable. Broadly, the cities are witness to a perverse simultaneity: hypertrophy – relentless production of the built environment – accompanied by declining housing affordability and growth of housing stress and homelessness. A broad tenurial shift sees a rising share of tenants and declining home ownership in the major cities, especially amongst younger middle-income households (Birrell and McCloskey, 2016). The increasingly visible and distressing disaster of urban homelessness is the manifest tip of a much larger and swelling estate of people in generally precarious economic and social circumstances (Witte, 2017). A 'precariat' has also been pointed to internationally, referring to a widening social stratum that is especially vulnerable to endemic features of neoliberal change, notably cost increases in housing and services, degrading employment conditions and tightening of welfare eligibility (Wacquant, 2014).

Despite institutional enthusiasm for long established policy ideas like 'social mixing', the combined effect of unfettered private housing markets, malnourished human services, rising living costs and mean labour markets is to herd the poor, the ill and the disabled into shifting urban netherworlds (NCOSS, 2014; Stone and Reynolds, 2016; Witte, 2017). These shadowlands include last resort public housing estates; mouldering walk-up private flats in middle-ring areas; ageing, about-to-go caravan parks; and weedy, wind-blown neighbourhoods on the metropolitan edges. In a dark parody of the social mixing ideal, drug dealers share public housing towers with devout Muslim refugees; single mums and kids congregate with the angry, the disturbed and the dispossessed in cheap rentals on the metro fringe; and disability pensioners mingle with solo dads and 'mental health consumers' in decrepit trailer parks (Gleeson, 2013).

Precarity evokes many threads of lesser vitality, of incapacity and confusion – social disabilities laying witness to the failures of deinstitutionalization and the creaking, fracturing capacities of human service systems. Initiation of the National Disability Insurance Scheme is expected to generate a surge of demand for affordable housing which the stressed social and public housing sectors simply cannot provide (Wiesel *et al.*, 2017). In Victoria alone, the scheme will produce an estimated increase of 20,000 to 30,000 people needing supported housing. Adding to the social precariat are new potent morbidities, such as the ice plague and the epidemic of gender and family violence that is sending shockwaves through urban fabrics. Migration is frequently a short track to vulnerability. As related to a 2016 Senate inquiry, short-term migrants and student visa holders are part of a sizeable and seemingly growing pool of low-paid, frequently exploited, urban service workers (Commonwealth of Australia, 2016).

The decline of older Fordist metropolitan mobilities was noted earlier. A general revival in public transport use in Australian cities has been observed since the mid-1990s (Mees and Groenhart, 2014). This is a modal shift surely welcomed by the narrative of the compact city, but it is driven by changes far outside our weak planning systems. Ever more extensive, complex and stressful journeying, including on public transport, betrays the dislocation of housing and labour markets in our cities and the life imbalances this imposes on many. Just as young people are, with astonishing speed, redefining mobility in Australia by not taking up licences or owning cars (Delbosc, 2015), so too are the underhoused, the excluded and the seemingly incapable citizens of our cities exercising and flexing new mobilities and capacities in their everyday lives (Gleeson, 2013). The rising modal shares of our public systems reflect more than the happy scripted shift of car users to trains, trams or buses. They also tell the story of the stressed and the marginal for whom car ownership is out of the question.

On the other side of the ledger, cities are stages for a proliferation, concentration and securitization of urban wealth. Intensification has seen gilded and securitized towerscapes produced by high-end redevelopment, as well as the deepening superannuation of urban advantage enjoyed by inner- and middle-ring residents with ready access to highly centralized quality employment and services. Wiesel *et al.* (2017) refer to these groups as the 'housing elite' whose wealth, influence and locational advantage has further entrenched their affluence during a period of widening social disparity. The elites include Australian and foreign investors producing an ever larger share of new housing, some of it entirely severed from the idea of use value. Troy and Randolph (2016) report:

> At the last census there were nearly 120,000 empty dwellings in the greater Sydney region alone, representing nearly one fifth of the projected new housing demand to be met by 2031, or equivalent to nearly five years of projected dwelling need. When this is combined with under-utilised dwellings, such as those let out as short-term accommodation, the total number of dwellings reaches 230,000 in Sydney, and 238,000 in Melbourne.

A story to be told is how cosmopolitanism and fracturing are now intersecting in complex, unexamined ways: consider the example of rising poverty and marginality amongst foreign students, especially those enrolled in the shadowy private training sector (Cook, 2015). Finally, further social fracturing is imminent given continuing manufacturing decline and rising housing stress. This will occur in a context of urban intensification which means generally poorer ratios of infrastructure and amenities to population, even for some affluent areas (especially towerscapes). As noted in Chapter 4, 'a by-product of the transition to a more compact city has been a more unequal city, in that lower income and disadvantaged communities are becoming increasingly marginalized' (Bunker *et al.* in this volume, p. 96). This lamentable change looks set to continue.

The Parallel Universe Problem

Critical scholarly assessment, echoed in rising social and political apprehensions, suggests that Australian cities are a long way from realizing the ideals of compact urbanism, notably sustainable ecology, social justice, efficient resource use and an innovative, inclusive economy. In 2006 Forster memorably depicted two 'parallel universes' in metropolitan Australia, those of urban planning and of urban reality, with plans portraying 'an inflexible, over-neat vision for the future that is at odds with the picture of increasing geographical complexity that emerges from recent research on the changing internal structure of our major cities' (Forster, 2006, p. 173).

The compact city vision that has guided Australian metropolitan strategy for at least three decades was intended to realize these aspirations in a morphology that departed from the extensive, car dependent monocentrism of the post-war metropolis (Forster, 2006). And yet, the metropolitanization processes observed in this account suggest that planning has not been the principal directional force for urbanization during the neoliberal preponderance. Instead, other modalities have shaped the course of urban change including national policies (especially immigration, taxation and financing), technological innovation, cultural shifts, political economy (notably neoliberal governance) and increasingly unrestrained market power. This set of transformational 'furies' has been grouped under the rubrics of intensification and pluralization. While it cannot be denied that they have produced many welcome and stimulating changes in our cities, the current course of metropolitanization, if left uncorrected, will potentially drive Australian cities further away from the ideal of sustainable urbanism.

Metropolitan planning regimes remain weak in authority and poorly resourced, largely bystanders to the amplification and dispersion of the urban form. As presently constituted they cannot hope to realize the basic morphology of the compact city, let alone its underlying ideals. In many contexts planning regimes are locked in a stand-off with communities unsettled and angered by metropolitanization, especially intensification driven by foreign investment. Their injury and opposition is heightened by the tendency of policy elites to dismiss them as self-interested NIMBYs. Some relief will likely come not from improved planning but via changes to federal and state rules and taxes that will dampen direct foreign investment in metropolitan property markets. After three decades of neoliberal governance, planning appears weak and unpopular; hollowed out by reform and, perversely, blamed by communities for imposing unwelcome change on cities and neighbourhoods.

The Metropolitan Prospect: Corporatism in the Wings?

What then is the Australian metropolitan prospect? Given the above, a democratically planned transition to sustainable urbanism seems unlikely. And yet, with rising urban friction and dysfunction, including in some parts worsening law and order, there will doubtless be increasing political compulsion to manage the urban process. This perhaps explains the recent emergence of conservative (largely Liberal party) support for federal urban policy and thus what appears to be an unprecedented bipartisan consensus on the need for urban management at the national level. The Turnbull government has established two principal new urban policy settings: 'smart cities and suburbs' and 'city deals' (Australian Government, 2017). The language and content of both programmes are revealing of the technocratic, econocratic characteristics of contemporary neoliberal urbanism, in Australia and globally. Genuflection is made to current policy nostrums such as 'liveability' and 'resilience' but the real idol is economic productivism: the Smart

Cities Plan is intent on 'building an agile, innovative and prosperous nation' (2017, p. 3). The values and qualities of democratic planning are hardly discernible. Increasingly, state and metropolitan level planning evince little difference to the new federal regime.

What of metropolitan governance in a time when the urban process calls for stronger management as dysfunctionality mounts? The splintered urbanism bequeathed by decades of neoliberal reform will surely not serve the cause of stronger management. History teaches that a period of worsening social disorder and paradox is usually resolved through the assertion of socio-political power. The contemporary course of Australian metropolitanization towards further conflict, contradiction and impasse in the urban process suggests that an alternative to raw neoliberalism is waiting in the near wings of history.

First stage responses to urban unmanageability have been made, still largely anchored in the public realm – such as the establishment of a Greater Sydney Commission in 2015 and, briefly, a Melbourne Planning Authority (2013–2016). The emphasis in such instances has been on improved growth management rather than stronger economic and social governance for the cities. The purview of reform has been narrow, confined to strategic and regulatory planning, leaving aside the increasingly privatized drivers of metropolitan change, urban infrastructure and services. Clearly planning reform cannot solve the paradoxes cast up by hypertrophic metropolitanization. The cause of stronger metropolitan management must eventually extend to the large and growing areas of the urban process that lie outside formal state ownership and control.

If Australian metropolitanization enters a period of crisis, authority will surely emerge to stem social, economic and natural disorders and restabilize the political economy. One scenario sees mounting urban terrorism and civil disorder engendering political reaction against cultural pluralization. Increasingly, surveillance and control are exercised in technically enhanced ways and with a new granularity – NSW Police has now established a 'fixated persons unit' that will 'focus on those who are marginalised but not on [the] counter-terrorism radar' (Farrell, 2017). In other words, the radar of terrorism surveillance now extends to the growing ranks of the urban precariat, an increasingly residual and, it seems, hostile stratum that bears witness to the social injuries of neoliberalism.

The 'resilience project' describes the growing presence and reach of resilience rhetoric and practice in Australian urbanism. Resilience thought is generally freighted with instincts to enclose and defend vulnerable systems such as cities. The project has emerged as an alternative to mainstream planning, and has been promoted and resourced by NGOs such as the Rockefeller Foundation in the face of state failure to make cities safe from manifold social, economic and ecological threats (Wilkinson *et al.*, 2010). Both Sydney and Melbourne have resilience frameworks that have emerged from a new fusion of state, elite NGO and corporate power (Resilient Melbourne, 2016; Resilient Sydney, 2016). They may be auguries of a new securitization of increasingly vulnerable and unmanageable cities. The dissolution of one urban regime of power (the post-war public city) is preface not to endless decomposition and liberty but surely to the reconcentration of power, this time in the hands of the private consortia and non-state interests that now shape the neoliberal city.

The climate emergency alone has the power to overwhelm existing capacities to manage urban systems in any potential setting. There are insufficient resources in the withered liberal democratic state to counter or prevent heat stress, resource disruption and collapse, new disease pathologies, and sudden panicked intrusions and extrusions of populations. In any case, these maladies call forth new diagnoses and treatments that were never developed as modern state capacities. Political and state responses to catastrophic declines in human (and non-human) wellbeing will of course be inevitable if likely to differ widely across metropolitan contexts. But what will surely rouse state force with greatest priority and effect is the threat these shocks pose to accumulation, now an innately urban project (Harvey, 2014).

Can we see the tracings and rousings of new state authority, perhaps even authoritarianism, in the Australian metropolitan process? Arguably yes, if we pay attention to the earlier essayed perturbations and paradoxes in metropolitan urbanization and urban governance. The long absence of effective metropolitan administration is increasingly problematical given the mounting problems of growth management, and of governability generally, in the cities. The capacity dilemmas facing weakly resourced municipalities and hollowed-out state administrations are increasingly apparent. Metropolitan dysfunction now raises serious barriers to realization. Lobbies such as the Property Council of Australia, Committees for Sydney, Adelaide, Perth and Melbourne and Infrastructure Partnerships Australia prosecute the cause of an increasingly perturbed urbanized capital. A resolution must be found, but not in new socio-technical fixes such as smart city urbanism or place management. The urban resolution must be political, though technically realized and enhanced.

A major cause of state incapacity – relentless privatization of urban services, infrastructure and technical capability – suggests the form of this resolution, a fusing of private ambition and resources with government power; viz., corporatism, meaning – in short – a new corporate state born of urban necessity and with unprecedented authority to address disorders. We may discern its prefiguration already in the rising assertions, indeed arrogations, of the privatized urban monopolies that control ever larger parts of Australia's metropolitan estates. Instances abound: new formal avenues for unsolicited proposals to state administrations which effectively privatize strategic and infrastructure planning; continuous proposals for concession extensions which greatly enhance and entrench monopoly power; development deals that suspend or bend process and deliver unprecedented windfall gains to monopoly interests; a failure to monitor, cost or even meaningfully regulate private concessions; and the ever swelling ranks of the 'shadow state', the army of consultants, advisers and technocrats that does the work of the state outside the formal bounds of the public administration but which is increasingly directive of, not just responsive to, civil strategy. As private ambitions strengthen and government capacities weaken further (the NSW government has just sold its land registry and Victoria and South Australia plan to do the same), the emergence of a corporate state seems inevitable and may be hastened by step changes in urban disorder; for example, terrorist actions and climate induced shocks. Such a state would surely need to take metropolitan forms to assert what may prove to be increasingly authoritarian control of the urban process.

Can the emergence of an urban corporate state be prevented? Could the trajectory of change be redirected towards re-establishment of democratic planning and governance for the cities, converging each and every thread of positivity that surfaces in this volume? To take us at least towards realization of that ideal would require a profound overhaul of many contemporary policy settings at all levels of government, and a new political economic consensus that mandated planned urbanization. Part of this must be a dispersal of monopolistic and other privately concentrated power and a reassertion of collective control over the urban process. This raises, of course, the wider necessity of redirecting global capitalism away from the fires of default that commentators such as Harvey (2014) and Streeck (2014, 2016) now see as inescapable. Regrettably, considering the dwindling animus and legitimacy of progressive politics, the likelihood of this redirection appears remote at best. We should perhaps accept Streeck's counsel and 'be thankful for every passing year that is good and peaceful' (Chakraborty, 2016).

References

ABS (Australian Bureau of Statistics) (2017) 3412.0 – Migration, Australia, 2015–16. Available at: http://www.abs.gov.au/ausstats.

Australian Government (2017) *Smart Cities Plan*. Available at: https://cities.dpmc.gov.au/.

Birrell, B. (2017) Universities too heavily reliant on foreign students. *University World News*, Available at: http://www.universityworldnews.com/article.php?story=20170531095918961.

Birrell, B. and McCloskey, D. (2016) *Sydney and Melbourne's Housing Affordability Crisis Report 2: No End in Sight*. Australian Population Research Institute. Melbourne: Monash University.

Buxton, M. (2016) *Liveable Melbourne: Is It Really?* Available at: https://www.rmit.edu.au/news/all-news/2016/september/liveable-melbourne.

Carey, A. (2017) 2000 people per train: Metro's standing room-only future revealed. *The Sunday Age*, 29 May. Available at: http://www.theage.com.au/victoria/2000-people-per-train-metros-standing-roomonly-future-revealed-20170528-gwettp.html.

Chakraborty, A. (2016) Wolfgang Streeck: the German economist calling time on capitalism. *The Guardian*, 12 December. Available at: https://www.theguardian.com/books/2016/dec/09/wolfgang-streeck-the-german-economist-calling-time-on-capitalism.

Coleman, S. (2016) *Australia State of the Environment 2016: Built environment*. Independent report to the Australian Government Minister for the Environment and Energy, Australian Government Department of the Environment and Energy, Canberra.

Commonwealth of Australia (2016) *A National Disgrace: The Exploitation of Temporary Work Visa Holders*. Education and Employment References Committee, Canberra: The Australian Senate.

Cook, H. (2015) Hungry students queue with the homeless. *The Age*, 15 February. Available at: http://www.theage.com.au/victoria/hungry-students-queue-with-the-homeless-20150213-13efjz.html.

Davison, G. (2016) *City Dreamers: The Urban Imagination in Australia*. Sydney: UNSW Press.

Delbosc, A. (2015) Why are young Australians turning their back on the car? *The Conversation*, 5 January. Available at: https://theconversation.com/why-are-young-australians-turning-their-back-on-the-car-35468.

Dodson, J. (2009) The 'infrastructure turn' in Australian metropolitan spatial planning. *International Planning Studies*, **14**(2), pp. 109–123.

Dow, A. (2015) Plans to use MCG as shelter for Melbourne's heatwave refugees. *The Age*, 16 February. Available at: http://www.theage.com.au/victoria/plans-to-use-mcg-as-shelter-for-melbournes-heatwave-refugees-20150213-13em74.html.

Farrell, P. (2017) NSW police establish 'fixated persons' unit to help counter lone wolf terror attacks. *The Guardian*, 26 April. Available at: https://www.theguardian.com/australia-news/2017/apr/26/nsw-police-establish-fixated-persons-unit-to-help-counter-lone-wolf-terror-attacks.

Forster, C. (2006) The Challenge of Change: Australian Cities and Urban Planning in the New Millennium. *Geographical Research*, **44**(2), pp. 173–182.

Glaeser, E. (2011) *The Triumph of the City: How Our Greatest Invention Makes Us Richer, Smarter, Greener, Healthier, and Happier*. Harmondsworth: Penguin.

Gleeson, B.J. (2012) 'Make no Little Plans'. Anatomy of planning ambition and prospect. *Geographical Research*, **50**(3), pp. 242–255.

Gleeson, B.J. (2013) Collins St 3pm. The end of the line. *Griffith Review*, **41**, July, pp. 42–52.

Gleeson, B.J. (2014) *The Urban Condition*. London: Routledge.

Gleeson, B.J. and Beza, B. (2014) The public city: a new urban imaginary, in Gleeson, B.J. and Beza, B. (eds.) *The Public City*. Melbourne: Melbourne University Press, pp. 1–11.

Gleeson, B.J., Dodson, J. and Spiller, M. (2012) Governance, metropolitan planning and city-building: the case for reform, in Tomlinson, R. (ed.) *Australia's Unintended Cities*. Melbourne: CSIRO Publishing, pp. 117–134.

Graham, S. and Marvin, S. (2001) *Splintering Urbanism: Networked Infrastructures, Technological Mobilities and the Urban Condition*. London: Routledge.

Hale, R., McSherry, B., Paterson, J., Brophy, L. and Arstein-Kerslake, A. (2017) *Consumer Transactions: Equitable Support Models for Individuals with Decision-making Impairments*. Melbourne: Melbourne Social Equity Institute, The University of Melbourne.

Hamnett, S. and Freestone, R. (eds.) (2000) *The Australian Metropolis: A Planning History*. Sydney: Allen and Unwin.

Harvey, D. (2014) *Seventeen Contradictions and the End of Capitalism*. Oxford: Oxford University Press.

Hodyl, L. (2014) To Investigate Planning Policies that Deliver Positive Social Outcomes in Hyper-Dense, High-Rise Residential Environments. Report to The Winston Churchill Memorial Trust of Australia. Available at: https://www.churchilltrust.com.au/media/fellows/Hodyl_L_2014_Social_outcomes_in_hyper-dense_high-rise_residential_environments_1.pdf.

Hollis, L. (2013) *Cities are Good for You: The Genius of the Metropolis*. London: Bloomsbury Press.

Lewis, M. (1999) *Suburban Backlash: The Battle for the World's Most Liveable City*. Melbourne: Bloomings Books.

Lucas, C. (2017) High-rise apartments are bad to live in and bad for society says respected architect. *The Age*, 29 August. Available at: http://www.theage.com.au/victoria/highrise-apartments-are-bad-to-live-in-and-bad-for-society-says-respected-architect-20160828-gr39nf.html.

Mees, P. and Groenhart, L. (2014) Travel to work in Australian cities: 1976–2011. *Australian Planner*, **51**(1), pp. 66–75.

Murray, C. (2017) The mystery of why investors leave homes vacant. *The Age*, 6 April, p. 18.

NCOSS (The Council of Social Service of New South Wales) (2014) *Cost of Living. Who's Really Hurting?* Surry Hills, NSW: NCOSS.

OECD (2010) *Measuring Globalisation: OECD Economic Globalisation Indicators*. Paris: OECD.

Randolph, B. (2013) Wither urban research? Yes, you read it right first time! *Urban Policy and Research*, **31**(2), pp. 130–133.

Resilient Melbourne (2016) *Strategy*. Melbourne: City of Melbourne.

Resilient Sydney (2016) *Preliminary Assessment Strategy*. Sydney: City of Sydney.

Salt, B. (2017) Brisbane, Adelaide, Perth: smaller capitals' population pause. *The Australian*, 1 June. Available at: http://www.theaustralian.com.au/business/opinion/bernard-salt-demographer.

Stone, J., Ashmore, D. and Kirk, Y. (2017) *Protecting the Long Term Public Interest in Melbourne's Rail Franchise*. MSSI Issues Paper No. 8. Melbourne: Melbourne Sustainable Society Institute, The University of Melbourne.

Stone, W. and Reynolds, M. (2016) *Children and Young People's Housing Disadvantage*. Melbourne: Swinburne University of Technology.

Streeck, W. (2014) *Buying Time*. London: Verso.

Streeck, W. (2016) *How Will Capitalism End?* London: Verso.

Thrive (2017) *Living Well Apartments: Comfort and Resilience in Climate Change*. Thrive Research Hub. Melbourne: The University of Melbourne.

Tomazin, F. (2017) City on the move all night, at weekends. *The Sunday Age*, 23 April, p. 17.

Troy, L. and Randolph, B. (2016) Negative gearing has created empty houses and artificial scarcity. *The Sydney Morning Herald*, 28 March. Available at: http://www.smh.com.au/comment/negative-gearing-has-created-empty-houses-and-artificial-scarcity-20160324-gnqoeb.

UN-Habitat (2010) *Cities for All: Bridging the Urban Divide: The State of the World's Cities 2010/2011*. Nairobi: UN-Habitat,

Wacquant, L. (2014) Marginality, ethnicity and penality in the neo-liberal city: an analytic cartography. *Ethnic and Racial Studies*, **37**(10), pp.1687–1711.

Webb, L.B. and Hennessy, K. (2015) *Projections for Selected Cities*. CSIRO and Bureau of Meteorology, Australia. Available at: https://www.climatechangeinaustralia.gov.au/media/ccia/2.1.6/cms_page_media/176/CCIA_Australian_cities_1.pdf.

Wiesel, I., Whitzman, C., Bigby, C. and Gleeson, B. (2017) *How will the NDIS Change Australian Cities*. MSSI Issues Paper No. 9 Melbourne: Melbourne Sustainable Society Institute, University of Melbourne.

Wildie, T. (2017) Climate change: model predicts Australia to lose famous sites in new sea-level rise. Available at: http://www.abc.net.au/news/2017-05-23/coastal-areas-at-risk-new-climate-study-reveals/8549934.

Wilkinson, C., Porter, L. and Colding, J. (2010) Metropolitan planning and resilience thinking: a practitioner's perspective. *Critical Planning*, **17**, pp. 25–44.

Witte, E. (2017) *The Case for Investing in Last Resort Housing*. MSSI Issues Paper No. 10. Melbourne: Melbourne Sustainable Society Institute, The University of Melbourne.

World Bank (2010) Cities and Climate Change: An Urgent Agenda. Urban Development Series Knowledge Papers No. 10. Washington DC: The World Bank. Available at: https://openknowledge.worldbank.org/handle/10986/17381.

Index

Figures and tables are indicated by page number in italics

2020 Vision (Metropolitan Adelaide, 1992) 46
20-minute city 62, *64*, 65, 200; *see also* cities; neighbourhood planning
30-Year Plan for Greater Adelaide 110–114, *111*, 114
30-Year Plan for Greater Adelaide Update 114, *115*, 116–119

Abbott, John 152
Abbott, Tony 10, 89–90
Abbott Liberal-National Coalition Government 10, 12
Abercrombie, Patrick 35, 39
ACT Planning and Land Authority (ACTPLA) 180–181, 183; *see also* Planning and Land Management Agency
activism 41, 58, *141*, 144, 180; *see also* green bans; social policy and reform
Activity Centres for Perth and Peel 136, 138
Adelaide 4, 6–7, 13, 17, 27–8, 30–1, *35*, 39, *40*, *45*, 46, 101–105, *108*, 109–112, *113*, 114–119, 197–198
  Barossa region 111
  Buckland Park 111
  CBD (Central Business District) 113, 118–119
  Elizabeth 40, 102
  Mount Barker 111
  population 102
  Riverbank area 112
  Roseworthy 111
airport cities 178, 181; *see also* business parks

airports 17, 87, 89–90, 95–97, 138, 178
Albrechts, L. 2
Allmendinger, P. 17
Andrews, Daniel 56
apartments 9, 70, *70*, 126, 132–133, 201; *see also* densification, flat/unit development; high-rise development
Arman, M. 94
Asia 5–6, 203
Australasian Association for the Advancement of Science 28
Australia 1–6, 11, 20, 31, 34, 36, 41, 46, 195–197, 207–208
Australian Capital Territory 177–178, 181, 183, 185; *see also* Canberra; Queanbeyan
  land development 177
  self-government 170–171, 176–177, 190
Australian Capital Territory (Planning and Management) Act (1988) 177
Australian Government 4, 10, 18, 34, 44–45, 84, 87, 89, 119, 142, 158, 171, 175–176, 178, 184, 190, 206–207
  Commonwealth Housing Commission (CHC) 34
  Department of Post-War Reconstruction 34
  Department of Urban and Regional Development 43
  Minister for Cities 12
  public service 5, 13, 171, 176, 183
Australian National University 188
Australian Security Intelligence Organization (ASIO) 182
authoritarianism 208–209
automobiles *see* motor car

Baillieu, Ted 56
Baillieu/Napthine Liberal-National Party Coalition Government 56, 60
Baird, Mike 90–91, *90*
Bannon Labor Government 104, 119

Barangaroo Delivery Authority 88
BASIX (Building Sustainability Index)
  94
Beattie, Peter 152, 156
Beattie Labor Government 152–153
Beaudesert 149
Beenleigh 160
Beerwah East 160
Bennett, Edward H 29
biodiversity 44, 107, 142, 153–154,
  157–158, 161, 163, 165–166
Bjelke-Petersen, Joh 152
Bland, William Dr 28
Bligh Labor Government 158
Boas, Harold 32
Borbidge, Rob 152
Borbidge National–Liberal Coalition
  Government 152
Bracks, Steve 56
Bracks Labor Government 56, 66
Brisbane 30–31, 33, 35, 37, 45, 148–149,
  155, *159, 163*
  CBD (Central Business District) 152
Brisbane City Council 33, 153; *see also*
  Greater Brisbane Council
Brown, A.J. 33–34
Brumby, John 56
Brundtland Report 43
Building a Better Planning System (WA)
  135
Building Better Cities Program (1991–
  1996) 11, 44
Bunker, Raymond 42–43, 46, 119, 138
Burke, M. 10
Burnham, Daniel 29
Burns, Tom 152
business parks 82, 178–179; *see also*
  airport cities
Buxton, M. 38

Cairns 151
Canada 32, 182
Canberra 7, 40, 45–46, 170–171,
  172–173, 173–176, 182–183,
  186–187, 188–190, *189*, 198; *see also*
    Queanbeyan
  Belconnen 188
  Braddon 188
  CBD (Central Business District) 175,
    181, 188
  City to the Lake 188
  Civic 184
  Gungahlin 188
  identity 174
  Kings Avenue 181
  Kingston 188
  Lake Burley Griffin 177, 182
  Murrumbidgee 188
  New Acton 188
  Northbourne Avenue 188
  Parkes Way 181–182
  parliamentary zone 177
  Woden 188
Canberra Airport 178, 181
Canberra Plan 179–180, 184; *see also*
  National Capital Plan; Spatial Plan;
  Territory Plan
capital cities 6–8, 7–8, 26–8, 37, 52, 68,
  91, 112, 124, 170–171, 179, 182–
  183, 191, 195, 200
  population growth 8, *8*, 101, 124–125,
    148, 197
capitalism 143, 209
Carr Labor Government 81
census data 6, *8*, 52, 54, 78, *78*, 102,
  112, 132, 205; *see also* population
Central Activities Districts (CADS,
  Melbourne) 60, 63–65
central business district *see* Adelaide;
  Brisbane; Canberra; Melbourne;
  Perth; Sydney
China 5–6, 127, 203
Cities 119
cities 12, 26–30, 43–44, 87, 91, 94, 136,
  138, 196, 200–202, 204–206; *see also*
    capital cities; arts and culture 51,
    102, 118
  compact city; city beautiful

movement; garden city movement; gentrification; globalization; neoliberalism; regional planning; urban planning activity centres 9, 15, 19, 57–60, *57*, *62*, 63, 67, 70–71, 105, 116, 132, 138, *139*, 142, 156, 160, 174, 181

  roads and streets 10, 27, *30*, 31, 35, 39, 41, 64, 87, 89, 104, 112, 129, 175

  tourism 7, 15, 102

Cities and Automobile Independence 83

Cities for the 21st Century 80

Cities of Opportunity 91

City and Environs (Federal Capital Competition) *29*

City Beautiful Movement 29

City Deals (UK) 12

City of Brisbane Act 1924 31

City of Cities 80, *81–82*, 82–83, 87, 91, 93–94, 96

city planning, *see* cities; metropolitan planning; urban planning

City Renewal Authority 190; *see also* Land Development Authority (LDA)

Civics and Citizens Unit (CCU) 129

Clare, Kerry 201

climate change 2, 11, 63, 83, 109–110, 116, 156–157, 182, 202; *see also Tackling Climate Change*

Coffee, N. 68

commercial development 29, *32*, 56–58, 60, 67, 70, 88, 109, 176, 178–179, 203

Commonwealth Government *see* Australian Government

community consultation 41, 58, 60, 129–131, 144, 153, 158–159

community planning *see* neighbourhood planning, urban planning

compact city 4, 10, 15, 18, 20, 36, 39, 41, 43–44, 57, 76, 80, 83, 91–94, 96, 109, 111, 116, 118, 131, 136, 154–7, 179, 181, 201–202, 204–206; *see also* cities; urban form and function

Congress of Engineers, Architects, Surveyors, and Members of Allied Professions 28

Cook, Frederick 31

Coolangatta 160

Copenhagen 39

corporatism 20, 176, 206–209

Corridor Plan for Perth 129

cosmopolitanism 6, 179, 198, 203, 205

Costello, Frank 36

Council of Australian Governments (COAG) 11–12, 91, 183

County of Cumberland Planning Scheme 36, *37*, 46

County of London Plan 35

Crown Group 88

Cumberland County Council 36, *37*, 95

Cunningham, Nita 153

Darwin 5

Davidson, K. 94

Davison, G. 195, 197

densification 18–19, 71, 79, 93, 126, 133–134, *141*, 142, 200–201; *see also* apartments; flat/unit development; high-rise development; housing; urban density

Department of Environment, Land, Water and Planning (DELWP, VIC) 65, 71

Department of Infrastructure and Planning (DIP, WA) 157

Department of Transport and Urban Planning (SA) 108–109

development *see* commercial; industrial; land; residential

development assessment 45, 89, 94, 109, 114, 142

Development Assessment Panels 109, 114, 135–136, 142

Directions 2031 and Beyond (*Directions 2031+*, WA) 125, 129, 133, 136–139, 142–143

District Centre Policy (Melbourne) 58

Dodson, J. 10

economic development 5–6, 43, 45, 76, 80, 83, 107, 110, 117, 124, 135, 158, 164, 203; *see also* capitalism
Economic Development Board (EDB, SA) 107
economic rationalism 5, 176
employment 6, 10, 12–13, 15, 19, 60, 83, 91–92, 144, 164, 178, 205
    knowledge economy 5, 10, 12, 15, 102, 116, 118, 164
environment 1, 83, 107, 129, 148, 158, 201
    greening 64, 87, 165–166
    renewable energy 11, 65, 109
Environment Protection and Biodiversity Conservation Act 1999 (AUS) 142, 158
Environmental and Sustainable Development Directorate (ESDD) 183
Environmental Planning and Assessment Act 1979 (NSW) 89
Europe 2, 6, 29, 31–32, 203

Farrelly, Elizabeth 90–91
federal capital 28–29, *29, 189*; *see also* Canberra; national capital
Federal Government *see* Australian Government
Fensham, Pat 85, 91
FIFO (fly-in/fly-out) 127
Fitzgerald, John D 30–31
Flagstone 156
flat/unit development 127, 133, 204; *see also* apartments; densification; high-rise development
Fordism 196, 203–204
Forster, C. 13, 19–20, 205
Fraser, Malcolm 152, 176
freeways 41, 56, 61, 126, 175; *see also* metropolitan planning; motor car
Future Perth 130

Gallop, Geoff 129

Garden City Movement 28–30, 33, 103, 174
Gateway Project 188
General Motors Holden 102
gentrification 41, 71, 200
Germany 29
Gini coefficient 78
Gleeson, Brendon 5, 20, 46, 148
Global Financial Crisis (GFC) 5, 83, 87, 94, 102, 110, 128, 156
Globalisation and World Cities Research Group 91
globalization 3, 8, 43, 76, 91, 143, 195, 197, 203
Gold Coast 10, 45, 149, 151, 164, *165*
Goss, Wayne 152
Great Depression 32–33, 103
Greater Brisbane Council 151; *see also* Brisbane City Council; Local Government
greater city movement 31; *see also* Greater Brisbane Council; Greater Perth; Greater Sydney Council; metropolitan planning
Greater London Plan 35, 39
Greater Perth 131
Greater Perth 7, 125–128, *133–134*, 134, 197; *see also* Perth
Greater Sydney Commission 12–13, 20, 86, 95, 97, 207
Greater Sydney Council 33
green bans 41; *see also* activism; social policy and reform
Green Girdle and Satellites for Sydney *34*
greenbelts and wedges 30, 33, 35–36, *35*, 53, 57, 175, 185, 188
Griffin, Marion Mahony 28–29, 40, 170–171, 174, 179
Griffin, Walter Burley 28–29, 40, 170–171, 174, 179
Griffin Legacy 179–180, 182, 188
Griffin plan 174–175
Groenhart, L. 94

Growth Areas Authority (GAA, Melbourne) 63
Growth Centres Commission (NSW) 81
Guy, Matthew 60

Hansen, Roz 60
Hanson, Pauline 167
Harrison, Peter 36, 42
Hart, Stuart 39
Harvey, D. 209
Haughton, G 17
Hawke, Alan 183
Hawke-Keating Labor government 5, 11
Healey, Patsy 3, 15
Heatwave Response Plan 202
Hepburn, Alastair 38
heritage and conservation 16, 19, 36, 41, 44, 79, 83, 103, 152–153, 163, 166, 180
high-rise development 9, 41, 58, 116, 143–144, 199, 201; *see also* apartments; densification; flat/unit development
Hobart 5, 37, 112
Hodyl, L. 199, 201
Hong Kong 199
housing 9, 18, 34–35, 55, 63–64, 69, 86, 103, 116, 126–1228, 132, 139–140, 143, 164, 201, 203, 205; *see also* apartments; flat/unit development; high-rise development affordable housing 18, 39, 44, 64–65, 67, 79, 85, 88, 96, 109, 116, 128, 156, 159, 164, 200
    density 9–10, 18, 27, 38, 43, *44*, 57–*58*, 60, 66–67, 79, *79*, 82, 92–93, 97, 112, 117–118, 124–126, 133, 143–164, 149, *163*, 164, 175, 184, 198–202; *see also* densification
    home ownership 9, 79, 126, 203
    homelessness 200, 203–204
Howard, Ebenezer 28, 41, 175
Howe, R. 38
H-Plan 181–182; *see also* Y-Plan

Hu, R. 92
Hutchings, A. 119
hypertrophic urbanism 197–198, 200, 203, 207; *see also* intensification; urbanism

Ideas for Australian Cities 39
immigration 6, 37, 52–53, 102, 149, 203–204; *see also* migration
    visas 6, 203
India 6
industrial development 5, *32*, 38, 41, 63, 67, 93, 102–103, 129, 158
Infrastructure NSW 94
Integrated Planning Act 153–154
Integrated Transport and Land Use Plan (ITLUP, SA) 113–114
intensification 85, 181, 184, 198–203, 205–206
Ipswich 149

Jimboomba 156
Joint Regional Planning Panels (NSW) 89
Joyce, Barnaby 174

Kelly, J.-F. 55
Kelly, Paul 5
Keneally, Kristina 83
Kennett, Jeff 56
Kennett Liberal-National Party Coalition Government 56, 58, 66
Kerry, Michael 153
knowledge economy *see* employment

laissez-faire 27
land development 18, 81–83, 88, 107, 109–110, 114, 119, 143, 158, 176, 178
    brownfield 15, 18–19, 86, 116, 130
    greenfield 13, 15, 28, 58, 63, 68, 70, 80–81, 86, 92, 112, 118, 129, 132, 154, 163, 166–167, 177–178, 181, 184, 188, 190

infill 18, 41, 82, 111–112, 116, 118, 129, 134, 136, 143–144, 154, 163–165, *163*, 200–201

Land Development Authority (LDA) 181, 188, 190; *see also* City Renewal Authority; Office of Asset Management; Suburban Land Agency

Land Management Corporation (SA) 110, 112; *see also* Urban Renewal Authority (SA)

Landcom 88, 93; *see also* UrbanGrowth NSW

Landcorp 143

landscape planning 125, 153, 157, 161, 174, 177; *see also* open space; parklands

Land-Use Transportation Study 175

legislation *see* planning legislation and controls

Lend Lease 88

Lewis, M. 202

Light, William Colonel 103

Local Environment Plans (LEPs, NSW) 88, 96

Local Government 17, 31, 114, 119; *see also* metropolitan planning; regional planning
  New South Wales 33, 36, 78, 82, 89–90
  Queensland 149, *150*, 151–152, 154–5, 158–162, 164, 166–167
  South Australia 109, 114, 119
  Victoria 56, 63, 66–68, 72
  Western Australia 126, 129–130, 135, 139–140, *141*, 142–143

Local Growth Management Strategies (LGMS, QLD) 155

London 28, 35, 39, 82, 87, 91, 155, 195

Loudon, John Claudius 28

Low, N. 5

McCosker, A. 3

McGuirk, P. 9, 17, 82–83

McInnis, Ronald 36

Mackay 36

McKell, William 33

Mackenroth, Terry 153, 156

Maginn, Paul J. 134

Mahattanization 200–201

Mahjabeen, Z. 83

manufacturing *see* industrial development

Mees, Paul 10, 94

Megalogenis, George

Melbourne 7–9, 27–28, *27*, 30, 32–33, *32*, 40, 43, *44*, 46, 51, *52–53*, 55, *57*, 62, *62*, 67–68, *70*, 71–72, 197–202, 205, 207
  CBD (Central Business District) 53, 55, 60
  Chadstone 58
  Cranbourne East 53
  Docklands 53
  Fitzroy 58
  Highpoint West 58
  Mitcham 58
  Monash 63
  Parkville 63
  population 51–53
  Port Phillip Bay 53
  South Morang 53

Melbourne 2030 56–59, *57*, 61, 63, 70–71

Melbourne@5Million 56, 59, *59*, 63

Melbourne@5Million: Urban Growth Boundary Map *59*

Melbourne Let's Talk about the Future 60

Melbourne Metropolitan Board of Works (MMBW, VIC) 28, 37–38, *38*, *44*

Melbourne Planning Authority 207

Melbourne Strategic Framework Plan *44*

METRONET (WA) 138

Metroplan (WA) 129–130, 134, 137

Metropolitan Canberra 185, *187*; *see also* National Capital Plan

metropolitan condition 5, 20, 195–198, 201, 205; *see also* metropolitanization

Metropolitan Development Plan
(Adelaide) 40
Metropolitan Local Government
Review Panel (WA) 135
Metropolitan Plan for Sydney 2036 80, *81*,
83–84, *84*
metropolitan planning 1–4, 11–13, 16,
18–20, 36–37, 39–40, 42–44, 46, 56,
60, 71–72, 77, *84*, 96, 101, 104, 119,
136, 143, 174, 196; *see also* regional
planning
corridors 30, 39–43, 53, 58, 60, 68,
80, 82–83, 85, 92, 96, 129, 132–134,
142, 161, 181, 184
governance 2–4, 11, *14*, 20, 77, 81,
83, 91, 94–96, 135–136, *137*, 143,
185, 197, 199, 206–209
public-private partnership 10, 15, 88–
89, 104, 162, 179–180, 188, 190–
191, 196, 202
spatial 1–2, 13, 15, 20, *29*, 39, 43, 92,
107–108, *108*, 180–181, 199–200
sustainability 11, 15, 43–44, 76, 83,
94, 129–131, 179, 181–182, 202
terrorism 91, 207
Metropolitan Planning Authority
(MPA, Melbourne) 63, 65, 67; *see also*
Victorian Planning Authority (VPA)
Metropolitan Redevelopment Authority
(MRA, WA) 127, 135, 143
Metropolitan Region Improvement Tax
(MRIT, Perth) 129, 136
Metropolitan Region Scheme (Perth,
WA, 1963) 39, 126, 129, 136
Metropolitan Regional Planning
Authority (Perth) 40, 129
Metropolitan Spatial Framework
(Adelaide) 107, *108*
Metropolitan Town Planning
Commission (Melbourne) 31–33, *32*
Metropolitan Town Planning
Commission (Perth) 126, 128–129
metropolitanization 197–200, 203, 206–
208; *see also* metropolitan condition

migration 78, 110, 124, 149–151, 197–
200; *see also* immigration
Miller, C. 17
mining *see* industrial development;
resources boom
modernism 41, 179, 199–200
Moreton Regional Coordination
Council (MRCC, QLD) 152
Moreton Regional Organisation of
Councils (MROC, QLD) 152
motor car 4, 10–11, 83, 102, 112, 117,
119, 144, 157, 175, 189, 200, 204–206;
see also freeways, uber-ization
multiculturalism *see* cosmopolitanism

Napthine, Denis 56
national capital 5, 34, 170–171, 182,
185, 188–189; *see also* federal capital
National Capital Authority (NCA)
178–179 188, 190; *see also* National
Capital Development Commission;
National Capital Planning Authority
National Capital Development
Commission (NCDC) 40–41, 171,
174, 177, 179, 181; *see also* National
Capital Planning Authority; National
Capital Authority
National Capital Open Space System
(NCOSS) 175, 185–186
National Capital Plan 177–178,
180, 184–185, *185–186*, 188; *see
also* Canberra Plan; Metropolitan
Canberra; Territory Plan
National Capital Planning Authority
177; *see also* National Capital
Authority; National Capital
Development Commission
National Disability Insurance Scheme
204
National Employment Clusters 63
neighbourhood planning 30, 36, 58, 62–
63, *64*, 65–67, 91, 94, 115–116, 118,
126, 202, 204, 206; *see also* 20-minute
city

neoliberal governance and planning 9, 16, 20, 80, 91, 190, 199, 206

neoliberalism 2–3, 5, 16–17, 43–45, 56, 66, 77, 89, 96, 101, 119, 135, 143, 176, 188, 190, 196, 199, 204, 206–208

Network City (WA) 13, 125, 129–134, *132*, 136–137

New South Wales *42*, 78, 209; *see also* State and Territory Government

New South Wales Local Government (Town and Country Planning) Amendment Act 1945 36

new towns 35, 175–177, 179, 185, 188–189

New York 31, 33, 82, 87, 91, 199

Newcastle 88

Newman, Campbell 155, 158

Newman, Peter 83

Newman National–Liberal Coalition Government 158

NIMBY 142, 206

Noosa 160

Northern Territory 8

Norwest Business Park 82

O'Malley, King 174

office development *see* commercial development

Office of Asset Management (ACT) 177, 181; *see also* Land Development Authority

Office of Urban Management (QLD) 153, 156–158

Olympic Dam Copper-Uranium Mine 102, 110

Olympic Games (Sydney, 2000) 81, 89

One Nation Party 167

open space 19, 28, 30–31, 36, 39, 41, 64, 83, 94, 96, 129, 142, 152–153, 165, 201–202; *see also* greenbelts and wedges; landscape planning; parklands

Orchard, L. 17

Organisation for Economic Co-operation and Development (OECD) 6, 170, 179

Packer, James 88

Palaszczuk Labor Government 158–160

Park Ridge 156

parklands 27–28, 30–33, 39, 62, 87, 126, 129, 179 ; *see also* greenbelts and wedges; landscape planning; open space

Peck, J. 135

Peel 13, 133, 136–137, 139, 142; *see also* Perth

Peel Region Scheme 136

Perth 7, 13, 30, 32, 37–40, 124, 126, 128, 130–131, 133, *137*, 138–140, *139–140*, 142, 144; *see also* Greater Perth; Peel

Bayswater 140

Canning 140

CBD (Central Business District) 133

Dalkeith *141*

Fremantle 129

Glendalough 127

Greater Bunbury 136

Jolimont 127

Joondalup 138

Melville 140

Northbridge 127

population 124–127, *125*, 131–132, 134–135, 138, 140

Stirling 127, 139–410

Subiaco 127

Swan River 142

Victoria Park 140

Yanchep 138

Perth Airport 138

Perth and Peel @ 3.5m (WA, 2015) 136, 142–143

Plan First (NSW) 81

Plan for Growing Sydney 80, *81*, 85–87, *85*, 95, *95*

Plan Melbourne 56, *62*, 63–64, 66–68, 71

Plan Melbourne 2017–2050 65, 67, 69, 71

Plan Melbourne Activity Centre *62*

Plan Melbourne Refresh 56, 63–64, *64*, 67

Plan of Chicago 29

Plan of General Development 31
Planning and Development Act 2005 (WA) 136
Planning and Development Act 2007 (ACT) 182
Planning and Development Review (SA) 110, 116
Planning and Environment Act 1987 (VIC) 66
Planning and Land Act 2002 (ACT) 180
Planning and Land Management Agency (PALM) 177, 179–180; *see also* ACT Planning and Land Authority
Planning Assessment Commission (NSW) 89
Planning, Development and Infrastructure Act (SA, 2016) 114
planning, evolution of 26–28, 33, 36–37, 41, 46–47, 119, 174, 190, 197–198; *see also* town planning; urban planning
   1930s 33–34
   1940s 34–36
   1950s 37–39
   1960s 39–41
   1970s 41–42
   1980s 42–43
   1990s 43–45
   nineteenth century 26–27, 125–126, 195
   twentieth century 3–5, 11, 20, 27, 29, 46, 103–104, 124, 126, 150–151
   twenty-first century 2, 4, 13, 26, 44, 47, 101, 118, 142, 151, 184, 189, 205–209
Planning Institute of Australia 67, 107, 112, 153
planning legislation and controls 36, 65–67, 72, 88–89
Planning Makes it Happen: A Blueprint for Planning Reform 135
planning reform 16–17, 56, 89–90, 101, 104, *106*, 119, 134–136, *137*, 144, 207
Planning Strategy Priorities *105*
pluralization 198–199, 203, 206–207

politics 46, 66, 71, 109, 117, 134, 142–144, 155, 158, 166–167, 170–171, 173–174, 179–180, 183, 189–190, 196–197, 200–201, 206–209
population 1, 6–7, 51–53, 102, 107, 109, 111–112, 116, 134, 150–151, 197; *see also* capital cities; census data; metropolitan planning
indigenous 6, 131
Port Kembla 88
post-war planning and reconstruction 11, 26, 34, 37, 46, 53, 103, 174–175, 196–199, 208
poverty 33, 205
PriceWaterhouseCoopers 91
privatization 17, 20, 43, 46, 176, 178–180, 199, 202, 208
Property Council of Australia 166
Prosperity through People 107
public participation *see* community consultation
public realm 88, 90–91, 199, 207
public services 148, 151, 162, 165

Queanbeyan 171; *see also* Australian Capital Territory; Canberra
Queensland 8, 17, 148, 150–153, 156–158, 164, 166; *see also* South East Queensland; State and Territory Government
Queensland Town Planning Association 33

Randolph, Bill 9, 19, 196, 205
Rann, Mike 101, 105, 107, 109, 112
Rann Labor Government 105, 109, 112
Rasmussen, Steen Eiler 39
Reade, Charles 30–31
Real Estate Institute of Western Australia (REIWA) 128
Regional Open Space System (QLD) 152
Regional Plan for New York 31, 33
regional planning 33, 61, 130–131,

140, 142, 148–149, 151, 156–158, *157 see also* cities; local government; metropolitan planning

governance 152–153, 156, 158–162, 166–168

Report on the Metropolitan Area of Adelaide 39

residential development 15, 66–68, *66*, 109–111, 128–129, 132, 165–167, 179, 202

Residential Metropolitan Development Program (SA) 107

resources boom 124, 127–128, 134, 143, 151

retail development *see* commercial development

roads and streets *see* cities

Rockefeller Foundation 207

Rogers, D. 80

Rowley, S. 71

Royal Commission for the Improvement of the City of Sydney and Its Suburbs 29–30, *30*

Rudd, Kevin 11

Rudd Labor Government 11

Salt, Bernard 149, 200

Sanitary Reform of Towns and Cities 28

satellite towns 30, *34–35*, 35–36, 38, 175, 181; *see also* planning, evolution of

Save Our Suburbs 58

Scenarios of Our Future – Challenges for Western Australian Society 130

Searle, G. 3

Shaftesbury, Lord 27

Shaping Sydney's Future 80

Smart Cities 12, 206–207

social life and conditions 9–10, 29, 41, 203–205; *see also* cities

social policy and reform 5, 34, 78, 101, 204; *see also* urban policy and reform

South Australia 8, 101–104, *105*, 107,

108, 109–110, 114, 116, 119–120, 209; *see also* State and Territory Government

South Australian Housing Trust (SAHT) 33, 103

South Australian Urban Land Trust 104

South East Queensland 1, 4, 148–153, *154*, 155–159, 162, 165–168, 197; *see also* Queensland

South East Queensland Growth Management Program 158

South East Queensland Infrastructure Plan and Program (SEQIPP) 156–157

South East Queensland Regional Coordination Committee 153, 156

South East Queensland Regional Organisation of Councils 153, 155

South East Queensland Regional Plan (SEQRP) 152–160, *154*, 156, *157*, *160*, 164–168

Southport 160

Spatial Plan (Canberra) *180*, 180–184, 188 *see also* Canberra Plan; Metropolitan Canberra; National Capital Plan; Territory Plan

spatial planning *see* metropolitan planning; strategic planning

Spearritt, Peter 153

Spencer, A. 155

Spiller, M. 55

Stapley, Frank 31

State and Territory Government 13, 15, 18–19, 33, 35–36, 44, 52, 77

Australian Capital Territory 171, *172–173*, 177–179, 182–184, 188, 190

New South Wales 33, 77, 80–81, 85–86, 88–91

Queensland 151–153, 156–158, 160, 164

South Australia 103–105, *106*, 107–108, 110, 116, 119–120

Victoria 55–56, 59, 65–68, 72

Western Australia 129–130, 134–136, 138, 142–144

State Development Areas (QLD) 166
State Environmental Planning Policies (NSW) 88
State Infrastructure Strategy (NSW) 86
State of Australian Cities 4
State of the Environment 201
State Planning Authority of NSW 40
State Planning Commission (SA) 114
State Planning Framework Policy, No1: State Planning Policy (WA) 134, 143–144
State Planning Strategy (WA) 136
State Sustainability Strategy (WA) 129–130
Steele, W. 148
Stephenson, Gordon 38–39
Stephenson–Hepburn Plan (WA) 126, 128–129
Stokes, Rob 90
Strategic Infrastructure Plan for South Australia 108, 114
strategic planning 2–4, 16, 18, 34, 39, 43, 51–52, 56, 66–68, 70–72, 76–77, 80, 86, 96–97, 101, 105–108, 111–112, 114, 124–125, 129–131, *132*, 135–138, 142–144, 155, 166, 170, 178–179, 181, 183, 190, 207–208; *see also* metropolitan planning; regional planning
Streeck, W. 209
Stretton, Hugh 18, 39, 118
Suburban Land Agency (Canberra) 190; see also Land Development Authority (LDA)
suburbanization 9, 16, 31, 46, 118–119, 125–126, 195; *see also* suburbs
suburbs 9–10, 12, 16, 18–19, 27–30, 37, 41, 53–55, 58, 63, 67–68, 71, 78–79, 101–102, 109, 113, 115–119, 126–127, 133, 138, 140, 142, 149, 182, 189; *see also* suburbanization
Sulman, John 28, 31
Sunshine Coast 45, 149
sustainability *see* metropolitan planning

Sustainability Policy Unit (SPU, WA) 129
Sustainable Future Program (ACT) 182–183
Sydney 7–9, 17, 27–28, 31, 33, 35, 37, 41, 43, 45, 54, 76–77, *78*, 80, 82, *84*, 85, *85*, 88, 91–95, 197–198, 200–202, 205, 207
  CBD (Central Business District) 19, 79, 82
  Badgerys Creek 87
  Barangaroo 19, 88
  Burwood 78
  Kogarah 78
  Liverpool 82
  metropolis of three cities 95, *95*
  North Sydney 82
  North West and South West Growth Centres 81, 92
  Parramatta 9, 82, 84–85, 87, 92–93, 95
  Penrith 82
  population 51–52, 77, 86, 93
  Strathfield 78
  The Rocks 79
  WestConnex 87, 89–90, 93
  Western Sydney 19, 83–87, 92–93, 97
  Western Sydney Airport 87, 90, 96
Sydney Harbour 85, 87–88
Sydney Metropolitan Development Agency 88
Sydney Region Outline Plan 40, 80
Sydney Regional Plan Convention 33

Tackling Climate Change 107, 109; *see also* climate change
Tasmania 8
Taylor, N. 143
technology and change 12, 76, 164, 178, 182, 197, 199
Territory Plan (ACT) 177–178, 182–185: *see also* Canberra Plan; National Capital Plan; Spatial Plan
The Australian Metropolis: A Planning History 4–5, 11, 26, 196

The Canberra Plan: Towards Our Second Century 182
The End of Certainty 5
The Future Canberra 40, 175
The Laying Out of Towns 28
The Metropolitan Problems of Sydney 30
Tice, A. 9
Tickell, A. 135
Time to Talk, Canberra 2030 182
Tokyo 87, 199–200
Tomorrow's Canberra 41
Tonts, M 127
Toowoomba 149, 160
tourism *see* cities
Towards a Vision for Perth in 2029 130
town and country planning 33, 35–36, 37, 40, 46; *see also* metropolitan planning; planning, evolution of; regional planning; urban planning
Town and Country Planning Association (SA) 40
Town and Country Planning Board (TCPB, VIC) 35, 40
Town and Development Act 1928 (WA) 126
town planning 29–33, 39, 43, 46, 126, 128; *see also* metropolitan planning; planning, evolution of; urban planning; town and country planning
Town Planning Association of Victoria 31
town planning associations 29, 31, 33
Town Planning Commission Report (WA) 39
town planning commissions 31–33, *32*, 39, 46, 126, 128
town planning movement 43; *see also* planning, evolution of
Townsville 151
Trad, Jackie 159–160
transport 1, 10, 18, 38, 61, 85–87, 138
    connectivity 84, 86, 91, 139, 164–165, *165*
    corridors 10, 15, 39–41, 53, 60, 84–85, 93, 111, *111*, 117, 129, 181, 184

public 41, 55, 87, *165*, 104–105, 108, 132, *165*, 175–176, 200, 204
rail *30*, 84, 86–89, 113, *113*, 129, 165, 188–189
roads *30*, 35, 39, 41, 64, 87, 89, 104, 112, 129, 165
Troy, L. 138, 205
Turnbull, Lucy 95
Turnbull, Malcolm 10, 90
Turnbull Liberal-National Government 12, 174, 206

uber-ization 144; *see also* motor car
United Kingdom 12, 33, 38–39, 46, 119
United States of America 1, 31–33, 46
urban consolidation 8–9, 41, 43, 56–57, 68, 92–93, 105, 126, 139, 143, 165, 167, 179, 184, 188, 201–202; *see also* urban form and function; urban design
urban density 9–10, 18, 60, 107, 117–118, 155, 160; *see also* densification
urban design 16, 19, 58, 82, 94, 162, 181–182
Urban Design and Places Panel 162
urban development 12, 27, 34, 43–44, 71, 76–77, 104, 107, 118–119, 143, 171, 173–175, 179, 181–182, 188–189
Urban Development Institute of Australia 118, 128, 153
urban form and function 4, 6, 9, 18, 20, 28, 31, 41, 43, 45, 57, 82, 103, 116–118, 128–129, 155, 157, 163, 165–166, 179, 181–182, 184, 199–200, 202, 206, 208; *see also* compact city; urban consolidation; urban design
urban growth boundaries 15, 18, 36, 57–60, 63, *69*, 105, 114, 118, 126, 130, 133, 136, 163, 181, 184; *see also* urban sprawl
Urban Growth Boundary (UGB) 57, *59*, 60, 63, 67–68
Urban Growth Monitor (WA) 136
Urban Management and Infrastructure

Coordination Committee (UMICC) 153

urban planning 3, 32, 41, 148, 205; *see also* cities; metropolitan planning

urban policy and reform 9, 12, 16–18, 28–29, 45, 202, 206; *see also* social policy and reform

urban renewal 9, 11, 36, 41, 46, 55, 62–63, 76, 81, 84, 88, 93, 96, 112, 118, 126–127, 188, 201

Urban Renewal Authority (SA) 112, 118; *see also* Land Management Corporation (SA)

urban sprawl 27, 107, 131, 133; *see also* urban growth boundaries

vertical sprawl 201

UrbanGrowth NSW 88, 93; *see also* Landcom

urbanism 15, 76, 126, 144, 197–198, 201, 205–208

urbanization 7, 9, 185, 195–196, 198, 200, 206, 208–209

Victoria 6, 8, 17, 70, 72, 204, 209; *see also* State and Territory Government

Victoria Planning Provisions 56, 60, 66, 71

Victorian Civil and Administrative Appeals Tribunal (VCAT) 58

Victorian Planning Authority (VPA) 65, 72; *see also* Metropolitan Planning Authority

Victorian Planning System Ministerial Advisory Committee (VPSMAC) 66

Vietnam War 41

Voorhees, Alan 41

Weatherill, Jay 101, 112

Weatherill Labor Government 112, 119

Weekes, Norman 33

WestConnex 87, 89–90, 93

Western Australia 8, 124, 127, 135, 142–143; *see also* State and Territory Government

Western Australian Planning Commission 114, 126, 129–131, 134–136, 143–144

Western Sydney Infrastructure Plan 90

Whitlam Labor Government 11, 41, 103–104, 176

Wiesel, I. 205

World War One 31

World War Two 26, 34, 196

Wynne, Richard 63

Yarrabilba 156, 160, *161*

Y-Plan 41, 175, 177, 181; *see also* H-Plan

zoning 9, 31–33, *32*, 36–38, 64–65, 67, 88, 118, 129, 177, 188, 201; *see also* land development; planning, evolution of